COOL COLLEGES

for the Hyper-Intelligent, Self-Directed,

Late Blooming, and Just Plain Different

COOL COLLEGES

for the

HYPER-INTELLIGENT,
SELF-DIRECTED,
LATE BLOOMING,
AND JUST PLAIN DIFFERENT

2ND EDITION

Donald Asher

TEN SPEED PRESS
Berkeley | Toronto

Ten Speed Press
Box 7123
Berkeley, California 94707
www.tenspeed.com

Distributed in Australia by Simon & Schuster Australia, in Canada by Ten Speed Press Canada, in New Zealand by Southern Publishers Group, in South Africa by Real Books, and in the United Kingdom and Europe by Publishers Group UK.

Cover design by Catherine Jacobes
Book design by Paul Kepple & Timothy Crawford @ Headcase Design
Production by Jeff Brandenburg

Thank you to the following for granting permission to use their work:

"Secret to Finding Scholarships—There Isn't One" by Jane Bryant Quinn (p. 34–36) copyright © 1999, the Washington Post Writers Group. Reprinted with permission.
Excerpt from *Looking Beyond the Ivy League*, revised edition, by Loren Pope (p. 48) copyright © 1990, 1995 by Loren Pope. Reprinted by permission of Penguin Books and the author.
"Western Colleges Finally Get Their Due" (p. 53–55) copyright © 1999 by Janet L. Holmgren. Reprinted with permission.
Excerpt from *Colleges That Change Lives* by Loren Pope (p. 84) copyright © 1996 by Loren Pope. Reprinted by permission of Penguin Books and the author.
"On College Counseling for the Intellectual Student" (p. 109–116) copyright © by Laura J. Clark. Reprinted with permission.
Narrative evaluation (p. 140–141) used by permission of New College of the University of South Florida.
"What is Intelligence?" (p. 147–150) copyright © by Ruby Ausbrooks. Reprinted with permission.
"Why Kids Aren't Happy in Traditional School" (p. 157–160) copyright © by Ruby Ausbrooks. Reprinted with permission.
"The Big Meeting" (p. 175–176) copyright © by Crystal Finkbeiner. Reprinted with permission.
"The Filene Center for Work & Learning" (p. 179–182) copyright © by Dan Golden. Reprinted with permission.
"A Life of Work and Learning" (p. 212–213) copyright © by Dennis Jacobs. Reprinted with permission.
"Why I Finally Chose to Attend an Historically Black College" (p. 240–241) copyright © by Amelia R. Shelby. Reprinted with permission.

Library of Congress Control Number: 2007922323

Printed in the United States of America
First printing, 2007

1 2 3 4 5 6 / 12 11 10 09 08 07

For

Lisa Bertschi

CONTENTS

ACKNOWLEDGMENTS

Nobody writes a book like this by himself or herself. Many, many people helped out in ways great and small. First and foremost I must thank my research assistant, Denise Rhiner, of Pyramid Communications in Seattle, who worked tirelessly to track down thousands of pesky details. There are still plenty of errors in this book, but they are all mine. Denise never makes a mistake. Thanks to my publishing team at Ten Speed, Phil, Lorena, Fuzz, and Hal. Also, very special thanks to Jeff for all his work on the interior of the new edition, and Catherine for an awesome new cover. Also, a few thousand people in higher education helped me to research and compile this book, including college presidents, deans and directors of admission, and public affairs officers. My surveys elicited warm and thoughtful comments from the best and the brightest at institutions all over North America, and I am grateful for their contribution. Special thanks to Kate Goldberg, college planning counselor, French-American International School in San Francisco; Laura J. Clark, college planning counselor, Ethical Culture Fieldston School in the Bronx, New York; Larry Large, president, Oglethorpe University in Atlanta; Janet Lavin Rapelye, dean of admission, Wellesley College; Janet L. Holmgren, president, Mills College; Fred Hargadon, dean of admissions, Princeton University; Marlyn McGrath Lewis, director of undergraduate admissions, Harvard University; and Dr. Dan Golden, director, the Filene Center for Work & Learning, Wheaton College in Norton, Massachusetts. Special thanks to L. M. Boyd, the trivia meister, author of "The Grab Bag" syndicated column, and the original source for a number of the academic trivia items in this volume. Very special thanks to Mr. Steve Old Elk, who rescued me when I needed it most. My greatest appreciation goes out to Dr. Judy Jones, one of my earliest mentors, who set this train in motion. Likewise to my mother, Dr. Ruby Ausbrooks, who was in school, like, forever, and my older brother, Bill, and younger brother, Clyde, who proved to me that anything is possible. I also need to acknowledge Professor Walter Englert, classics, Reed College, who is a credit to the profession of professing; and Tom Francis, director of career services, Swarthmore College, a true friend and a fine wrecker of boats.

WHERE THIS BOOK CAME FROM

I didn't really fit in at high school. The classes moved along at a glacial pace, until I felt that I'd just pull my hair out one strand at a time out of sheer boredom.

The dean of students had a personal vendetta against me. I'd be in a crowd of students and he'd see Don Asher and some nice young people. It was probably some kind of pattern recognition thing. Like that time I wore a Native American getup to Western Day, and got sent to the principal's office for my lack of "spirit," whatever that was. I never did really understand school spirit. I always thought school was about learning, and this spirit stuff was usually some blatant glorification of the very students who weren't learning anything. It seemed like a perverted recognition system to me. I didn't fit expectations. Sometime in high school I began to realize that systems in general were not designed for me.

I was not alone. My friends and I were always doing the "challenge" problems in the math books (and sometimes we'd even remember to turn them in). We talked in puns, collected oxymorons, read ahead in the books, wrote poetry, and drew cartoons in class. We gloried in discovering the historical inaccuracies of our texts, and had long arguments about minutiae, often bringing in outside references our teachers knew nothing about. We didn't always get the top grades. We were "difficult." We were trying so very hard to stay interested in an educational system that clearly was not designed for us.

Then I discovered a program whereby I could go straight into the largest university in the state without graduating from high school! All I needed were three things: the right grades (had 'em), the right SATs (had 'em), and a letter of recommendation from my high school principal. The only thing standing between me and this blessed event was a recommendation from my high school principal. He was a thin, bald man, who left all troubles to the dean of students. I knew the dean well, but I'd never actually spoken to the principal. Would he write me a letter? Would he release me? "I'd be glad to," he said, with a smile I couldn't interpret.

And so I went to college. Heaven at last, I thought. A university! Where they'll treat me like an adult! Where learning is the raison d'être for the entire institution!

The first week of classes the dean of students' secretary called me and said, "The dean wants to see you in his office. Would you be available on Wednesday at two?" What had I done now? I wondered. I thought all deans were alike, and I thought maybe my high school dean had called this university dean and warned him about me.

When I got there I was literally shaking. I had to wait only a few minutes before I was ushered into the dean's office. He motioned for me to take a chair with an authority that could not be denied. Then he spoke. I couldn't have been more shocked when he said, "I've been going over your file and I just want to say how delighted we are that you chose this university. We need a thousand students like you, and it's critical that you adjust well and stay here. If you ever need anything, you let me know. I want you to consider me your personal friend." I was terrified of him, and just nodded a lot and left as quickly as I could.

But I did not adjust well. I was shocked that my fellow students were more interested in dating, sports, and avoiding the real world for four years than they were in learning. Students openly discussed cheating, and professors routinely dismissed class well before the scheduled end. I was so disappointed I dropped out after one semester. So I was technically a high school dropout with one semester of perfect college grades.

My dad was livid. I was going to become a bum, he thought. I was going to fall in with a bad crowd. I was throwing my life away. In fact, I was on a mission, and that mission was to find a place in this world where I would fit in, where I was the norm, where I was welcome, and where I felt at home. After three years of research, I found it, in one of the schools in this book. It is absolutely not true that all colleges are the same, or that "the college experience" is largely similar throughout the country. There are very real differences between institutions, and even some wonderful experiments in higher education in America. I found the perfect place *for me.*

I hope you find your college, too, a perfect place *for you,* a place where you'll be happy, excited, welcomed, appreciated, and productive, a place that will launch you into the rest of your life like a trampoline. You deserve this. From the bottom of my heart, I wish you good luck. I wrote this book for you.

RESEARCH METHODOLOGY, BIASES, AND LIMITATIONS

The most important part of research is passion. My passion for this topic, choosing the right college when you are hyper-intelligent, self-directed, late blooming, or just plain different, carried me across a full decade of inquiry. My first vision of this book was that I'd design a methodology to identify cool, and then list and describe the "most cool" colleges in some ordinal ranking until I got to a reasonable number of schools or pages, whichever came first. I naively blundered into this endeavor expecting it to be easy. It proved very difficult after all, and in the end, this book became a hobby I worked on over a ten-year span.

Occasionally I advise young people on college choice, especially when they are hyper-intelligent, self-directed, late blooming, or just plain different, but that is not my main career. I am a self-employed business writer and public speaker specializing in careers and higher education. I guest-speak at undergraduate and graduate schools from coast to coast, usually about career development and graduate study issues. I am not a college administrator or a faculty member, but as part of my job I visit some 100 campuses each and every year. Part of my motivation for finally completing this book is that I have a daughter and a stepdaughter who are both making college decisions as I write. (As is typical, neither is the least bit interested in the contents of this book—

one says she doesn't want to go to college at all, and the other says she's going to school in Europe.)

In 1990, when I first began this project, there were very few college guides and they were all as dull as a televised fundraising marathon. From my own early research, I knew of a few dozen of the more interesting and innovative colleges in the United States. But I also knew that I didn't know much. So I wrote to a few thousand college presidents, deans, and directors of admission, explaining my endeavor and asking for their advice.

They were wonderful! They told me about schools I'd never heard of, suggested criteria, alerted me to trends that were underreported in the national media, decried the intellectual dishonesty of the most popular ranking system, applauded my efforts, and predicted, almost every last one, that my project was doomed from the outset.

The problem, according to them, was that the culture of a college, its very ethos, defies depiction. The environment of a college might be described, but it could never be measured. In short, I'd never be able to design a methodology to identify and quantify whatever it meant to be "cool."

I worried about this, but at the same time I noticed clear patterns in the schools they were recommending for study. The same schools kept showing up over and over in the surveys. So I made a list of the most nominated schools and sent out another wave of letters, asking college presidents, deans, and directors of admission to vote on which institutions should be further investigated.

This was unfair, of course, because I was asking them to vote for schools that were both good *and* innovative, without formally defining either term. Although most people can see the problem with formalizing a definition for "innovative," many would argue that "good" ought to be easy to define. However, it is not, unless you want an easy but not very meaningful definition. The problems lie in quantification and practicality. A good college has what overt, measurable aspects? (See p. 60 for a discussion of inputs and outputs.) For example, what calipers would you put on a professor to see if he or she is really a good professor? Does she prepare students for graduate school? Or to be good citizens? Does he have a talent for reaching the chronic underachiever? Or does he spend all his energies on the brightest students? Does she excel at conveying the intellectual traditions of a discipline? Or does she ignite dynamic, new, creative approaches to classic problems? A truly outstanding professor might have any of these aspects, and even if you focus in on certain ones, always and necessarily at the expense of others, you will still face the challenge of quantifying qualitative matters.

Even supposing an elaborate methodology for measuring these issues, I projected that problems of access and cost, to say nothing of multistage validation studies, would doom the endeavor. Cost alone would be prohibitive. Even the most basic inquiry into the quality of an institution would involve a host of factors.

So how, then, do the national ranking systems work? They rely on self-reporting of existing data, i.e., they conduct zero original research at any institution. The data they collect is already quantified, collected by the institution for its own purposes, which in almost all cases was never meant to address qualitative issues at all. In the words of programmers everywhere, "garbage in, garbage out." I wanted to get at what it was like to study and live at a certain school, and I didn't think an institution's financial data were going to be particularly illustrative.

In spite of the transparent inadequacies of my surveys, I always got plenty of votes. So whatever "good" and "innovative" means at the institutional level of colleges and universities, it must fall into that "I know it when I see it" category. At least presidents and deans seemed comfortable making decisions based on common understandings of those words.

There are other problems with the "voting" methodology I used in my early research (often derisively known by social scientists as a "beauty contest survey"). Suppose, as is frequently the case, a very good and very innovative school is poorly known. Other schools, perhaps only slightly good and slightly innovative, will receive many more votes. So I conducted further research on schools that were least known but had promising reports on the innovative scale. For example, someone wrote to me about a school called Thomas Aquinas College, where intellectual inquiry is almost a religion. My correspondent wrote, "The president of the college sometimes has the *entire student body* over to his house to discuss ideas. These meetings can take hours, and have nothing to do with the regular class load." Hmmmm. It doesn't take a genius to realize that a school like that belongs in a book like this, regardless of the number of votes it gets.

Finally, there was another problem, and it was not a small one. Not only is it extremely difficult to figure out what makes up the culture of an ever-evolving institution, one student's experience at that institution will always be uniquely individual in any case. For example, the student in Smith Hall 107 may love the institution for reasons A, B, and C, while the student in Smith Hall 108 hates it for reasons A, X, and Z, and the student in Smith Hall 109 loves it for reasons X, Y, and Z. Not only are schools different from one another, but students are different too. Students like and dislike different things. So my solution was simple: provide information on A, B, C, and X, Y, Z, and let the students decide for themselves.

In fact, that is why I decided to consider a few hundred schools instead of a few dozen—sometimes by discussing a type of school and then listing all the members of that category. My original plan was to profile in detail very few schools, and omit those that did not receive enough votes. This proved silly when I kept finding out about really cool classes and programs at institutions that were otherwise absolutely ordinary. The more students I spoke with the more I realized that almost any college or university is "cool" to somebody. Sometimes the reasons are incomprehensible such as that of one student who told me she picked a particular school "because it had two swimming pools," but nevertheless, each and every student has a rationale. Ultimately, I decided to include every accredited four-year institution in the United States and Canada.

(By the way, two of the most influential factors in the college choice decision are the attractiveness and persuasiveness of the tour guide. This is not logical since prospective students are not likely to ever see this person again, even if they do decide to attend the institution.)

To complete my research, I visited several hundred colleges and universities. I did not visit every one of the schools I recommend in this book, but I did visit enough to be able to translate promotional rhetoric and gossip into very accurate predictors of what I would find if I did, indeed, visit. Visits, while helpful, were more useful for eliminating colleges from further consideration than for ensuring their inclusion.

Over time I became more sophisticated in my understanding of colleges and universities. From more than thirteen years of inquiry, three years on my own behalf and ten years of working on this book, I have come to trust my own judgment. I discovered that some of the schools that educators favored were long past their prime. Others, hardly visible on the national scene and known only to a small circle of faculty and currently enrolled students, were doing exceptional work. A purely statistical methodology of any kind would not reveal these differences, yet a trained observer can spot them immediately. I became a trained observer.

In the end, the colleges featured in this book were chosen by me. They were originally proposed by college presidents, deans, and directors of admission, but if they made the final cut it was a purely subjective decision by one person.

In ten years of tracking this issue I collected thousands of articles and press releases, and like anyone else, was subject to manipulation by particularly skilled (or unskilled) public affairs officers. That is, I might be swayed by their presentation of information. One bias that I do not claim: As much as possible, I did not reward or penalize a school because of interactions with any one administrator. As enticing as it might have been to remove a school because an administrator was rude (or include a school because an administrator was particularly solicitous), I avoided doing so.

Here are my biases as I know them. First of all, I am not sixteen anymore. I am a Baby Boomer, like it or not, and have a different point of view than young people today. I am idealistic to the point of being corny. My daughters and their friends think I am "quaint," and perhaps you will, too. I think education can liberate a soul, and that social meritocracy and individual success can be attained by means of education. (I have tons of data to support this point of view, but that is not the point. The point is that I have this point of view, rather strongly.) I believe in citizenship and responsibility, and have a "right is right" and "wrong is wrong" attitude. These are beliefs I grew up with and I couldn't shake them if I wanted to. That's a bias. In fact, that's nearly the definition of a bias.

Second, I don't think large universities are good places for young people as undergraduates. Again, I have very good reasons for this bias, and I've tried to present some of them in this text, but it is a bias just the same. Just because in large universities students are more likely to report being lonely and isolated, more likely to drop out, more likely to be taught by a graduate assistant than a professor, more likely to cheat, more likely to be unable to name even one friend from college ten years after graduation, less likely to go to graduate school, more likely to be unable to get needed classes, more likely to work more than ten hours a week, and more likely to go through all four or five years of their education without really being changed by it shouldn't create bias, but in my case it has.

Third, I've studied at two large universities, two small universities, and one college mentioned in this text. I'd like to think I've succeeded in being objective about them (if anything I've been overly critical), but nevertheless, my experience must color my report somehow.

Fourth, upon reconsideration of this text, I discovered that I tend to favor some of the lesser-known institutions. I think this provides a service, since we all know about Harvard, Princeton, Yale, and Stanford. This guide is not meant to be the primary guide in a counselor's office, nor the only guide a student should consider. One of my explicit goals is to provide information not readily available everywhere.

Fifth, I did not research college cost while preparing this book. I find the subject obtuse, labyrinthine, and illogical, but those are not the reasons I decided not to cover it. Any statement a college makes about its own cost is intentionally misleading. When the overwhelming majority of students at any institution receive complex and multilayered financial aid, and when even wealthy families are negotiating discounts, the sticker price is meaningless. I'd like readers of this book to look for a good college fit. Every student should apply to his or her dream college or university, and make the financial decision when you have the financial data, i.e., after you have aid offers. For more on this topic, read a book that specifically addresses the issue of college financing, such as Bruce G. Hammond's *Discounts and Deals at the Nation's 360 Best Colleges* (Golden Books Publishing Company).

IS IMPORTANT INFORMATION MISSING FROM THIS BOOK?

In spite of the fact that I wrote to almost a thousand schools a minimum of four times each, some of them didn't provide me with so much as a viewbook. One wrote back, "We as an institution have made the decision not to participate in surveys such as the one you are conducting." Nice. If you have information that belongs in this book, whether you are an alumnus, an alumna, a currently enrolled student, or a member of faculty or administration, I welcome it for the next edition. As you can see, there are a wide range of topics covered. If you know of a way that your favorite school stands out from the crowd, I'd be delighted to hear about it:

Donald Asher • Cool Colleges Project • c/o Ten Speed Press • P.O. Box 7123
Berkeley, CA 94707 • Fax: 775-557-2525 • donasher@ix.netcom.com

You should be careful about believing everything you read in college guides, even this one. Writers can be mistaken or, even worse, intentionally misled either by overzealous school officials or by bad data. For example, at a top liberal arts college students got together twice to intentionally mislead national magazines, both times filling out surveys as if they were taking drugs and binge drinking every single day. This was a big joke to them, but the school suffers from this lingering reputation. The irony is that it would be impossible for students to succeed academically at this school if they even remotely participated in these parties fabricated as a prank.

Finally, I know of a nationally ranked business school that hands out "suggested responses" for filling out quality surveys, and reminds students that the cash value of their graduate business education depends on the school's continued high rating in national rankings. Wow. Think about that.

Sixth, I did not research the issue of admissibility. That is, this is not really a book about how to get into college; it is a book about cool colleges one might want to get into. There are many other books on improving your chances of getting into a highly competitive program. I will tell you this, however: the best way to get into an elite school is to be the son or daughter of wealthy alumni.

One final limitation of this book is that it groups together schools in a way that is, ultimately, arbitrary. For example, it has a chapter called "Schools Where Scholarship Is Honored," and another one titled "The Great Books Programs." The decision to put St. John's College in the chapter on Great Books programs was, for me, an agonizing one. It very strongly belongs in the chapter "Schools Where Scholarship Is Honored." The school is extraordinary in its curriculum (Great Books), but even more extraordinary in its ethos (very scholarly). Tough call. Creating a taxonomy of schools, at least for the

Q. Why are some listings in this book in reverse alphabetical order?
A. I was touring a rather undistinguished institution in the middle of nowhere, whose name begins with an A. I was struck by the number of international students and the number of students from distant states. When I asked the dean why the school had such draw, she said, "We think it's our name. Students start making a list, and we're at the top of it." Since I thought this was a singularly poor reason to choose a college, I resolved to mix up the organization of my listings. I'd do them in random order, but people do want to look quickly and see if one they know of by name is on any given list. Thus, some are in alphabetical order, and some are in reverse alphabetical order.

Q. Why is there no standardized methodology in this book?
A. Finding the right college should be a process of discovery. One profile or even one item of information should be the trigger for you to investigate further and find your dream school. If the descriptions of schools in this book were all alike, even the most avid and serious student's eyes would glaze over shortly. I wrote thousands of letters to research this book, read thousands of letters and e-mails, read hundreds of viewbooks, visited several hundred schools, interviewed thousands of currently enrolled students, and researched comparative data until I was seeing spreadsheets and tables in my sleep. Then I thought about what stood out from the background noise. Whether one college has five thousand more books in its library than another is irrelevant. Physical books are themselves increasingly irrelevant. The culture or feel of a campus cannot be reduced to a ranking or a unilinear measure of any kind. The vitality and creativity of a student body is not visible in mean incoming SAT scores. Whether a professor will help *you* learn cannot be revealed by the number and prestige of his or her almae matres. I invite you to see through the chaos of this book to see that there *is* a methodology, and to see what that methodology suggests to you. Where will you be happy? Where will you learn the most? What is important to you? How can you find out more?

purposes of organizing this book, was not a pleasant task. Many outstanding and unique schools are lumped into groups. How do you create a taxonomy of unique items anyway? They defy organization.

Then, there was something that I came to call "The problem of Earlham." Earlham is a fantastic college in Richmond, Indiana. I have visited this school, and I know that it is a truly wonderful institution. The students are enthused and engaged. The faculty is smart and caring. The school as a whole has a coherent philosophy of education and service. It has an attractive campus and a solid physical plant. And yet it was hard to find the right spot for it in this book. Do I describe it by itself as the twenty-third example of a liberal arts college? You, dear reader, would go glassy-eyed with that approach, and yet it seemed quite unfair to simply list it as an iteration of a category.

So as you read this book, please be aware of its limitations. Its organization is imperfect, and a little like organizing a car lot by putting all the blue cars and trucks in one corner, and all the red cars and trucks in another. If you're interested in four-wheel drives, you're going to have look all over the lot.

HOW TO USE THIS BOOK

There are three ways to use this book:

Method Number One: I call this the smorgasbord approach—just open it up anywhere and read any amount you want. Fool around with it; don't work at it. To look for interesting items, try the index and the table of contents. If you're not applying to college right away, the best thing you can do with this book is put it in your bathroom and glance through it when the opportunity presents itself. If your parents have their own bathroom, get them their own copy.

Method Number Two: If you are applying to school soon and want to make sure you don't make an egregious, life-ruining mistake by missing the chance to apply to a college you'd really love but have never heard of, then use the table of contents to methodically investigate schools in the chapters that most interest you. Read about all the schools in those chapters that match your personality and approach to education.

Method Number Three: Look up the schools you're interested in, and pay particular attention to the schools listed in the "Cross Apps" feature. This section will lead you from schools you already know a little about to similar schools that you don't know much about, but may like better. This is like surfing the Web—and all you need is one school you're interested in to get started.

SOME FINAL, *VERY* IMPORTANT DISCLAIMERS

This book purports to provide information on every accredited institution in the United States and Canada. You need to know that we have made every effort to identify every accredited institution at the time this book went to press, but it is entirely possible that an institution may have become accredited after this book went to press, or we may have missed an accredited institution through error on our part or on the part of the accrediting authorities, or there may be an accrediting authority that is unknown to us but carries weight for a certain type of institution. Also, we may have listed an institution as accredited when it is not, through error on our part or on the part of accrediting authorities. We made the decision not to mention those institutions that are on warning from their accrediting authorities, as it is very unusual for an institution to be delisted, and many infractions are minor and/or of an administrative sort.

We would be remiss if we did not state forcefully that the institutions listed herein are of vastly differing missions and quality. Just because an institution is described in this book does not mean that it will provide the quality and type of education that you seek. Sometimes students will focus on some aspects of a college that are very attractive, and fail to notice other aspects of that same college that make it a poor match.

Finally, although it is true that there is sometimes only one college in the world that seems to be a perfect match for a student, particularly an unusual student, it is not good strategy to apply to only one college, no matter how strongly you feel about a school you may discover in these pages. We recommend that you make your college choices in close collaboration with your parents, teachers, college counselors, and other advisors, and that you apply to several colleges.

For every accredited college and university in the U.S. and Canada go to www.donaldasher.com/colleges

Education is what survives when what has been learned has been forgotten.

—B. F. Skinner

Chapter One

Three PREP COLLEGES

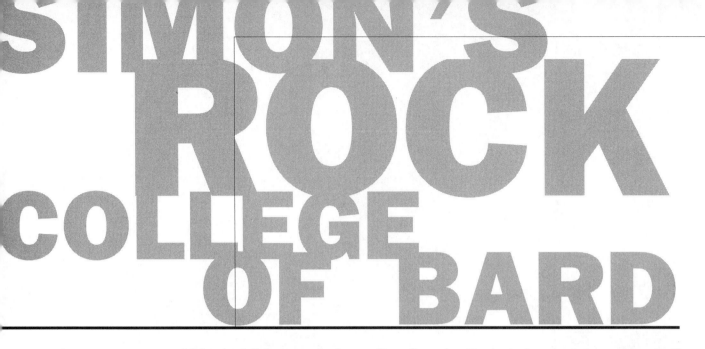

SIMON'S ROCK COLLEGE OF BARD

early entry program • **no high school diploma required** • *quality college education beginning at age 16, 17, or even 15, if you have what it takes* • **350 students: 60% women, 40% men** • *beautiful environs* • **a unique chance to get on with it**

Simon's Rock is one of the few schools in the nation to seek out students who have *not* finished a high school curriculum. It offers an early start at college for those students who are ready for college before most colleges are ready for them. Strictly speaking, Simon's Rock is not just a prep college, as many students do complete all four years there. Deep Springs is a two-year school like no other. When you think about two-year programs, you're probably not thinking about Simon's Rock and Deep Springs. These two schools are listed first in this book just to give you an idea of some of the different approaches to higher education that are out there once you think beyond the nearest large state university. The third school, Landmark College, is a terrific school with a highly trained staff that are sensitive to the needs of students with learning challenges such as dyslexia and AD/HD. The questions under consideration in this chapter will be: Should you go to a large or a small institution? What about scholarship scams? Are there really totally free schools out there?

**An old pond
A frog leaping in
The sound of water**

—Matsuo Basho

SIMON'S ROCK COLLEGE OF BARD

Some people are too bright for high school. Is this you? Do you find the level of academic endeavor at your high school slightly beneath sea level?

Are you drowning intellectually while you wait, wait, wait for the day when you can escape and join a real college?

Well, you are not alone. All over North America smart young people are bored out of their minds by high schools that de-emphasize academics and emphasize sports and a warped view of adolescent social life.

Here's the really important question: Are you ready for college now? There are four main parts to this question, really:

- Do you have the intellectual capacity to perform at the college level today? Are you ready to write college papers and do college-level scientific work and tackle college-level mathematics? This is a question of intellect.
- Are you academically prepared? That is, do you know enough to benefit from college now? This is a question of accumulated knowledge.
- Are you mature enough to perform on your own? Are you able to get out of bed in the morning, manage your own time, and meet your commitments?
- Have you gotten all your high school has to offer you? Not perhaps all your high school has to offer, but all your high school has to offer *you*?

If you can answer an unequivocal yes to each of these four questions, you should consider the early entry program at Simon's Rock College of Bard in Great Barrington, Massachusetts.

Simon's Rock admits students of demonstrated promise straight out of high school. Except for this one fact, it is in most other senses just an innovative New England liberal arts college. It has a carefully designed curriculum emphasizing mastery of critical thinking skills, followed by increasing specialization and the design and execution of a major research project before graduation with a bachelor's degree. You can start a classic liberal arts education here, then transfer after two years to another school—or stay and complete your bachelor's degree.

At the end of the sophomore year, students complete what the school calls the Lower College program, and are awarded an associate of arts degree. At this point,

> **❝ It's a really great school for kids who are too bright to do well in high school. ❞**
>
> —*Independent college counselor*

I recently went to my high school reunion. Everybody who was really cool in high school was now selling vacuum cleaners door to door while everybody who had been down with the out crowd was a scientist or a college professor or a dot-com millionaire. It was almost a biblical reversal of fortune. Weird.

two-thirds of Simon's Rock students opt to complete their studies at another college or university. This was the way the college was originally designed to work, as a sort of early entry prep college for young scholars who were bound for other schools after completing Lower College. Simon's Rock students find admission to such colleges and universities as these:

American University, Washington, DC

American University in Paris, France

Bard College, Annandale-on-Hudson, New York

Barnard College, New York, New York

Bates College, Lewiston, Maine

Berklee College of Music, Boston, Massachusetts

Boston University, Boston, Massachusetts

Brandeis University, Waltham, Massachusetts

Brown University, Providence, Rhode Island

Bryn Mawr College, Bryn Mawr, Pennsylvania

Carleton College, Northfield, Minnesota

Carnegie Mellon University, Pittsburgh, Pennsylvania

Case Western Reserve University, Cleveland, Ohio

Claremont McKenna College, Claremont, California

Clark University, Worcester, Massachusetts

Colgate University, Hamilton, New York

Colorado College, Colorado Springs, Colorado

Columbia University, New York, New York

Cornell University, Ithaca, New York

Dartmouth College, Hanover, New Hampshire

Drew University, Madison, New Jersey

Duke University, Durham, North Carolina

Emory University, Atlanta, Georgia

Eugene Lang College of the New School for Social Research, New York, New York

Evergreen State College, Olympia, Washington

Fisk University, Nashville, Tennesee

George Washington University, Washington, DC

Goucher College, Baltimore, Maryland

Hampshire College, Amherst, Massachusetts

Harvard University, Cambridge, Massachusetts

Hood College, Frederick, Maryland

Howard University, Washington, DC

Hunter College, New York, New York

Johns Hopkins University, Baltimore, Maryland

Knox College, Galesburg, Illinois

Lehigh University, Bethlehem, Pennsylvania

Lewis & Clark University, Portland, Oregon

Macalester College, St. Paul, Minnesota

Massachusetts Institute of Technology (MIT), Cambridge, Massachusetts

Michigan Technological University, Houghton, Michigan

Mills College, Oakland, California

Morehouse College, Atlanta, Georgia

Mount Holyoke College, South Hadley, Massachusetts

New York University, New York, New York

Oberlin College, Oberlin, Ohio

Parsons School of Design, New York, New York

Pitzer College, Claremont, California

Pomona College, Claremont, California

Reed College, Portland, Oregon

Rensselaer Polytechnic Institute, Troy, New York

Rice University, Houston, Texas

Royal Holloway College of the University of London, England

Rutgers University, New Brunswick, New Jersey

San Francisco Art Institute, San Francisco, California

Sarah Lawrence College, Bronxville, New York

Savannah College of Art and Design, Savannah, Georgia

School of Oriental and African Studies of the University of London, England

Skidmore College, Saratoga Springs, New York

Smith College, Northampton, Massachusetts

Stanford University, Stanford, California

State University of New York, Albany, New York

State University of New York, Binghampton, New York

"No one has ever written to me to say he or she was sorry to have earned a college degree."

—Dear Abby

State University of New York, Buffalo, New York

State University of New York, Purchase, New York

State University of New York, Stony Brook, New York

Stevens Institute of Technology, Hoboken, New Jersey

Swarthmore College, Swarthmore, Pennsylvania

Syracuse University, Syracuse, New York

Trinity College, Dublin, Ireland

Tufts University, Medford, Massachusetts

University of Arizona, Tucson, Arizona

University of California, Davis, California

University of California, Irvine, California

University of California, Los Angeles, California

University of California, Santa Cruz, California

University of California, San Diego, California

University of Chicago, Chicago, Illinois

University of Colorado, Boulder, Colorado

University of Illinois, Urbana-Champaign, Illinois

University of Maryland, College Park, Maryland

University of Massachusetts, Amherst, Massachusetts

University of Michigan, Ann Arbor, Michigan

University of Minnesota, Twin Cities, Minneapolis, Minnesota

University of North Carolina, Chapel Hill, North Carolina

University of Pennsylvania, Philadelphia, Pennsylvania

University of Rochester, Rochester, New York

University of Utah, Salt Lake City, Utah

SIMON'S ROCK AND BARD

Is Simon's Rock part of Bard, or what? You'd think this would be a simple question to have answered, but it is not. According to the public affairs office of Simon's Rock College of Bard, "Simon's Rock is an independent college with its own board of directors, but it has the same president as Bard, Leon Botstein. Bard is the parent college, but Bard does not 'own' Simon's Rock." Whatever that means. You figure it out. Leon Botstein is one of the most interesting people in higher education today. See the sidebar on his book, which makes a case for the abolition of high school as we know it.

University of Washington, Seattle, Washington

Vanderbilt University, Nashville, Tennesee

Vassar College, Poughkeepsie, New York

Washington University in St. Louis, St. Louis, Missouri

Wellesley College, Wellesley, Massachusetts

Wesleyan University, Middletown, Connecticut

Williams College, Williamstown, Massachusetts

Yale University, New Haven, Connecticut

> ❝❝ **We pick up a fair number of home-schooled students. They tend to do well here.** ❞❞
>
> —*Simon's Rock administrator*

C o O l   B o O k   A l E r T !

Jefferson's Children: Education and the Promise of American Culture by Leon Botstein (Doubleday)

Eighteenth-century optimism has been lost in a national morass of pessimism, Botstein contends. Weighing an assemblage of evidence, he charges that we no longer believe we can educate our children to create a better world. Leon Botstein was the youngest person to assume such a post when he became president of Bard College. Now the longest-serving college president *and* director of the American Symphony Orchestra, he makes a bold indictment of present practices in public education. "The American high school is obsolete," he declares, characterizing schools as "breeding grounds for violence, for drug and alcohol abuse, vulgarity, and a totally thoughtless, rampant expression of sexuality," and where the "best are influenced by the weakest." Yet, Botstein portrays public education as doing a better job than political rhetoric would have us believe, despite the deleterious effects of bureaucratic regulations, defensive teachers' unions, and parents more concerned with school prayer than with education. He offers concrete ideas, some of them certain to raise hackles, for creating renewed institutions of learning.

Also check out Stanley Aronowitz's *The Knowledge Factory: Dismantling the Corporate University and Creating True Higher Learning* (Beacon Press), in which the author calls modern universities "glorified employment agencies." If you want even more fun books along this line, read Martin Anderson's *Imposters in the Temple* (Hoover Institution Press), Charles Sykes's *ProfScam: Professors and the Demise of Higher Education* (St. Martin's Press), and Richard Huber's *How Professors Play the Cat Guarding the Cream* (George Mason University Press).

One-third of students decide to complete the bachelor's degree at Simon's Rock by completing the Upper School. The college emphasizes interdisciplinary study and independent study, with strengths in some areas, such as environmental studies and most of the liberal arts, and weaknesses in others. If a student is interested in an area the college feels it cannot support, the student is encouraged to transfer to complete her or his undergraduate program at a more appropriate institution. Students can cross-register with nearby Bard College, and many do. A central part of the Upper School degree program is a year-long independent study leading to the writing of an undergraduate thesis. Expectations are high, and success in this degree program is excellent preparation for graduate study.

Recent thesis projects include:

An Investigation of the Possible Synergistic Mutagenic Effect Created In Vitro by Potassium Chromate and Meta-Stable Barium

My Room: An Exploration of Non-Traditional Performance Art

Whipworms and Water Filters: An Investigation of Intestinal Parasites in Children Living in a Temporary Home in Tegucigalpa, Honduras

Harlem Rising: The Contributions of African-American Music to American Culture during the Harlem Renaissance

Art or Artifact? Historicizing Ancient Egyptian Archaeology

Once Upon a Thesis: An Original Fairy Tale and Dance Narrative

Mud and Myrabolam: An Exploration of Pattern, Fabric, and the Woodblock Printing Traditions of Jaipur, India

The Legacy of French Colonization in Côte d'Ivoire

The Why of Y: An Analysis of Morphological Variation in the Unisexual-Bisexual Nactuspelagicus *Complex (Reptilia: Gekkonidae)*

DOWNSIDE: Many parents are shocked to have their children interested in an early entry program. The student may feel that the program is perfect and a salvation, but the parents may be financially and emotionally unprepared for the student to leave home for college. Can your family afford a school like Simon's Rock? The majority of students at Simon's Rock are on financial aid, and the college grants twenty full-ride merit scholarships every year in national open competition. For more information, contact the college. In short: It may be a lobbying job to convince your parents that you

At first I was relieved. There were a lot of strange people like me. It was the first time I'd ever really felt at home. After a while I realized I wasn't strange at all.

—*Simon's Rock alumna*

should take an early-entry option. On the other hand, your parents may jump at the chance to see you happy and challenged in school.

Also, it is important to understand that Simon's Rock is a college, not some kind of boarding school on steroids. Students thrive here who are able to manage their time well, who welcome intellectual challenge, and who are mature and independent. Many young people, fifteen to eighteen years old, overestimate their maturity and self-motivation. Does your mother wake you up? Drive you to school? Nag you about the due dates on assignments? Wash your clothes? Your mother's probably not going to be around, so how would you really do without this type of support?

Here's what one administrator told me: "The student who thrives here is very self-directed, has an inner set of values, and is somewhat sure of himself or herself." Let's face it, this is not the typical sixteen-year-old, no matter how smart he or she is.

CROSS APPS: If you're interested in early entry programs, you should know that before the American high school was invented it was the norm for students to enter college at fifteen or sixteen years of age. For years, Simon's Rock was a lone voice in this wilderness, championing the early-entry option. Now, more programs are coming on line. Some states, such as my home state, allow early entry under special circumstances, but it's not always that great an advantage to be just thrown into the regular university system. Check out the early-entry program for women at Mary Baldwin College in Staunton, Virginia, the summer program at Johns Hopkins University's

> **&&Everyone is born a genius.&&**
>
> —*R. Buckminster Fuller*

ARE YOU GIFTED?

Are you a brilliant young person going brain dead in a regular school but not feeling old enough to enter a regular college? There are many opportunities for you in talented and gifted programs. One new, truly amazing program is affiliated with the University of Nevada-Reno and the Washoe County Public Schools. The Davidson Academy was launched in 2006 and funded by Jan and Bob Davidson, software entrepreneurs. This is a free boarding school for students who score above the ninety-ninth percentile on intelligence tests. You can download testing and application information from www.DavidsonAcademy.UNR.edu, or write to Davidson Academy of Nevada, 9665 Gateway Drive, Suite B, Reno, Nevada, 89521.

To hook up with a huge underground movement toward better schooling for talented and gifted youth, go to Hoagies' Gifted Education Web Page at www.hoagiesgifted.org and discover you are not alone.

And, while you're at it, consider whether you want to live with the "gifted" label at all. Read *Drama of the Gifted Child* by Alice Miller (Basic Books) for a discussion on the costs of being identified as hyper-intelligent or being pushed to excel at an early age.

THE EAST COAST?

Dr. Orland Maxfield, professor emeritus of geography at the University of Arkansas, Fayetteville, used to give a lecture every year on the wonderful attributes of "The Coast of Vermont." Most years he got all the way through the lecture without protest. Students dutifully took notes on what they thought would be on the test.

10 LARGEST COLLEGES/UNIVERSITIES

University of Phoenix-Online — 115,794
Everywhere

Arizona State University, Tempe Campus — 49,171
Tempe, Arizona

Miami Dade College — 57,026
Miami, Florida

University of Florida — 47,993
Gainesville, Florida

Ohio State University, Main Campus — 50,995
Columbus, Ohio

Michigan State University — 44,836
East Lansing, Michigan

University of Minnesota, Twin Cities — 50,954
Minneapolis, Minnesota

Texas A&M University — 44,435
College Station, Texas

University of Texas, Austin — 50,377
Austin, Texas

University of Central Florida — 42,465
Orlando, Florida

(Source: MSN Encarta)

12 SMALLER COLLEGES/UNIVERSITIES

Deep Springs — 26
Deep Springs, California

Cincinnati College of Mortuary Science — 125
Cincinnati, Ohio

Webb Institute — 72
Glen Cove, New York

American Indian College of the Assemblies of God — 64
Phoenix, Arizona

The Curtis Institute of Music — 160
Philadelphia, Pennsylvania

College of the Atlantic — 262
Bar Harbor, Maine

Thomas More College of Liberal Arts — 95
Merrimack, New Hampshire

San Francisco Conservatory of Music — 287
San Francisco, California

Shimer College — 100
Chicago, Illinois

Thomas Aquinas College — 332
Santa Paula, California

West Suburban College of Nursing — 105
Oak Park, Illinois

Manhattan Christian College — 336
Manhattan, Kansas

(Source: original research)

❝ I went to Texas A&M and majored in psychology. I didn't have a single class in my major with fewer than 200 students in it. ❞
—*Aggie alumna*

Center for Talented Youth, The University of North Texas-Denton's Texas Academy of Mathematics and Science, and the University of Washington-Seattle's Students in Transition School. These are outstanding programs designed for this type of student. See also the National Research Center on the Gifted and Talented at www.gifted.uconn.edu and the National Association for Gifted Children at 202-785-4268 or www.nagc.org.

If you're interested in the idea of doing an undergraduate research project and/or thesis, be sure to read the section on Reed College, beginning on p. 68, and New College of Florida, beginning on p. 136.

Simon's Rock is particularly strong in environmental studies. If this is of interest to you, see also Evergreen State College in Olympia, Washington; University of California, Santa Cruz; Prescott College in Prescott, Arizona; Green Mountain College in Poultney, Vermont; and College of the Atlantic in Bar Harbor, Maine, among many others.

If you're interested in a school that can see you're smart in spite of some iffy grades, also check out St. John's College in Annapolis, Maryland, and Santa Fe, New Mexico, and to some extent, Reed College in Portland, Oregon. All of these schools will look beyond your overall GPA, but don't overinterpret this as a license to quit worrying about your GPA. They will be looking for certain grade patterns that might be misleading in aggregate. For example, they may look for many very high grades offset by a few very low grades, with no grades in the middle (a smart nonconformist), or all As in some years and mediocre grades in other years (a smart student who gives up). No school is going to agree with

> **The greatest shortcoming, I believe, of most attempts at liberal education today, with their individualized, unfocused, scattered curricula, and ill-defined purpose, is their failure to enhance the students' understanding of their status as free citizens of a free society and the responsibilities it entails.**
>
> —*Donald Kagan, (Chronicle of Higher Education)*

IN TODAY'S LESSON, CLASS, WE EXPLORE THE INCREASING ISOLATION OF THE INDIVIDUAL IN SOCIETY.

you that your collection of Bs and Cs really should be counted as As, no matter what your rationale. Remember, all schools are looking for concrete reasons to admit you, real evidence you can perform, rather than mere claims of such ability. You can't be all potential and no actualization. By seventeen years of age, you should have done something that can serve as evidence of your abilities.

If you're interested in Simon's Rock's small size, see Marlboro College, p. 161; New College of Florida, p. 136; College of the Atlantic in Bar Harbor, Maine, p. 130; or Deep Springs, p. 25, which is truly small with only twenty-six students, all male. Deep Springs is also a two-year prep program leading to entry to the most elite colleges and universities in the nation. (See the next page for a complete description of Deep Springs.)

Simon's Rock College of Bard

84 Alford Road

Great Barrington, MA 01230

413-528-0771

www.simons-rock.edu

For every accredited college and university in the U.S. and Canada go to www.donaldasher.com/colleges

COLLEGE PLANNING DIFFERS BY FAMILY INCOME

Lower-income families and upper-income families have entirely different concerns when it comes to college planning and college counseling. Lower-income families want to know how to pay for college, and if they can pay for college at all. That is their number one concern, eclipsing all others. Upper-income families want to know how to improve their students' chances of getting into the most competitive colleges. They want to know what techniques or tips or angles will give their students the biggest "boost" over equally prepared competitors. This results in too-high placement of upper income students, relative to their abilities, and too low placement of lower income students, relative to their abilities. All too seldom, at either end of the scale, is the number one concern to find a good match between a student's preparation and interests and a college or university's greatest institutional strengths. Whether you are wealthy or not, brilliant or not, your first concern should be to find a college or university where you will be truly happy and thrive.

DEEP SPRINGS COLLEGE

26 students · *all male* · on a working ranch · *students run everything* · unbelievably strong two-year program ·
prep here, then finish at almost any top college or university · campus is 80 square *miles* · *oh, and it's free*

Many colleges and universities claim to be "unique" or "distinctive," but Deep Springs is a college like no other. This tiny men's college is built upon three pillars: scholarship, self-governance, and labor. The founder, a visionary named L. L. Nunn, started the college in 1917 as an educational experiment, an "idealistic vision of what an education should be." With a student body limited to twenty-six young men, the college is a bastion of brilliant eccentricity in the "rising tide of mediocrity" that is higher education in this country today.

Deep Springs's isolation is quite intentional. Located between Death Valley and Yosemite National Park, the college is precisely in the middle of nowhere. It is a place so remote that the mail gets delivered to a post office in another state. The campus is in fact an eighty-square-mile cattle ranch and organic alfalfa farm. L. L. Nunn thought that cities were a distraction to the academic studies of young men, and morally corrupting, so he sought a place where such distractions would be at a minimum.

The ranch itself is quite a distraction, however, as the students run it—fish, tarp, and spindle. They provide the labor, from sowing to reaping, and are charged to wring

> **Hey, we've got the Internet. We're global.**
>
> —*Deep Springs student*

The school has a perennial debate about whether to go coed. In fact, the school has a perennial debate about everything, but this is one of the more serious issues that keeps coming up.

a profit out of the "living endowment" of the ranch. The labor is one cornerstone to the educational experience that is Deep Springs. Students need to keep up with their chores while studying one of the most demanding curricula available anywhere (more on that in a moment). The ranch work is not for the overly squeamish, as it includes the grunt work of neutering steers and slaughtering stock, as well as entering production figures on a computerized spreadsheet. Nevertheless, the student body usually includes some vegetarians, who somehow find a way to do their part.

Students run Deep Springs. Like labor, self-governance is a cornerstone of the college. The students are completely responsible for the conduct of their own numbers as well as for the governance of the college and the ranch. I interviewed a first-year student who was a member of the board of trustees, a sworn fiduciary of the college, a member of the curriculum committee, a member of a faculty search committee, and a member of the committee planning the next year's academic calendar. (Remember, this is a student, who presumably finds time to study as well.) Nunn wanted his college to build citizenship

GET THE NAME RIGHT!

When you're looking for a college or university that you know only a little about, be careful to get the name right! Several people have told me that upon hearing for the first time that "Penn" was an Ivy League school, they thought of Pennsylvania State University, especially if they heard this in casual conversation. Pennsylvania State University-University Park is in State College, Pennsylvania, and "Penn" is the University of Pennsylvania in Philadelphia. Very different.

Also, many state universities sound alike. There are twelve institutions calling themselves "Rutgers." Check it out. And Washington University in St. Louis changed its name from Washington University to "Washington University in St. Louis" in 1976 to keep this strong national university from being confused with the eighteen other schools in the country with "Washington" as part of their name.

There's a Saint Francis College in Loretto, Pennsylvania, and another one in Fort Wayne, Indiana, as well as a St. Francis College in Brooklyn Heights, New York. Then there's St. John's College in Annapolis, Maryland, and her sister campus in Santa Fe, New Mexico, and a totally different institution by the exact same name in Winnipeg, Manitoba, and the St. John's University in Jamaica, New York, and the Saint John's University in Collegeville, Minnesota, a St. John's Seminary College in Camarillo, California, and another one in Brighton, Massachusetts, not to be confused with St. John Vianney College Seminary, in Miami, Florida, to say nothing of the St. John Fisher College in Rochester, New York.

There's a great little liberal arts college called Wheaton in Norton, Massachusetts, and a great little liberal arts college called Wheaton in Wheaton, Illinois. One is a Christian college, and one is famous for its career development program (see p. 165). I suppose it matters whether you want most to advance in this life or the next, but it would pay to get it right either way.

and leadership, and viewed Deep Springs as an incubator for mastering those qualities.

Finally, Deep Springs academics are second to none. The school sets the highest standards for students and faculty. Classes are small, ranging from one student to maybe twenty. (Obviously the largest possible class, under any circumstances, is twenty-six.) The workload is heavy, and there is certainly no way to fake it or coast in an environment where everybody knows everything about everybody's business. The school accepts approximately one applicant out of twenty, making it, arguably, the most exclusive and competitive college in the nation.

The curriculum changes annually, depending on the interest of the students and the available faculty. "We do not have a Great Books program," says one student. "We pretty much follow the Western canon, but it is not a Great Books program per se. We try to keep a balance of social sciences, humanities, French literary theory. Right now, for example, we have a class in Marcel Proust's *In Remembrance of Things Past,* a class on nationalism in the twentieth century from an anthropological perspective, and classes on postmodernism and literary theory, James Baldwin, geology, sustainable agriculture, natural moral philosophy (taught by a professor from Oxford who is coming here just to teach that class), ancient Greek language, patristic theology, ecology, and history of higher education, taught by our college president, Jack Newell." The classes move along at a blazing speed, with a year made up of six seven-week terms. The only required course is public speaking, which every student takes every term.

There is no tenure at Deep Springs, and the faculty rotate in from places like Stanford and Swarthmore for periods from one to five years. Even the presidency tends to rotate. Half the student body changes every year. A running joke on campus is that the longest-lasting residents on campus are the dogs. The real winner is a cat, rumored to be twenty years old, older than many of the students.

Who goes to Deep Springs? Very smart, very motivated male students who want to have a very different college experience. Those who are admitted need no outdoor experience at all, but they must want to participate in the working agrarian community that is Deep Springs. Last year's incoming class included one sixteen-year-old, one student who worked for three years after high school before even applying to college, and

> **Nunn was a self-made man in the storybook way, a poor man who worked hard and became a multi-millionaire industrialist. He observed in the late 1800s that the country was being run by an old boys' club, and decided that those who would become members of that club needed some moral training. The original student body were the sons of wealthy industrialists, sent here to keep them from becoming spoiled.**
>
> —*Deep Springs student*

Deep Springs is bigger than the City and County of San Francisco, yet it exists to serve just twenty-six students. Institutional continuity is an issue. But somehow the school has stayed remarkably consistent over the last eighty years.

a couple of transfers, so out of an incoming class of thirteen, roughly one-third were not traditional eighteen-year-old high school graduates. However, the average combined SAT is "about 1500" according to the dean of academic affairs, making this an elite student body indeed.

Deep Springs is free. Tuition, room, and board are absolutely free. A student's only expenses are books, travel, and a laptop if he wants one.

L. L. Nunn wanted to create a place with democratic self-governance to develop respect for democracy and justice, manual labor to develop character, and strong academics to sharpen the mind and reasoning capabilities. If this appeals to you, apply.

DOWNSIDE: This is an intense college choice. Any man who could get in here could probably go anywhere else, so this is obviously a place students choose, rather than just accept. The admissions process is grueling, including a visit where you will have to try to be yourself while interacting with your future peers, who are in fact your admissions committee, too. If you go to Deep Springs, you'll never have a simple answer to the question, "Where'd you go to college?" If you've been coasting through high school to make straight As, that won't work here. And finally, they are dead serious about the work aspect. Students work like ranch hands at Deep Springs College—because they are.

MORE UPSIDE: Students who complete the two-year degree program at Deep Springs are generally able to write their own tickets to any top college. In the world.

CROSS APPS: Deep Springs does not have any meaningful cross apps. It is simply not like any other school.

Deep Springs College
Off California Highway 168
Deep Springs, California
c/o HC72 Box 45001
Dyer, NV 89010
760-872-2000
www.deepsprings.edu

Deep Springs may have the best food in higher education. They grow their own organic vegetables, slaughter their own beef and pork, and make their own cheeses. Not exactly cafeteria food.

LANDMARK COLLEGE

for students with dyslexia, AD/HD, and other learning challenges • **fully accredited** • *rigorous curriculum* • **not dumb-ed down** • *completely individualized learning programs* • **associate's degree** • *many go on to four-year colleges* • **5 to 1 faculty-student ratio!**

Landmark College is a lifesaver for students who suffer with learning disabilities or those with a strong feeling of being out of sync with factory schooling in America. Once a student's learning differences are diagnosed and treated or accommodated, many find education attractive for the first time in their lives.

The faculty at Landmark understands learning differences, and the Landmark library has one of the largest collections of works on this subject available in the United States.

The academic curriculum—and the individualized, holistic accommodation, coaching, and training that each student receives—is designed to prepare students for transfer to four-year colleges with the skills, discipline, and self-understanding necessary for continued success.

Landmark also has a bridge program to help high schoolers with learning differences prepare for entry into other colleges and universities.

Landmark College
River Road South
Putney, VT 05346
802-387-6718
www.landmark.edu

> **Landmark wasn't easy, but it changed my life. And it was great just to have friends who understood me.**
>
> —*Landmark alumna*

ON CREDIT

You no doubt have a credit card. You may have several. There is no finer thing you could do for your long-term welfare than to destroy those cards immediately. College is always financially difficult. No matter how much you've saved or how much your family supports you, you will not have enough money. Worse than that, you may be shoulder to shoulder in school with others who *do* have seemingly unlimited access to cash. The temptations will be constant. A consumer item here, a car repair there, a "celebratory" dinner for some triumph, a dollar here and a fiver there, and just like in Congress, pretty soon you're talking about real money. Get a debit card if you like the convenience or, even better, get a credit card with your name on it that really belongs to a parent. Then, if you have an emergency, you've got a card, but you're not likely to abuse the privilege, as your parents will get that bill every month and notice how many "emergencies" you were having.

First, don't dream for even one moment that your parents will bail you out if you run up your cards. They're going to be spending a fortune on your college education, and your credit line with them is very likely to dry up before you graduate. Your parents' financial advisors are busy telling them *not* to pay off your credit cards, so you can "learn from" your mistakes.

Second, you will have real trouble after you graduate trying to rent an apartment and buy a car if your credit is wrecked. You may land a great job and be in a really embarrassing bind because you don't have adult access to credit. No apartment, no car, no business clothes, and you'll look like a jerk.

Third, you will have trouble getting financial aid for graduate school if you accumulate credit card debt. Student debt, even tons of it, is factored in to graduate school financial aid, but consumer debt never is, even if you only bought books with those credit cards.

Fourth, credit card companies make the most money from the least creditworthy customers, and that means you. You'll face high interest rates and punitive late fees, and that's just if you have a reputable card provider. The unscrupulous ones have devised more ways than you can imagine to squeeze money out of people who get in over their heads. Why enrich them?

These credit card companies should be banned from campus. If a drug dealer came and set up tables and gave away free T-shirts, the whole academic community would be up in arms. But credit card companies do it every day with impunity, offering free sign-ups and fancy enticements reminiscent of the drug dealer's clichéd come-on, "Here, try one of *mine*. No charge the first couple of times." They're extending thousands of dollars of credit to people *most of whom don't even have a job*.

They know that no matter how high the interest rate and how many fees they pile onto your account, sooner or later you're going to need new credit bad enough to clean up your old account. And that's how they get paid. Oh, and by the way, even after you pay them off, you still have bad credit on your record. That means more years of higher interest rates.

Your goal: Don't get involved with them at all. Get a debit card, or get a card in your name on your parent's account. If you do get your own account, pay it off every month and *always* pay off 100 percent of your credit card debt before the first day of school every year. If you fail, burn the card and live without it. Don't let it get any worse.

Warning signs of credit problems

Using credit cards to get cash advances.

Using credit cards to pay rent.

Using credit cards to buy groceries.

Using credit cards to pay off other credit cards.

Getting dinged with late fees.

Failing to pay off your outstanding balance every month.

Making only the minimum payment every month.

Borrowing money from others to make credit card payments.

Bumming money from your parents to pay off credit card bills.

Running out of money before you run out of month.

Lying about your debt.

If you run up $2,000 and then stop, you could make the minimum payment every single month for the rest of your life and, if you were never late once, *every year you would owe more than the last.* Wow, is that dumb.

Don't even get started.

For more on this, get the Real Credit Cost Reminder Kit from Access Group, Inc., www.accessgroup.org, 800-282-1550.

AN UNUSUAL APPLICATION ESSAY

3.A. Essay.

IN ORDER FOR THE ADMISSIONS STAFF OF OUR COLLEGE TO GET TO KNOW YOU, THE APPLICANT, BETTER, WE ASK THAT YOU ANSWER THE FOLLOWING QUESTION: ARE THERE ANY SIGNIFICANT EXPERIENCES YOU HAVE HAD, OR ACCOMPLISHMENTS YOU HAVE REALIZED, THAT HAVE HELPED DEFINE YOU AS A PERSON?

I am a dynamic figure, often seen scaling walls and crushing ice. I have been known to remodel train stations on my lunch breaks, making them more efficient in the area of heat retention. I translate ethnic slurs for Cuban refugees, I write award-winning operas, I manage time efficiently.

Occasionally, I tread water for three days in a row.

I woo women with my sensuous and godlike trombone playing, I can pilot bicycles up severe inclines with unflagging speed, and I cook Thirty-Minute Brownies in twenty minutes. I am an expert in stucco, a veteran in love, and an outlaw in Peru.

Using only a hoe and a large glass of water, I once single-handedly defended a small village in the Amazon Basin from a horde of ferocious army ants.

I play bluegrass cello, I was scouted by the Mets, I am the subject of numerous documentaries. When I'm bored, I build large suspension bridges in my yard. I enjoy urban hang gliding. On Wednesdays, after school, I repair electrical appliances free of charge.

I am an abstract artist, a concrete analyst, and a ruthless bookie. Critics worldwide swoon over my original line of corduroy evening wear. I don't perspire. I am a private citizen, yet I receive fan mail. I have been caller number nine and have won the weekend passes. Last summer I toured New Jersey with a traveling centrifugal-force demonstration. I bat .400.

My deft floral arrangements have earned me fame in international botany circles. Children trust me.

I can hurl tennis rackets at small moving objects with deadly accuracy. I once read Paradise Lost, Moby Dick, and David Copperfield in one day and still had time to refurbish an entire dining room that evening. I know the exact location of every food item in the supermarket. I have performed several covert operations for the CIA. I sleep once a week; when I do sleep, I sleep in a chair. While on vacation in Canada, I successfully negotiated with a group of terrorists who had seized a small bakery. The laws of physics do not apply to me.

I balance, I weave, I dodge, I frolic, and my bills are all paid. On weekends, to let off steam, I participate in full-contact origami. Years ago I

A FEW THOUGHTS ON THE LARGE VS. SMALL DECISION

If you play a sport in high school and you'd like to continue to play it in college, consider a smaller college. There probably won't be a scholarship for it, but there will be field time and the camaraderie and the competition and the excitement that you've come to love about your sport. At a large university, you're either a national-level contender, or you don't play.

If you want to write for the newspaper at a small college, all you have to do is find the editor and propose an article. Boom, you're a reporter, maybe even a columnist. At a large university, you'd probably have to be a journalism major, and even then a lot of the newspaper jobs are actually full-time, paid positions.

If you want to be a DJ for the campus radio station, at a small college all you have to do is find the station manager and ask to come on board. You'll start with the worst time slot, but it'll be your show. You can play rockabilly, gospel, and have poetry readings, all on the same show probably, if that's what you want. At a large university, you'd have to follow the playlist.

At a smaller institution, you can more easily become captain or founder or czar of something, compared to major universities where student senate campaigns have a media budget. You can be the lead in a play without being a theater major. You can go on biology field trips without being a biology major. You can play cello in a quartet without taking a single music class. You can *try lots of things out* without specializing yet.

If you want to get to know your professors, and have them know you, it's sure a lot easier if there are ten or twenty students in a class, than if there are one hundred or two hundred.

Suppose you want friends. Maybe you think that on a campus with fifteen thousand students you'd have ten times as many people to know as on a campus of fifteen hundred students. This is like the saltwater sailor's lament, "Water, water everywhere, and not a drop to drink." The larger the campus, the less interaction outside of class. At a large school, you won't know the one thousand people in the student union at any given moment. At a small school, you're likely to know *all* of the few dozen students in the student union at any given time. Also, at large schools, the overwhelming majority of students live off campus. They go home after class, and lots of them go home between classes. You'll see them, alright, walking past you to find their cars.

The most important factor in creating a school's on-campus atmosphere is on-campus living. It is absolutely essential to creating a bond between students and between students and the institution. Very few universities succeed in providing this—Yale, Princeton, and Rice are the only that come to mind—but practically *all* the smaller colleges do.

discovered the meaning of life but forgot to write it down. I have made extraordinary four-course meals using only a mouli and a toaster oven.

I breed prize-winning clams. I have won bullfights in San Juan, cliff-diving competitions in Sri Lanka, and spelling bees at the Kremlin.

I have played Hamlet, I have performed open-heart surgery, and I have spoken with Elvis.

But I have not yet gone to college.

NOTE: This essay has appeared all over the Internet, and undoubtedly belongs to an actual student, who is also undoubtedly a politician by now. Do not copy or even imitate this essay. Believe me, the original was the best that ever will be. However, do be encouraged by this student's bravery and creativity, and see that you can be brave and creative in your essay as well.

SECRET TO FINDING SCHOLARSHIPS— THERE ISN'T ONE

by Jane Bryant Quinn

I dialed a toll-free number and heard a cheerful, recorded voice.

"Hi! And thanks for calling the College Funding Seminar Hotline," it chirped. "Discover the little-known, inside secrets to getting the most money possible to pay for your child's education. . . . Receive all the details at our next, upcoming free seminar that's saving other parents just like you thousands of dollars."

Oh, dear. The old "secret scholarship" game, updated for the seminar age. The postcard promoting this particular seminar promised the "Shocking Truth!" about

Near the end of my freshman year I got a letter informing me that I had won an academic scholarship based on "demonstrated and sustained merit and recommendation of the faculty." It was for $1,000. I was proud about earning this scholarship. I even began to think about how I could use this $1,000 to pay my account at the bookstore. In fact, I went to the bookstore and charged a couple hundred dollars in books in anticipation of receiving an actual check for $1,000. Two days after that I got a letter from my financial aid officer, informing me that he was reducing my overall financial aid award by $1,000 due to my recent good fortune. Ouch. Thanks for nothing. The scholarship "money" went from one ledger to another without ever leaving the business office. And I worked all summer to pay off my bookstore account.

scholarships and claimed it would disclose "amazing facts . . . never before revealed!"

Why, one wonders, would colleges want to keep scholarships secret? Why would the facts be revealed only to a seminar company that bulk-mails postcards with no return address? Why would you think these amazing facts would be revealed for free?

Maybe something's fishy here.

I left a message on the hotline, saying who I was and asking someone to call. No one did. So I can't tell you more about this particular seminar.

But I can tell you this: There are *no* secrets—amazing or otherwise—to unearthing student financial aid. You'll find all you need to know below.

The Federal Trade Commission sees an upswing in seminars offering scholarship information and advice. You'll get a piece of junk mail at home saying that your student is "scheduled for an interview" on college costs or "has been identified" as eligible for aid.

But the so-called interview "isn't so much educational as it is a sales pitch," says attorney Gregory Ashe of the FTC's Bureau of Consumer Protection.

At the meeting, a salesperson may imply that thousands of hidden scholarships lie within your grasp. To find out where, however, you'll have to pay.

Alternately, you might be told that you can win more federal aid dollars by rearranging your assets to appear more needy. Most of these asset-protection methods involve costs, such as taking loans or buying annuities. And there's no guarantee that you'll get a larger student grant.

Yet other seminars offer to help you with college and aid applications. But you still have to gather all the information for the application, which is the hardest part of the paperwork.

If paperwork is your problem, your high school guidance office often will help you, at no cost. So will www.finaid.org (a Web site that has lots of other good information, besides).

Among the sales tactics to be wary of, according to the FTC: claims that you can't get this information anywhere else (false!); pressure to sign up for the paid service now, now, now; testimonials from people who say they got big scholarships (they might be paid shills); money-back guarantees hedged with lots of conditions.

Pitches to worried parents are commonplace during the precollege years. Telemarketers get your student's name from lists of people who buy yearbooks, order class rings, and show up in student directories. You get a mass-mailed postcard urging you to call a toll-free number.

The FTC recently shut down eight companies that, for a fee, "guaranteed" they could find you $1,000 or more in private student aid. They charged $10 to $400 up front and delivered a lot of useless information.

After the FTC actions, scholarship companies quit "guaranteeing" money, Ashe says, and switched to "identifying" $1,000 to $5,000 scholarships for which you supposedly qualify. But the information you get might be inappropriate or out of date.

No legal action has been brought yet against any seminar operations, which cost in the $750 range. But the FTC's Project ScholarScam is still functioning, so one can assume that the field remains under observation.

Here's the real "Shocking Truth" about finding college aid: It's easy to locate for free. You high school guidance office (or www.ed.gov) has the government forms and timetables. The colleges do the rest after you apply.

"Between 90 percent and 95 percent of all student aid, including federal aid, is packaged for you by the college you attend," says Bruce Hammond, a college counselor at Sandia Preparatory School in Albuquerque, New Mexico, and author of *Discounts and Deals at the Nation's 360 Best Colleges*.

Most of the remaining aid comes from corporations, in the form of employee benefits.

Those "secret" private scholarships account for no more than 2 percent of all college aid money, Hammond says. You can locate them yourself, through www.finaid.org.

But guess what? If you find a $500 private scholarship, many colleges deduct $500 from your aid package, leaving you no better off. You'd pay a seminar for that?

TOTALLY FREE COLLEGES AND UNIVERSITIES

What does free mean? It certainly doesn't mean that a school will have no cost for students and their parents. Free means tuition-free, but it does not mean that you won't have expenses for living, books, and travel to and from home. California, for years, had the ruse that its colleges and universities were "free," but they charged thousands of dollars in "fees" until it was the same thing as tuition. It is important to realize that many expensive private colleges and universities are cheaper than many seemingly inexpensive public universities, because their financial aid awards are comprehensive, that is, they take your total college expenses into account (tuition, room, board, books, fees, travel). Most public university awards amount to a waiver of all or part of the tuition, leaving a student to patch together monies to cover the other parts of college costs. Unfortunately, the only way to tell how much a college will cost you is to apply, and be accepted. There is a book purporting to provide X-ray vision into the process, however: Bruce G. Hammond's *Discounts and Deals at the Nation's 360 Best Colleges* (Golden Books Publishing Company). The following schools are tuition free. Each provides an outstanding education. And with some planning and some hard work, it is possible to enter some of these schools without any more than a summer's savings, and graduate debt free in four years.

TUITION-FREE INSTITUTIONS

Alice Lloyd College

(No tuition for individuals from select mountain counties in Kentucky, Ohio, Tennessee, Virginia, and West Virginia— only small fees and room and board; students outside these counties pay $4,000 per year.)
100 Purpose Road
Pippa Passes, KY 41844
606-368-2101
www.alicelloyd.edu

Berea College

101 Chestnut Street
Berea, KY 40403
800-326-5948 or 606-986-9341
www.berea.edu

College of the Ozarks

Opportunity Avenue
Point Lookout, MO 65726
800-222-0525 or 417-334-6411
www.cofo.edu

Cooper Union for the Advancement of Science & Art

(Has "mandatory student fee" of $500 per year.)
30 Cooper Square
New York, NY 10003
212-254-6300
www.cooper.edu

Curtis Institute of Music

1726 Locust Street
Philadelphia, PA 19103
215-893-5262
www.curtis.edu

Deep Springs

Off California Highway 168
Deep Springs, California
c/o HC72 Box 45001
Dyer, NV 89010
760-872-2000
www.deepsprings.edu

Olin College

Olin Way

Needham, MA 02492

781-292-2300

www.olin.edu

(Olin is a new school, and accreditation is expected this year or next; see www.olin.edu for accreditation details.)

United States Air Force Academy*

2304 Cadet Drive

Colorado Springs, CO 80840

719-333-1110

www.usafa.af.mil

United States Coast Guard Academy*

31 Mohegan Avenue

New London, CT 06320

860-444-8444

www.cga.edu

United States Merchant Marine Academy

300 Steamboat Road

Kings Point, NY 11024

800-732-6267 or 516-773-5000

www.usmma.edu

United States Military Academy*

(The whole city is the academy and military base.)

Stony Lonesome Road

West Point, NY 10996

914-938-4200

www.usma.edu

United States Naval Academy*

121 Blake Road

Annapolis, MD 21402

410-293-1000

www.nadn.navy.mil

Webb Institute

(A school of naval architecture and engineering)

Crescent Beach Road

Glen Cove, NY 11542

516-671-2213

www.webb-institute.edu

*Post-baccalaureate active-duty service commitment of five to six years. See the section on "The Military Academies," p. 204.

(Source: Web searches and a partial list provided by U.S. News & World Report at the following location: www.usnews.com/usnews/edu/dollars/howtopay/dsfree.htm)

CoOl ScHoLaRsHiP!

The Collegiate Bass Anglers Association offers bass-fishing scholarships. There are 23 institutions with bass-fishing clubs.

(Source: Chronicle of Higher Education)

Chapter Two

THE IVY LEAGUE AND MORE

> **When any Schollar is able to understand *Tully*, or such like classicall Latine Author *extempore*, and make and speake true Latine in Verse and Prose, *suo ut aiunt Marte*; And decline perfectly the Paridigm's of *Nounes* and *Verbes* in the Greek tongue: Let him then and not before be capable of admission to the Colledge.** 🙶

—Harvard's admissions requirements, circa 1636, as cited by Ernest L. Boyer in College: The Undergraduate Experience in America *(Carnegie Foundation for the Advancement of Teaching)*

What is the Ivy League? What are your chances of getting into an Ivy League school? What would improve your chances? There used to be no greater cachet in American higher education than to attend an Ivy League college or university. Unfortunately, there are some significant challenges involved in applying to these schools due to the overwhelming competition from other outstanding students applying from all over the world. What do you think of a school that rejects the majority of students who apply with a perfect SAT score (800 Math, 800 Verbal)? What do you think of a university that rejects more than 20,000 students *every year*? In spite of these increasingly oppressive statistics, parents still push for an Ivy League or other big name school. Obviously, it is time for students to educate themselves and their parents on what "highly competitive" means in higher education today. A great education is available at hundreds of schools, but only a handful of schools attract this level of attention. Where did the name "Ivy League" come from, anyway?

THE IVY LEAGUE

The Ivy League was originally a football conference between eight venerable Northeastern schools close enough together to play intercollegiate games: Harvard (formed in 1636), Yale (1701), Pennsylvania (1740), Princeton (1746), Columbia (1754), Brown (1764), Dartmouth (1769), and Cornell (1853). Over time, the name came to refer to the schools themselves, rather than to the football conference. There is a tremendous mystique to the Ivy League schools. They are now, in effect, a collective brand identity.

The name allows them to continue to attract very good students and very wealthy benefactors. For example, Harvard's endowment of more than $30 billion makes it one of the larger fiduciary entities in the world. (Bill Gates, a Harvard dropout, has more, but Bill Gates has more money than God.) The schools are really quite different from one another. Cornell is best known for its engineering and technical programs, and certainly has one of the most regal and beautiful campuses in the world. Columbia is in

In a recent year, Harvard rejected 89 percent of applicants. The applicant pool included:

3,000 class valedictorians

11,000 students in the top 10% of their graduating class

2,100 students with a perfect 800 on Math Level II

400 students with a perfect SAT score (double 800s)

New York City, and is inseparable from that fact. The University of Pennsylvania, almost always known as Penn, is also an urban school, set in Philadelphia. Dartmouth used to be known as a bastion for politically conservative students, although it has been busy distancing itself from that reputation. Yale is known as the most liberal and socially conscious; students belong to colleges within the university, giving it a small feel for a large school. On the cool scale, Brown is the coolest Ivy League school. It doesn't have any distribution requirements whatsoever (which means there aren't any required classes), some classes can be taken credit/no credit, and the students are more laid-back and open than at the other Ivy League schools. Princeton and Yale are arguably the most willfully intellectual, as in intentionally and self-consciously intellectual. Of course, these are gross generalities. One thing I've learned about these schools is that the department you're in makes all the difference in the world. You may go to Harvard or Dartmouth or Yale, but whether you are happy or not will depend on your relationship with the faculty in your department.

A lot of people consider Stanford (1885) to be the ninth Ivy League school, but that's not what it says in the dictionary. Incidentally, Stanford was started by Jane and Leland Stanford, with a railroad fortune. Stanford's original fortune came from selling mining supplies to forty-niners suffering from gold fever. Leland Stanford became one-quarter of the Big Four, who built the Central Pacific Railroad from California over the Sierras to Promontory Point, Utah. At one time, the Big Four owned the entire town of

Completing a minimum of two years of foreign language study as an undergraduate is required for admission to most graduate programs, and learning a market language is beneficial in any career. (Market languages are Chinese, Japanese, Spanish, Arabic, French, Indonesian, and any language used as a lingua franca by a region of the world.) Learning a foreign language is difficult in three classroom hours a week. If you really want to learn a foreign language, take a language or literature course every semester, spend a lot of hours in the language lab, join a conversation group, live in the language dorm, spend a semester or year abroad among native speakers, and spend your summers and breaks the same way. (Just for trivia: They still speak Latin in the Vatican.) Some of the best programs try to recreate an immersion environment. For example, Beloit College in Beloit, Wisconsin, has a summer languages institute providing intensive, nine-week, residential immersion programs in Arabic, Chinese, Japanese, Russian, Portuguese, and other languages. Check it out. Also, if you're really into languages, you've got to look at the Monterey Institute of International Studies, Monterey, California. It is the preeminent foreign language-focused institution in the United States. Its strengths are education in spoken foreign language, interpreting, translating, diplomacy, international trade, international business, commercial diplomacy, and international environmental policy.

Reno, among their other vast holdings. Leland dedicated his quarter of the fortune to found Stanford University. There is an unsubstantiable story that Leland and Jane originally tried to give a gift to Harvard University in the name of their son, Leland, Jr., who had died tragically. Neither institution has any interest in this story being true, and both call it an urban legend. Stanford was started on the site of Stanford's Palo Alto stock farm, and is still affectionately called "The Farm." (Incidentally, Harvard Yard was originally a cattle lot, too.) If you want to really tease a Stanford student, remind him or her that the institution's official name is Leland Stanford Junior University.

The Ivy League schools have far more applicants than they need. One of the problems with higher education enrollment management today is that students are becoming a national commodity without becoming savvy to national levels of competition. That is, students are looking past their local and regional schools and concentrating on national schools, but they and their parents are downright naive about the admissions process. The result of this is that students vastly overestimate their admissibility to these elite schools. The ugly truth is that very bright and capable students are rejected by these schools every day. Students with a 4.0 GPA are routinely rejected. Students with a 4.0 GPA and two sports and six hobbies and three community service activities are *routinely* rejected. Basically, everyone in North America is applying to the same ten or fifteen schools, creating a classic market imbalance of supply and demand. It is not really the school's fault that they are forced to reject the overwhelming majority of applicants.

High school counselors call these schools "lottery schools." If a student gets in to one of these institutions, it's partially a matter of chance. You can improve those chances, however, by being born to an alumna mother or an alumnus father, which would make you a legacy (that's the term). According to the *Wall Street Journal,* that will increase your chances by approximately 15 percent. You might start your application essay with this line: "My uncle, for whom your library is named. . . ." That might work. You also can play sports that are favored by these schools, such as lacrosse or

Princeton's commencements are still delivered in Latin, and students are instructed in a set of signals when to laugh or applaud or gasp or express other crowd emotions, so that their parents and guests are convinced they understand Latin. This innocent ruse has been going on for at least a hundred years. Presumably, before then, Princeton graduates did not need signals to know when to laugh in Latin.

crew. (Interesting that these are the same sports favored by elite private high schools in the Northeast. So much for valuing diversity.)

Students and their parents need to know these data. Students with a connection, or a particularly strong attraction, to a specific Ivy League school should of course apply to that school. Truly outstanding students should of course apply to some of these schools. But students without a nearly perfect record should think twice before racking up a stack of rejections from these hypercompetitive institutions. A better idea all around is to go out there and learn how many good schools there are that you've never heard of, places that would be delighted to admit you, fund you, care for you, and send you out into the world with a first-rate education.

These are certainly all good schools, but that doesn't mean that you'll thrive at one of them. Well, that said, here is the Ivy League:

Brown University
45 Prospect Street
Providence, RI 02912
401-863-1000
www.brown.edu

Columbia University
2960 Broadway
New York, NY 10027-6902
212-854-1754
www.columbia.edu

> 🙶🙶 Of all the young men who come to me with letters of introduction from friends in the East, the most helpless are college young men. 🙸🙸
>
> —*Leland Stanford, founder, Stanford University*

THE MOST COMPETITIVE SCHOOLS IN AMERICA

How hard is it to get in? In a recent year:

Harvard rejected 91%	Dartmouth rejected 88%	University of Pennsylvania rejected 82%	Swarthmore rejected 77%
Yale rejected 90%	Deep Springs rejected 86%	Swarthmore rejected 82%	Cornell rejected 76%
Columbia rejected 90%	Brown rejected 86%	Amherst rejected 81%	Williams rejected 76%
Princeton rejected 89%	MIT rejected 86%	Georgetown rejected 78%	University of California-
Stanford rejected 89%	Caltech rejected 83%	Rice rejected 77%	Berkeley rejected 76%
			Duke rejected 74%

Keep in mind that the average acceptance rate, nationwide, is three out of four, and many institutions have what amounts to an open door policy. So these schools are, indeed, difficult to enter.
Deep Springs is so small that this figure varies tremendously. In some years it is 95%.

Please note that conflicting numbers may exist due to reporting variances, use of wait lists, and timing of reporting; some schools own websites had conflicting data posted in different areas and at different times.

(Source: original research.)

Cornell University

410 Thurston Avenue

Ithaca, NY 14850-2488

607-255-2000

www.cornell.edu

Dartmouth College

East Wheelock Street

Hanover, NH 03755

603-646-1110

www.dartmouth.edu

Harvard University

(Technically Harvard College is the under-

graduate college; Harvard University

refers to the entire institution, including

all its graduate schools and affiliated

institutes.)

Massachusetts Hall

Cambridge, MA 02138

617-495-1000

www.harvard.edu

Princeton University

Princeton, NJ 08544

609-258-3000

www.princeton.edu

University of Pennsylvania

(almost always known as Penn)

34th and Spruce Streets

Philadelphia, PA 19104

215-898-5000

www.upenn.edu

Yale University

New Haven, CT 06520

203-432-9300

www.yale.edu

The Ivy League has wonderful professors, right? Well, yes, but maybe as an under-graduate you won't see much of them. "Undergraduates at Yale University are twice as likely to be taught by a graduate student or an adjunct instructor as by a tenured pro-fessor," says *The Chronicle of Higher Education*. Yale is hardly unusual in this practice.

In the last year for which complete data are available, Harvard University rejected 80 percent of the valedictorians who applied and the majority of the students with a *perfect* SAT score (double 800s). The best activities for applicants: those that are only really popular in the Northeast prep schools, such as lacrosse and crew. Bowling? Forget it. Also, it's easier to stand out if you excel in something a little unusual. "We're always looking for oboes," says Janet Lavin Rapelye, dean of admission at Wellesley. For more on this, see "Beating the Ivy League Odds," in the *Wall Street Journal*.

And undergraduate classes are often huge, with several hundred students sitting in large lecture halls.

THE YALE SYNDROME

Sometimes ambitious students pushed by ambitious parents will view admission to one of these schools as a major life goal, rather than education for its own sake or success in later life. The student may spend years preparing to be a good applicant to college, weighing every activity and endeavor by how it might look to an admissions officer. The parents may exacerbate this effect by speaking frequently about how much it would mean to them for the student to be admitted, and how much it would fulfill somebody's, usually not the student's, lifetime dream. The whole process is made much worse if some family member attended the school in question, or tried and failed to attend. Of course, the importance is magnified when the boy from up the street gets into Stanford, or the daughter of an office rival gets into Yale.

This creates an odd psychological horizon for a young person. Instead of fantasizing about future careers and professional and personal relationships with others, the student has a short chronological horizon: the event of college admission. Students may spend so much emotional and developmental energy preparing to apply that they may not develop a plan for actually being at a college or university. Further, if their decision-making processes have been colored by measuring every decision against its impact on admissibility, they can fail to successfully function in school after admission.

This is called the Yale Syndrome. Students afflicted with the situation described above need counseling to rediscover what it is that they themselves actually might care

> **How do we judge the quality of an undergraduate institution? We look at the athletic program. We have found an inverse relationship between the quality of a school's intercollegiate sports program and the quality of its academic program.**
>
> *—Yale Law School recruiter, perhaps in jest, perhaps not*

Q. What is the biggest warning sign of parental overinvolvement?

A. Pronoun confusion. If your parents say "we" got into MIT or "we" had an interview at Knox or "we" are wait-listed at Stanford, you've got a problem. How do you get help for overinvolvement? (1) If your parents are a problem, don't allow them to sit in on interviews with admissions counselors. (2) Arm yourself with information, so you can reassure them that you know what you're doing. (3) Ask your guidance counselor to ask them to back off. (4) Move in with your Uncle Bob until you turn eighteen. This is your life, and yes, they're probably going to pay for some of it, but you can't let anybody else make this decision for you. If you are happy in the place of your choice, you will thrive in college and succeed in life. If you are unhappy in the place of your parents' choice, you will lose joy in life, start to cut corners, become boringly predictable, and slide into a slimy pit of loathsome mediocrity. It's your life. What's it gonna be?

about. They feel lost, unmotivated, confused; they may report that life has become meaningless; many drop out.

The same thing happens when some people apply to medical school and law school. They may have made the decision to apply *years* prior and not reconsidered that decision. They drive and strive until they are admitted, and then feel guilty and conflicted and miserable to discover that they don't actually like medicine or law.

These are usually family-system problems. That is, it's not the students themselves who are driving this train. Think over your reasons for wanting to go to college, and find a college that can meet those needs. Think for yourself, because you are the one who is going to live this.

For students, parents, and counselors, here are a couple of great books touching on this topic: *Hand Me Down Dreams: How Families Influence our Career Paths and How We Can Reclaim Them* (Harmony Books) by Mary H. Jacobson, and *The Ambitious Generation: America's Teenagers, Motivated but Directionless* (Yale University Press) by Barbara Schneider and David Stevenson.

If you think you may be building a big case of the Yale Syndrome, show this passage to your school counselor and ask for help. This is serious. This is not a joke.

THE SEVEN SISTERS

All of the eight Ivy League schools were originally men's colleges. The Seven Sisters were a collection of women's colleges, some closely affiliated with certain men's colleges, and others always and wholly independent. It's not accurate to speak of Seven Sisters anymore, as Radcliffe has really merged with Harvard and Vassar has gone coed, but here they are, the original Seven Sisters, with notes on their status today:

At the University of California, Berkeley (aka Cal or Berkeley), the average GPA of the most recent incoming class was 4.16. That's right, *above* a 4.0. Advanced placement classes are weighted, allowing GPAs above 4.0. By the way, Berkeley rejects thousands of students every year who have a GPA of 4.0 or better. Imagine that. Thousands. Are you starting to understand the national market now? To keep Berkeley from howling, I should tell you that they admit many students with less-than-perfect GPAs because those students are interesting, passionate, involved in their communities, and good essay writers. But rejecting *thousands* of 4.0s? Wow. In all, Berkeley rejected 22,854 students in a recent application year.

Barnard College

(still a women's college;

cross-registration with Columbia)

3009 Broadway

New York, NY 10027

212-854-5262

www.barnard.edu

Bryn Mawr College

(still a women's college; cross-registration

with Swarthmore, Haverford, and others

in a Philadelphia-area consortium)

101 North Merion Avenue

Bryn Mawr, PA 19010

800-BMC-1885 or 610-526-5000

www.brynmawr.edu

Mount Holyoke College

(still a women's college, prides itself

on its strengths in math and science)

50 College Street

South Hadley, MA 01075

413-538-2000

www.mtholyoke.edu

Radcliffe Institute for

Advanced Studies

(the current iteration of what was once

Harvard's "Sister")

10 Garden Street

Cambridge, MA 02138

617-495-8601

www.radcliffe.edu

For every accredited college and university in the U.S.
and Canada go to **www.donaldasher.com/colleges**

It is very interesting to get hundreds of letters from college presidents. When I was writing to them asking them for nominations for this book, I included a running list of schools other presidents had recommended. My correspondents often criticized the choices of other college presidents, and advocated for their own choices, quite eloquently. Nevertheless, I noticed that the institutional knowledge of college presidents, and academicians in general, is geographically determined. They recommended schools closer to them, and criticized schools farther from them, as if they were infecting their neighbors with quality. Ernest L. Boyer, in his book, *College: The Undergraduate Experience in America* (Carnegie Foundation for the Advancement of Teaching), found that high school counselors were generally quite unknowing of institutions more than five hundred miles distant. I believe, really, that knowledge of academic institutions is regional, while the market for students has quietly become nationalized. So students are entering the national marketplace with advice, from parents, teachers, counselors, and even family friends in higher education, that is quite localized. This has allowed national rankings, whatever their limitations may be, to thrive. They are filling this vacuum of knowledge. Of course, rankings cannot determine which students will be happy at which schools. Ultimately, that task falls to the students themselves.

CoOl BoOk AlErT!

Looking Beyond the Ivy League: Finding the College That's Right for You (Penguin USA) by Loren Pope, Director of the College Placement Bureau and former education editor for the *New York Times*

In this pull-no-punches, take-no-prisoners book, Loren Pope attacks the myths of college choice. Here are a couple of typical passages:

"The university's oft-cited claim that having many fine research scholars affects the quality of undergraduate teaching is a false position that has misled the public too long. If the great scholar teaches undergraduates at all—and most teach few or none—he is likely to be only an animated book or a television performer in a big lecture hall."

"Every year brings more proof that a college's effect on one's life has little to do with its prestige, and that the university, with its worship of research and its cheating of undergraduates, should be sued—or at the very least chastised—for false and misleading advertising."

How's that for taking a stand? In the land of hyperpolite understatement that is academic journalism, Loren Pope is a breath of fresh air. This book is a must-read for students, parents, and educators. Here are his myths.

Myth One: An Ivy League college will absolutely guarantee the rich, full, and successful life.

Myth Two: If you can't make an Ivy, a "prestige college" is next best, because the name on your diploma will determine whether you do something worthwhile in life.

Myth Three: Eastern institutions are the best and most desirable.

Myth Four: The big university offers a broader, richer undergraduate experience.

Myth Five: A college you've heard about is better than one you haven't.

Myth Six: What your friends say about a college is a good indicator.

Myth Seven: The college catalog can help you decide if this is the school for you.

Myth Eight: You should make your college selection early in your senior year, before Christmas if at all possible.

Myth Nine: Your college should be bigger than your high school.

Myth Ten: Going more than 200 miles away from home will cost more and may result in isolation.

Myth Eleven: If you're in the top 10 percent of your class with SATs of 1300 or better, you belong in an Ivy or prestige college.

Myth Twelve: Ivy League schools are looking for students who don't have excellent grades.

Myth Thirteen: SAT scores are the most important thing; good ones will get you in and poor ones will keep you out.

Myth Fourteen: A coaching course will improve your SAT scores.

Myth Fifteen: A bad recommendation from a teacher or counselor will ruin your chances.

Myth Sixteen: Your choice of major will decide your career path, so the quality of the department should govern your choice of college.

Myth Seventeen: A high school diploma is needed to get into college.

Myth Eighteen: Going to a private prep school will enhance your chances of getting into a good college.

Myth Nineteen: Millions of dollars in unused scholarships are going begging every year.

Myth Twenty: A good college is hard to get into.

For a full explication of each point, you'll have to read his book.

Smith College

(still a women's college, has an

engineering department)

Elm Street

Northampton, MA 01063

413-584-2700

www.smith.edu

Vassar College

(now fully coed)

124 Raymond Avenue

Poughkeepsie, NY 12604

914-437-7000

www.vassar.edu

Wellesley College

(still a women's college,

but men are in some classes

through an exchange program)

106 Central Street

Wellesley, MA 02481

781-283-1000

www.wellesley.edu

Oh, and just for the record, women comprise the majority of undergraduates, and the majority of graduate students.

WHY WE STILL HAVE MEN'S, WOMEN'S, AND MINORITY-FOCUSED COLLEGES

All the Ivy League schools were originally men's colleges, and all of them have been coed for years. When men's colleges go coed, they can, for a period of time, be an awful place for women. The only men's college to go coed gracefully in recent years was Rose-Hulman Institute, a top engineering school in Terre Haute, Indiana. Rose-Hulman made an institutional commitment to *inviting* women to Rose-Hulman; it searched the nation for bright, well-prepared women who were interested in science, engineering, and math. It

SKULL AND BONES AT YALE

In addition to its residential colleges, which give Yale the intimate feel of a much smaller institution, Yale has a long history of student-run, student-managed secret societies. The rituals and practices of these societies are supposed to remain a tightly guarded secret. Duh! That's why they call them "secret societies." For some of them even membership itself is supposed to be kept secret, and members are supposed to deny that they are members. At least one former president blabbed to all the world that he was a member of Skull and Bones. Skull and Bones may have held a meeting in their clubhouse, a windowless building known as The Tomb, to discuss what censure would be applied to George Bush the Elder, our 41st president (or 40th, depending on whether you count Grover Cleveland twice). Their decision is, of course, unknown.

worked hard to bring large numbers of women to the campus all at once, rather than dribbling away at it over a period of years. It also explained to the students why the institution was going coed, and prepared the young men who were then enrolled in how to act like gentlemen, and what was expected of them.

The administration of Rose-Hulman Institute, now smoothly coed for years, ought to be applauded from the Atlantic to the Pacific for the good job they did in this transition.

Contrast this with The Citadel of Charleston, South Carolina, which was dragged kicking and screaming into compliance with a series of court orders. The Citadel

The highest paid employee on almost any major university's payroll is the head football coach.

allowed hazing and harassment of its first female cadet, Ms. Shannon Faulkner, to the point that she decided to withdraw.

Why are there still men's colleges and women's colleges? For several very good but also very divergent reasons. Although the students and admissions staff at these institutions can tell their own stories best, here are some things I know:

There are still women's colleges because men still hog the majority of attention in most classrooms. Read *How Schools Shortchange Girls* by the American Association of University Women (Econo-Clad Books), or just look around you. It is an established fact that men speak out more in class than women. It is an established fact that faculty (male or female) spend more time on and give more approval to the opinions expressed in class by men. It is an established fact that our greater society, beyond the boundaries of the ivory tower, is also male dominated. Women often feel that they are guests in the land of the men, strangers in a strange land that does not belong to them and that they did not design. This is easily established by a walk across campus

Rice University in Houston also has residential colleges patterned after the Oxford and Cambridge model, with faculty and students living together. With top-caliber students, strong science and engineering programs, and a cost close to half of the typical Ivy League college, it delivers real bang for the investment. Bruce G. Hammond, author of *Discounts and Deals at the Nation's 360 Best Colleges* (Golden Books Publishing Company), calls Rice "the nation's preeminent bargain among elite private universities."

at any women's college. Mills College, in Oakland, California, is a perfect example. The statues on the lawn are of women. The art on the walls is of and by women. The quotes posted on professors' and students' doors are primarily by women. There are women everywhere, studying, reading, talking, walking, exercising. In every class, all the students are women. If you are a woman, this is a new experience, and it can be a life-changing experience. Ever since Betty Friedan wrote *The Feminine Mystique* in 1963, it has been a tenet of gender theory that the nondominant gender does not even know the cost of living in nondominant status. In my opinion, every female in the world would benefit from living for a year in non-nondominant status. Every female in the world would benefit from going to a girls-only high school or a women's college for at least a year. *It can change your life forever.*

The exact same argument can be made for attending a college that serves a large proportion of your race. If you have spent your life living in a dominant white culture (or any other dominant culture), it can be a truly liberating experience to spend time at a college where your race or your culture is dominant. See the essay by Amelia R. Shelby of Howard University, "Why I *Finally* Chose to Attend an Historically Black College," on p. 240.

Further, there are many people, young men and young women, who would like to put off the whole question of sexuality for a few more years. They choose to spend their college years concentrating on their studies, and worry about sexuality at a later time. They choose a single-gender school because they find it less distracting. A tremendous amount of energy is spent on dating and partying at coed institutions, and not all students want to spend their time in this way.

Also, there are many religions and cultures in the world where men and women are commonly separated for education and worship. When people from these religions and cultures send their children to college, they prefer to send them to single-gender institutions. Many extremely powerful and wealthy families from other countries have sent generations of their offspring to the same U.S.-based, single-gender schools.

Applying to a large university? Be sure to use your full legal name, and put your social security number on everything. You *are* your social security number. According to the *Chronicle of Higher Education*, Truman Bradley of Boulder, Colorado, received a letter from Arizona State University that started out like this: "Congratulations on 345-62-2439's admission to Arizona State University!" Bradley decided to go elsewhere.

Furthermore, there are people who just prefer the company of their own gender, and that is reason enough for them. For most of history and in most of the world, this has been a common sentiment, requiring no further explanation.

FOUR SCHOOLS THAT ARE KICKING BUTT

Beloit College, Beloit, Wisconsin

Many of the prestigious old-line schools are on autopilot. Their reputations are based on glory from decades past. But Beloit College in Beloit, Wisconsin, is an "up and coming" college. The students at Beloit are happy and confident, the faculty are energized, the physical plant is in great shape, it's in a picture-postcard little town, and . . . I think you get the picture. I think it is the students, themselves, who stand out the most. They are the opposite of moody and depressed. Maybe it's that healthy Wisconsin air.

Whitman College, Walla Walla, Washington

Whitman is one of those gems that should be overrun with students from all over the country, but is not well known outside of its region. I asked an auditorium of sixty of their students, "How do you like this college?" Not one, *not one,* had a complaint about it. They all said: "It's great." "This place really supports you." "The professors here are excellent." And so on. I dare you to fill an auditorium at any school and get these kinds of endorsements. This was in the week before midterms, when most students are naturally grumpy. (Just for the record, the students were gathered to hear a guest speaker, and they were definitely not prepped by the admissions or public affairs offices.)

Washington University in St. Louis, St. Louis, Missouri

According to its students, Wash U. is the perfect size for a university. With about 5,000 undergraduates and a cloistered feel to the campus, students get the university experience without being lost in a faceless crowd. Students are showered with attention, the academics are excellent, and the administration is responsive. Students have been known to launch their own classes, which is very unusual for a university. Wash U. offers no athletic scholarships, so "if you were a starter in high school you'll probably get to play here, too." St. Louis, always a gateway city (that's what the arch is all about), is cross-fertilized, a little bit Southern, Northern, Western, and Midwestern. The campus is extremely well cared for, almost to country club standards.

Villa Julie College, Stevenson, Maryland

Villa Julie has been blessed by a visionary president and a visionary executive director of career planning who both had the same dream. The result is Career Architecture, an innovative career development program that infuses every aspect of the Villa Julie experience. This is not an ivory-tower program. Students build a values-based, strategic plan for their careers, starting in the freshman year, and use internships and service hours to supplement their academic advancement. Villa Julie graduates know where they're going.

And finally, some of these schools have massive endowments, and can provide full-ride scholarships for students who might otherwise not be able to afford to pursue a quality education.

So for these important reasons, we still have, and still *ought to have,* single-gender schools and schools that focus on serving specific minorities.

For more on this, check out these lists later in the book:

The Historically Black Colleges, p. 242.

The Hispanic Colleges, p. 252.

The Tribal, Indian, and Native American Colleges, p. 262.

The Women's Colleges, p. 267.

The Men's Colleges, p. 271.

WESTERN COLLEGES FINALLY GET THEIR DUE

by Janet L. Holmgren, president, Mills College

Higher education is hot again in the national press, as millions of American high school students—and older students, too—go through the challenging ritual of deciding to which colleges they will apply.

Two California independent/private higher educational institutions were recently ranked No. 1 by *U.S. News & World Report* and *Time/The Princeton Review.* Ranked as the top national university in *U.S. News's* "America's Best Colleges," The California Institute of Technology (Caltech) was recognized in part for spending more per student ($192,000) than any other college or university in the nation.

The University of Southern California (USC) was named *Time/Princeton Review's* college of the year in "The Best College for You," having transformed itself from a widely known party school to a committed partner helping to revitalize Los Angeles.

As president of Mills College (one of California's oldest institutions of higher education) and chair of the executive committee of the Association of Independent California Colleges and Universities, I am delighted to see long overdue recognition lavished on Western universities. While occasionally acknowledging Stanford and Berkeley, the national media often seem to have difficulty seeing beyond the Northeast corridor when covering higher education. However, it is a sign of our times that *Time/The Princeton Review* and *U.S. News* focused on the extremes of what a college education represents. While I believe national magazine rankings should play a minor role in the decision-making process, they can provide useful lessons about how institutions distinguish themselves.

Caltech values science and technology and recruits the nation's top students in these fields. These areas of study are expensive as well as valuable to society, and the students who go to Caltech are very well supported.

However, as in many research universities, the faculty is overwhelmingly white and male, and Caltech lags in the recruitment of women and people of color to the student body. USC was chosen college of the year because across the curriculum and throughout the university's hierarchy, USC has "discovered ways to inspire the quality of education everywhere," according to the editors of *The Princeton Review*.

The popularity of these rankings teaches us that the public is hungry for evaluations that will guide them about the merits of a variety of institutions. An undergraduate education can be an expensive proposition and researching the right college is crucial. Yet, with more than 2,000 baccalaureate-granting colleges and universities in the United States, and nearly 200 in California alone, how does one make sense of their strengths and weaknesses? And how does one find out what an institution values?

A Mills parent recently approached me at a reception and said that when she and her daughter visited many liberal arts colleges, they heard similar messages: the college would educate her daughter well, spend a lot of money on her, and support her to become a successful alumna. What they heard at Mills made the difference in their decision. We

"What I'd tell teenagers today: Pick a good liberal arts school, and learn how to think."

—R. Glenn Hubbard, dean,
Graduate School of Business, Columbia University

When Florida State University didn't like how they came out in a ranking by the *Princeton Review*, they gave the company the "Golden Gargoyle" award for The Most Bogus Survey in Higher Education. Said university president Sandy D'Alemberte, "There was a lot of competition for this award, so I think the *Princeton Review* should be proud." Reed College refuses to participate in *U.S. News & World Report*'s annual ranking surveys, saying that their methodology is "without merit."

told them that we educate women to make the world a better place. And, in addition to offering a first-rate, liberal arts education, we do everything we can to develop a student's leadership abilities, to engage her in meaningful community service, and to help her learn how to make responsible choices for using her education into the future.

Other colleges and universities articulate educational values similar to Mills', and it is important to consider written materials as well as personal encounters with the institutions, students, faculty, staff, and alumni to determine whether the institution "walks the talk." The faculty and students at any institution are drawn to it because of its values—its history and traditions, and its current orientation—as well as its academic strengths, physical facilities, and financial resources. So, before you make your final choice, find out what the college or university values and compare it to your own values and aspirations.

Reprinted by permission of the author.

CoOl BoOk AlErT!

The Public Ivys: A Guide to America's Best Public Undergraduate Colleges and Universities by Richard Moll (Viking Penguin)

THE PUBLIC IVYS

Miami University of Ohio
University of California at Berkeley
University of California at Davis
University of California at Irvine
University of California at Los Angeles
University of California at San Diego
University of California at Santa Barbara
University of California at Santa Cruz
University of Michigan at Ann Arbor
University of North Carolina at Chapel Hill
University of Texas at Austin
University of Vermont at Burlington
University of Virginia at Charlottesville
William and Mary College of Virginia

Worthy Runners-Up:
Georgia Institute of Technology at Atlanta
New College of Florida
Pennsylvania State University at University Park
State University of New York at Binghamton
University of Colorado at Boulder
University of Illinois at Urbana-Champaign
University of Pittsburgh
University of Washington at Seattle
University of Wisconsin at Madison

It is important to realize that most of these are very large and highly competitive institutions, perhaps much more appropriate for graduate education and adult commuters than for the benefit of traditional-age undergraduates. The exception would be New College of Florida, see p. 136.

Q&A WITH A DEAN OF ADMISSION: WHAT *HIGHLY COMPETITIVE* REALLY MEANS

with Janet Lavin Rapelye, Dean of Admission, Wellesley College

Wellesley College is a highly selective women's college in Wellesley, Massachusetts.

Q. What's it like to be a dean of admission?

Virtually everyone I know who is a dean of admission went into this work because he or she was committed to higher education, and to students in particular. At the height of the selection season, our jobs are all encompassing. The volume of material is relentless. We essentially give up our personal lives. We give up evenings. We give up weekends. Having said that, the reason it's exciting and the reason we do it is because behind every application is a student. Every piece of paper we get has a story behind it. It's incredibly humbling to read these applications, to read about these students' lives, whether they are traditional-age students or more experienced students applying as transfers. It is extremely hard work, and a huge responsibility.

Q. Students want to know, How do you make the decision?

Well, I can't answer for other schools. At Wellesley we make the decision by com-

SCHOOLS WITH MASSIVE ENDOWMENTS

Private Institutions

Woods Hole Oceanographic Institution ($1,708,889)

Princeton University ($875,321)

Grinnell College ($760,484)

Harvard University ($727,522)

Bryn Athyn College of the New Church ($721,910)

Webb Institute ($718,872)

Agnes Scott College ($692,914)

Rice University ($684,313)

Curtis Institute of Music ($674,036)

Public Institutions

VMI Foundation (Virginia Military Institute, $166,663)

Oregon Health Sciences Foundation ($126,036)

University of Texas System ($70,842)

University of Virginia ($65,842)

University of California at San Francisco Foundation ($55,640)

University of Michigan ($51,916)

University of Delaware ($50,404)

Endowment Association of the College of William and Mary ($50,038)

Texas A & M University System ($49,469)

Georgia Tech Foundation ($45,020)

(Figures show endowment per student. Source: Chronicle of Higher Education)

mittee. Our committee is made up of admissions professionals, faculty, administrators, and even some students. The faculty are elected to the committee by the Wellesley faculty, and the student members are chosen by the Wellesley students, and I think we are unusual in that. Ultimately, decisions are made by majority vote of this committee. There are no decrees. I can be outvoted by others, and have been, and the committee decision stands. We are choosing the next class of students, and it is truly a community process.

The decision about every student is made individually. We have no quotas, no set formula. Every single decision is made individually. Every file is read by three different readers, and then goes to committee for discussion and a vote. Sometimes a recruiter will champion a candidate. She may say, "I met this student on the road, and she impressed me as being incredibly mature, poised, and well spoken." She may try to sway the other members of the committee. Sometimes she can. Sometimes she can't, but we do value the ability to speak well and to write well. Can these arguments overcome a mediocre transcript? No. Will they override weak letters of recommendation? No. But we take everything into consideration.

Incidentally, if students or parents want to know how a college or university makes its admission decisions, I'd recommend they ask. Most schools will tell them.

Q. How much do grades and scores count? And how much do activities count?

I think admissions offices can always quantify their classes at the end of the process, how many admitted, average GPA, range of SAT, and so on, but this process is much more an art than a science. While we do have the transcript in front of us, which is the most important part, we ask: Has she taken the most challenging load? Has she done well in the more challenging classes? Has she taken advantage of everything her high school has to offer?

Then we're trying to measure the intangibles—the motivation, the creativity, the potential. We're looking for talents the student will bring to our campus. And we're looking for diversity in the broadest sense of the term, diversity of thought, diversity of backgrounds, diversity of talents. And that's why we rely on the committee process.

Swarthmore College and Occidental College do an outstanding job of attracting, retaining, educating, and graduating minority students in a small liberal arts college setting. Check them out.

Because certain things appeal to different readers. The essay is very important. In the essay we're looking for how well a student writes. But essays can be more or less appealing depending on the reader, and then again, that's where the committee process comes in.

Students are not just academics. They're not just numbers. Whether a person plays field hockey or the oboe matters to us. Art and music and theater and dance are all part of our curriculum. They're part of what we do. So they're not just "extra"-curricular for us.

So we look at the academic piece, and the talents, and the overall background, and then we look even further, for the intangibles. For example, leadership. Leadership is an intangible that is generally best articulated by someone else, besides the student in question. When you're talking about selective admissions, you have to talk about potential *and* performance. It can't be all potential. A student who has very high scores and low grades is probably not going to fare well in a selective admissions process. When a student says, "I have the potential for leadership," but they haven't really done it, they need to realize that there are a lot of other students out there who have done leadership, who have already demonstrated it.

Q. How competitive is it to get into a top school?

Most of the highly selective schools publish the range of students that they admit. We do. It's important for parents to look at the range, and look objectively at their own daughter. Most of the guides have this information, and most viewbooks are frank about the competition, and we're not kidding.

The problem is that most parents think that their child will be the exception in this process. They look to see if we admitted anybody at all with a statistical profile similar to their daughter's, and if so, they think that surely we'll see that we should admit her, too.

Selective admissions means that we don't have enough spaces for all the qualified candidates. That's exactly what it means. We have to turn down many qualified students each year. That's what makes our jobs so hard for us. We're not going to expand the size of the college, so we have to make decisions. These decisions are very hard to make, sometimes.

One administrator at a highly selective institution (not Wellesley) told me, "We don't need any more applicants. It will just cost us money to reject them." That's a pretty amazing statement. "Okay. I won't send you any," I promised.

It's very important for parents to be realistic about what their son or daughter looks like on paper. Like it or not, students will be judged by what they look like on paper, their transcripts, recommendations, grades, scores, essay, extracurricular activities, and how they put the application together. Applications that are done at the last minute look like applications that were put together at the last minute.

So a refuse decision does not mean that a student could not have succeeded at our school. But it does mean that I have to write her a letter denying her admission, a letter that feels very inadequate to me. I have to say that we simply do not have enough

SHOULD YOU GO TO THE BEST COLLEGE YOU CAN GET INTO?

How many times have you heard this: "You should go to the best college you can get into"? This is a really common belief held more by well-meaning parents than by most educators. If you somehow manage to get into a program vastly above your preparation and skill levels, you could be very poorly served by picking "the best" school you can get into. You may be frustrated and overwhelmed, or lose your confidence as a scholar. In general, it is better to pick a school where you will be challenged, where you will need to work very hard but not relentlessly, where you can earn grades you can take satisfaction in. The exact same student could be an admired scholar at one school or a reviled laggard at another. And grad schools are definitely going to be more interested in strong grades from a weaker school than weak grades from a stronger school. Upon thinking deeper, you will realize the whole question has a built-in fallacy. There is no such thing as a unilinear ranking of colleges. Therefore, there is no meaningful arbiter of good, better, best *across all departments* and *for every student*. Colleges and universities cannot be reduced to rankings like so many baseball teams. Departments will vary. Specific instructors will have more to do with your experience than any abstract notion of the overall quality of an institution. And what about the differences between students? You may fit in socially at one college and feel completely out of place at another. Your academic interests may be much better served by one college or another, but all of these factors are unlikely to have anything to do with any college's ranking on a "good, better, best" scale. Imagine this: Rank all the sports teams on the North American continent from "best" to "worst." Mix in NHL teams with MLB teams with NFL teams with NBA teams with women's Olympic soccer with two towns competing in a regional Mexican rodeo. Now tell me: Does that make any sense? Why not? They're all sports teams. This is exactly like the process of ranking undergraduate institutions in unilinear ordinal rankings. Finally, real-time quality lags reputation. You may pick a school because of some published ranking, and find that it has passed its prime. The academic officers and the professors that made the place special are no longer in charge. The administration no longer has a commitment to excellence. The current students are more bland and homogenous and predictable than the ones who helped build the reputation for excellence in the first place. I can name half a dozen highly ranked schools that haven't, together, generated a new idea in years. My tip: Start thinking for yourself. Start looking for a team you want to play on, where you can be a starter every day and at least occasionally a star.

INPUTS AND OUTPUTS

Most measurements of college quality are actually input measurements. For example, they measure the quality of students entering the college, not the quality of students exiting the college. Here are some inputs and outputs:

INPUTS	OUTPUTS
High School GPA	GRE Scores
SAT/ACT Scores	Satisfaction Surveys
Endowment	Student Debt at Graduation
Faculty Salaries	Career Placement
Spending per Student	Average Salary Offer
Freshmen in Top 10% Ranking	% Admitted to Graduate School
Faculty with Terminal Degree	% Who Get Ph.D.'s
Full-Time Faculty	Citation Analysis
Faculty-Student Ratio	% Who Tithe to Their Alma Mater
Parental Lifetime Income	Student Lifetime Income

Think of a college as a black box device, with high school seniors entering on one side and college graduates exiting on the other. It is clear that the "best" college would have the greatest difference between inputs and outputs, and the "worst" college would have the least difference between inputs and outputs. No national survey has taken this approach, but it would sure be interesting to see which colleges would win this ranking query.

As another example of input vs. output, an administrator at Wells College in Aurora, New York, told me, "We take a lot of A students here, but our greatest strength is taking a student who was maybe a B student in high school and turning her on to education, and making an A student out of her in college." In my opinion, that's an excellent college.

Some other measures are slightly less clearly an input or an output. For example, retention. Some would argue that retention is an output, for it is a result of the educational process itself. Thus, high retention leading to a high graduation rate could be seen as an indicator of quality. This is how it is treated by *U.S. News & World Report.* But Steve Koblik, former president of Reed College, told me he thinks otherwise. "Retention is not an indicator of academic rigor. Quite the opposite. If your program is truly challenging, some people are going to have a hard time with it. The idea that retention is a sign of academic rigor is—on the face of it—absurd." He does have a point.

When evaluating a college, remember that it is the output you'll have to live with. What kind of graduate school and career experiences do graduates have? That is the question. Because once you graduate, you're an output.

places at Wellesley College, and I'm sorry but we had other candidates who just had to come first.

It's very hard for that group just below the top group to understand why they weren't included. In fact, we believe they'll be terrific college students. Let me be clear. Selective admissions is not a decision about how worthy a child is. This is not a report card for parents on their parenting, nor is it a judgment call on a student's intrinsic value as a person or even as a candidate. As hard as it is to accept, it is a decision about what an individual student looks like on paper compared to the rest of the applicant pool of a particular college in a given year. It's as simple as that, and as complicated as that.

Q. Any final words of advice for applicants and their parents?

Well, two things. We're seeing an increase in the anxiety level of families about whether application materials have arrived in our office. If you mailed your application, or any piece of it, within the prior five days, it's entirely possible that it's in our office, but it's physically impossible for us to tell you whether it's here or not. Trust the process, but be sure to keep copies of everything.

It's very important that they fill out the forms to tell us how they would like us to contact them. If they prefer to use a middle name or even a nickname, we will honor

---

MEASURING THE VALUE OF AN IVY LEAGUE DEGREE

There is a famous and oft-cited study conducted in the sixties by Patricia Salter West while she was at Columbia University, that attempted to set a cash value for the Ivy League education. The study factored out socioeconomic status of incoming students, but failed to factor out academic preparation, intelligence, and drive (i.e., very important inputs), thus establishing nothing. Scores of studies since have suffered from the same methodological weakness. One would almost begin to believe that researchers had a systematic bias, i.e., a desire to find a high value for an Ivy League education. A more useful study is one done recently by Alan B. Krueger (Princeton) and Stacy Berg Dale (Andrew W. Mellon Foundation), sponsored by the National Bureau of Economic Research. Their findings: For the middle class student, going to a college with average SAT scores of 1000 will result in higher income later than going to a college with average SAT scores of 1200. Read that last sentence several times. Some factors to consider are these: Of two students who are otherwise equal, the one attending a slightly less selective institution will have a higher class rank, will stand out more to faculty, will probably earn higher grades, and will be more confident of his or her own abilities.

This study, like all the studies in this genre, is controversial and has its critics. For a discussion of many of the research projects on this topic, see "Measuring the Value of an Ivy Degree," in the *Chronicle of Higher Education*.

that, but they've got to let us know and they've got to be consistent in the application.

Finally, I have this to say: Virtually every student that we see coming through the process has wonderful qualities and talents and skills. They have the ability to push the intellectual limits of a college campus, and there's a right college out there for them. There's a place out there looking for them. Their goal should be to find that right campus.

Oh, and one final, final thing: If you're a bright young woman reading about this, we'd like you to consider Wellesley as possibly that right campus for you.

COLLEGE RANKINGS

The college rankings in *U.S. News & World Report* have been debunked by everyone from the *Washington Monthly* to the presidents of every single university I have ever interviewed. Amazingly, an internal report commissioned by *U.S. News & World Report* concluded: "The principal weakness of the current approach is that the weights used to combine the various measures into an overall rating lack any defensible empirical or theoretical basis." Wow.

So are there *any* useful rankings out there? Not many. Almost none of them measure any aspect of instruction or learning. (And instruction and learning are, after all, at the core of the college experience!) A student should be wary of *all* ranking systems. If you want to learn about more sophisticated and interesting college rankings, go to the

EASTERN OREGON UNIVERSITY

Eastern Oregon University is located in the middle of nowhere near the corners of Washington, Idaho, and Oregon. It is nestled in a quaint little town of La Grande, Oregon. They do not charge out-of-state tuition for students from Washington and Idaho. Why is this college in this book? Because it offers a much better education than most of the large universities near you. Almost all the students are undergrad, so the focus is on them. There is no big and distracting social scene revolving around big-time football and Greek Row. The pace is relaxed, but the students are engaged. Nobody has to go to college in La Grande, so the students I met were, in general, quite interested in getting the most out of their educational opportunity. In fact, that's the point: They viewed it as an opportunity. "People come here to go to school. There's not much else to do," said an administrator. "A lot of them play athletics, or they hunt and fish, or they hike and ski. It's a great place for those things, but many, if not most, just concentrate on school."

Eastern Oregon University • 1410 "L" Avenue • La Grande, Oregon 97850 • 541-962-3511 • www.eou.edu • admissions@eou.edu

reference section of any library and look at *Education Rankings Annual* (Thomson Gale). Or take a look at the National Survey of Student Engagement at http://nsse.iub.edu/index.cfm.

Here is just one example of a more valid ranking system: The *Wall Street Journal* analyzed the per-capita frequency of admission to the top professional schools. Here are the top fifty feeder schools to the most elite business, medical, and law schools in the country:

Amherst College

Barnard College

Bates College

Bowdoin College

Brandeis University

Brown University

Bryn Mawr College

Caltech

Case Western Reserve University

Claremont McKenna College

Colby College

Columbia University

Cornell University

Dartmouth College

Duke University

Emory University

Georgetown University

Grinnell College

Harvard University

Haverford College

Johns Hopkins University

Macalester College

Massachusetts Institute of Technology

Middlebury College

Morehouse College

New College of Florida

Northwestern University

Pomona College

Princeton University

Reed College

Rice University

Stanford University

Swarthmore College

Trinity College

Tufts University

United States Military Academy

United States Naval Academy

University of California, Berkeley

University of Chicago

University of Michigan

University of Notre Dame

University of Pennsylvania

University of Virginia

Vassar College

Washington and Lee

Washington University in St. Louis

Wellesley College

Wesleyan University

Williams College

Yale University

(Source: Wall Street Journal*)*

TOP TEN PER-CAPITA PRODUCERS OF PH.D.S

Suppose you aren't interested in graduate schools of business, medicine, or law? Here are the top ten per-capita producers of Ph.D.s in all fields:

Bryn Mawr	MIT	University of Chicago
Caltech	Oberlin	Yale
Carleton	Reed	
Harvey Mudd	Swarthmore	

(Source: Weighted Baccalaureate Origins Study, Higher Education Data Sharing Consortium. To see these data segmented by gender and academic discipline, go to http://web.reed.edu/ir/phd.html.)

Best Place to Grow a Woman Scientist?

About half of Oberlin College's students who earn Ph.D.s are women. What about Stanford, MIT, and Cornell? Not even close. The article "Small Colleges, Big Results" published by *Chronicle of Higher Education* stated these findings:

"Across the board in all fields, liberal-arts colleges sent a higher percentage of women on to get Ph.D.s than did doctoral institutions... The gap was most pronounced in the sciences."

Some of the reasons are smaller classes, more attention, and more women faculty to serve as role models. There may also be a cultural problem. "There's a disjunction often between what young women expect from college and what first-year science courses are like at big schools: the largeness, the impersonality, the pointless difficulty, the general meanness, the sense that we don't need you," says Barbara L. Whitten, professor of physics at Colorado College, in the article.

Why Distance Doesn't Matter, and All Schools Are Local

With email and IM and cell phones, students are never out of touch anymore. You can call your parents or best friend five times a day, if you want, no matter where you go to school. And here's the real shocker: It doesn't cost any more to go to school at the other end of the country as it does to go to school a short drive from home, and it may help you make better grades to move further away! The key is giving up a car in the freshman year. As mentioned elsewhere, students who live on campus make better grades than students who commute to campus, and students who don't have cars make higher grades than students who do own cars. Cars cost far more than most of us realize. With insurance running $200+ per month and gas sky high, you'll either have car payments or repair bills running at least $200 per month, on average. You may need to convince your parents of this, so I have provided this table:

SCHOOL IN NEXT TOWN	SCHOOL FAR AWAY
Gas/insurance/license/repairs or loan payments: $500/month x 9 months = $4,500	Air fare bought in advance for trip to school, plus return home for Thanksgiving, Christmas, and Spring Break, 4 trips @ $500 = $2,000 travel expenses
24-hour access to Mom and Dad and friends	24-hour access to Mom and Dad and friends
Risk of DUI: Real	Risk of DUI: Zero
Risk of accident: Real	Air travel: Absolutely the safest way to get from A to B
Drive to library, and won't	Walk to library, and will
Parking tickets (believe me, everybody gets parking tickets)	No parking tickets
Time to get home: 1 to 4 hours from a "nearby" school	Time to get home: 1 to 5 hours from any spot within the continental United States
Maybe not the best choice, academically	Maybe the best choice, academically

Saving Mom and Dad $2,500? That's *really* $2,500. Getting to go to your first choice school: Priceless.

The Best College Library in America

Where is the best college library in America? It is at Middlebury College. This library changed the culture and focus of the campus when it was opened in 2004. It took ten years to plan and build, and it is the epitome of what architecture can be when it is done right. It bills itself as a hub of technology, learning, and research—which it is—with every doodad and technological device imaginable. But really it is a cathedral of studying—inviting, welcoming, relaxing. Study areas are intermixed with the book collection, and students come early to nail down the best spots. Couches and chairs and nooks and alcoves encourage students to spend the evening. They can practice PowerPoint presentations, watch movies, teleconference with friends, or study in groups in private "boardrooms." And, of course, there's a coffee shop. During exam weeks the library is open 24 hours a day, and the coffee shop seating area is open 24 hours all the time as a gathering spot for night owls.

The library changed the center of gravity of the whole institution. Studying and socializing at the library is *the* thing to do at Middlebury. The library is the place to see and be seen, and students gravitate to it. College administrators come from all over the country to study this library, how it works, and how it influences the culture of an already studious campus.

Check it out at **Middlebury College** in Middlebury, Vermont.

" The true University of these days is a collection of books. "

—Thomas Carlyle

For every accredited college and university in the U.S. and Canada go to **www.donaldasher.com/colleges**

Chapter Three

SCHOOLS WHERE SCHOLARSHIP IS HONORED

What is the purpose of the college experience? Is it to prepare a student for a successful career? Or a meaningful life? There used to be a consensus in higher education in America that education was supposed to build citizens. That consensus is outdated, however, and nothing has stepped up to replace it. There is no longer agreement among institutions of higher education about the main purpose of those four or five or six years after high school. Worse yet, there is often dissent within a single institution about its own purpose. The schools in this chapter, however, have not lost their sense of identity and purpose. They believe that a student is not just a vessel to be filled like so many gallons in the tank. They believe an education should change the vessel as well as fill it.

Also in this chapter, a college president weighs in on the role of faculty, and we will continue our discussion of college choice with attention to college ranking systems and how college counselors provide guidance to the hyper-intelligent, the self-directed, the late blooming, and yes, even the just plain different.

a community of scholars • **all design and conduct a major research project, and write a thesis, before they can graduate** • *junior qualifying exam to advance to senior status* • **one of the only small liberal arts schools that is also outstanding in the sciences** • *used to be called The Reed Institute* • **has its own nuclear reactor** • *science seniors get their own labs* • **everybody takes the same humanities core** • *no Greek system* • **no football team** • *honor code* • **ski cabin** • *no published grades (weird!)*

If there were a way to quantify cool, Reed College would rank at the very top. The shortest way to describe this school is to say that it is an extremely liberal student body wedded to an extremely conservative curriculum. That's liberal in the old sense of free, and conservative in the old sense of guarding a known good.

The college takes the radical approach that it is admitting adults, who will conduct themselves accordingly. So it does not spend a lot of institutional energy on controlling the social and personal lives of its students. The students manage student life. On the other hand, the curriculum is sacrosanct. It has hardly changed since the college was founded. Students have almost no input to the curriculum. The faculty are the guardians of the canon, and interestingly enough, Reed students are content to let them be so. The faculty are not in the habit of tinkering with the curriculum, which is a classic liberal arts and Great Books program. At Reed, if it was good enough for the Greeks, it's good enough for students today. Every decade or so something is added, such as Chinese Humanities, but other than that nothing much changes.

In this day and age of treacly concern for "the whole student," Reed is not afraid to stand up and say it is interested only in the student's mind. This school exists for the life of the mind. Reed is the epitome of an ivory tower. It is a place where students and faculty have discussions for days over whether words can ever completely convey a personal reality, and whether calculus was invented or found. It is a place where ideas matter. A lot. For their own sake.

All students participate in a humanities core, whether they are majoring in chemistry or philosophy. With an emphasis on small group seminar discussions and reading original texts, the humanities core provides a common bond for students. But the thing to "get" about Reed is that there is an academic culture here that goes well beyond the classes. You could take all the classes that are offered at Reed at many other schools, but you wouldn't capture what happens at Reed. The very atmosphere at Reed is filled with discourse. If Reed students learn nothing else, they learn to present and defend their ideas.

An interesting thing about Reed is that it is a liberal arts college that is outstanding in the sciences. Harvey Mudd is also like this, but in reverse: It is a science school that is strong in the liberal arts. Usually science and engineering schools only give lip service to liberal education, but Reed and Harvey Mudd provide the type of education that serves as a real foundation to a scholarly life. Reed has its own nuclear reactor, which will give you an idea of the level of science done here.

The students manage their own affairs through an honor principle and a peer judicial board. The honor principle is simple. *"The members of the Reed College community believe that they should take upon themselves a responsibility for maintaining standards of conduct that ensure an atmosphere of honesty and mutual trust in their academic and social lives. Such standards of conduct rest upon a principle of honor rather than a constitutional system of right and law. This principle entails the unquestioned integrity of the individual in all areas of his or her intellectual activity, and a shared responsibility for enabling the college as a whole to achieve its highest aims as a community of scholarship and learning."* This code is taken very seriously, and there are

> ❝ **The most important skill to acquire now is learning how to learn.** ❞
>
> *—John Naisbitt, futurist*

CoOl WoRd LiSt!

---

coprolite • limivorous • emporiatrics • exobiology • newel • hierodule • mortmain • sural • vidette • wen • uroboros nimbus • menhir • acedia • confubuscate • hokey-pokey • scaffolder • sibilate • shvontz • oysvurf • boid • hippopotomonstrosesquipedalian • loganamnosis • kakistocracy

many ramifications to that fact. For example, there are no test proctors at Reed. Faculty assume that no student would ever cheat, so a common faculty practice is to pass out a test and then leave the classroom.

WHY REED DECLINES TO PARTICIPATE IN NATIONAL RANKINGS

Reed has refused for years to participate in national ranking surveys, taking the position that they are not meaningful. Even the schools that rank at the top of these lists find them controversial. The first year Swarthmore was ranked number one, there were protests on that campus about the questionable nature of the honor. Was Swarthmore honored by this association with *U.S. News & World Report,* or was *U.S. News* honored by its association with Swarthmore?

Reed's stance is self-serving, but not entirely disingenuous. Reed used to show up in any list of the top liberal arts colleges in the country before *U.S. News & World Report* started its rankings. As long as it showed up on the tops of the lists, Reed never complained. What changed? Reed, or the lists? Prior to *U.S. News,* most lists were surveys of academic reputation. A magazine or other interested party would survey college presidents or deans of admission or departmental chairs on what liberal arts colleges were of highest quality. Even *U.S. News* started its controversial rankings using this methodology. Reed's reputation among college presidents, especially, is exalted. Reed is a known original source for outstanding faculty, intelligent scholars who really care about teaching at the college level, and researchers who bring creativity and passion to their work. *U.S. News* surveys, however, focus on other, more quantifiable

In a survey on academic integrity at nine large public institutions, three quarters of respondents admitted to one or more instances of "serious" cheating on tests or examinations. (Research authors: Linda K. Trevino, Pennsylvania State; Kenneth D. Butterfield, Washington State; Don McCabe, Rutgers-Newark.) Those who cheated cited "pressure to succeed." Obviously, all three-fourths of these students are at the wrong institutions for the wrong reasons. When you are at the right college for you, your goal will be to learn and discover and compete against your own standards and expectations. Cheating probably exists on every campus, but it is rare indeed at some of the schools in this book. Who would cheat at St. John's, or Reed, or Thomas Aquinas, or Hampshire, or Prescott? The concept is almost absurd.

(Source: Chronicle of Higher Education)

data, such as size of the endowment, the percentage of alumni who contribute to the college, and so on. These data are then weighted, and combined into a single, unilinear ranking of best-to-worst schools.

This is not a trivial exercise, but it is of limited validity. If you happen to personally care about the exact same criteria to the exact same weight as the editors of *U.S. News & World Report,* then the rankings will be valid for you. If you care about different things, or care more and less about the same things, *U.S. News* rankings are simply not valid for you. Think about it. Finally, you need to know that from time to time they tinker with the criteria. They claim this is in response to input from college administrators, but if that were true, they'd stop calculating unilinear ordinal rankings altogether in favor of compiling and reporting categorical data, and letting students and parents decide what mattered the most to them. I believe the real reason they remain dedicated to the ordinal rankings is so that schools will move up and down in the rankings and generate controversy and publicity.

At a convention for the National Association for College Admission Counseling, I heard a senior *U.S. News & World Report* editor actually admit, "I realize our methodology excludes some important factors. I realize that it excludes what goes on in the classroom." *What's strong about Reed College is what goes on in the classroom.*

For every accredited college and university in the U.S. and Canada go to www.donaldasher.com/colleges

> **I taught at Reed for six years and found it a wonderful, quirky, and absolutely intense academic experience. The ethos of the college— to study hard and master fields—permeated not simply the classroom but every activity on campus.**
>
> —*Reed professor*

SIZE DOES MATTER

One of my post-undergraduate almae matres is one of the highest ranking public universities in the world. Although I was impressed with the quality of the professoriate, I was very disappointed in the student body. They were, statistically, brilliant. But you would never know that from sitting in class with them. They very diligently wrote down whatever the professor said. They seldom spoke. They never ran even five minutes of class discussion. Mind you, this was at the graduate level. When one professor was too busy being famous to grade his own mid-term, I decided to leave and pursue studies elsewhere.

One of my brothers went to one of the larger Ivy League universities. His freshman calculus class had hundreds of people in it. He watched the professor on a projection screen from an assigned seat near the back of an auditorium. It was a really good thing that he already knew calculus.

> **Basically the faculty here try to guide you but stay out of the way. In fact, if you ask me, the whole place is set up that way. The student has total access to the academic endeavor. I have keys to the chemistry building, and I work all night whenever I want to. A lot of us do.**
>
> —*Reed student*

If you're really interested in comparative data on colleges, go to more complex data and think for yourself. Check out *Educational Rankings Annual* (Thompson Gale), where Reed shows up on these lists:

U.S. colleges and universities

- offering the best overall academic experience for undergraduates
- where students study the most
- with excellent instructors
- with the most accessible instructors
- which produced the most papers cited and citations for papers published
- de-emphasizing varsity sports

Private, four-year undergraduate colleges and universities

- producing the most Ph.D.s in all fields of study
- producing the most Ph.D.s in life sciences, chemistry, computer sciences, economics, English, history, mathematics, physics, astronomy, political science and international relations, psychology, anthropology, and sociology
- top baccalaureate colleges for bachelors degrees awarded to science and engineering Ph.D.s
- innovative and/or unorthodox colleges

Whatever college or university you are interested in, I recommend you check it out in *Educational Rankings Annual*. It's a great resource and fun to surf through, or you can just cut to the index and find out as much as you can about a specific institution.

Reed is a prep college, which means that the curriculum is designed to prepare students to succeed in graduate school. All seniors design and conduct a major original research proj-

PHILOSOPHICAL DIFFERENCES

At many major universities, public and private, renowned and mediocre, undergraduate classes are taught by teaching assistants, that is, graduate students who may not have been undergraduates themselves a few months ago. One Ivy League school admitted that 60 percent of its classes were taught by tenure-track professors! There are notable exceptions, such as Caltech, but not many. Reed has no graduate assistants.

ect, write a thesis, and defend their entire undergraduate education in front of an orals board. Reed even has a comprehensive written exam at the end of the junior year just to qualify to *become* a senior. After passing these hurdles, most Reed students report that graduate school is easy.

In order to de-emphasize grades, Reed has one of the weirdest grading systems in higher education: students get regular A to F grades, but they are not reported to the students. Students have to make a specific type of appointment with a dean or a faculty advisor to learn their grades, and many go all four years without doing so. This is not wise, however, as Reed also has one of the toughest grading systems in the country, along with Harvey Mudd and Swarthmore. It is extremely difficult to make an A at Reed, and only four students have graduated with a 4.0 in the last sixteen years. One faculty member explained the rationale for this system this way: "We want students to

> **The lecture method of instruction: A process by which the notes of the professor are transformed into the notes of the student without passing through the minds of either.**
>
> —*Anonymous*

To: Friends & Colleagues

Re: Rankings

I really wish we could get past the idea that academic programs can be rated—as if all students interested in a particular field were identical. I'm teaching at a small school not often heard of nationally; are we *the best* at anything? Maybe not, compared nationally; but we're way ahead of some of the most prestigious schools in being able to help some of the students who seek us out (and who would have no chance to go to a prestigious school). And certainly size and resources have much to do with the ratings. My department simply can't offer all the courses that a major university department does, nor can we afford the large library acquisitions that state funding and huge endowments can. I nonetheless think that it is a superlative department, able to prepare students better than the two major (and ranked) state universities I attended as a graduate student.

Why not focus on making the best possible match between students with their particular circumstances, and schools most able to benefit them?

Maybe that would be *the best* for everybody.

Regards,

Phil Hey

English and Writing

Briar Cliff College

Sioux City IA 51104-2100

712-279-5477

hey@briar_cliff.edu

focus on faculty comments, not the letter grade. We want them to focus on the learning itself, not the measurement of it."

In keeping with its overall philosophy, Reed has no football team and no Greek system. Students manage a few intercollegiate teams, the most popular being men's and women's rugby, but the administration does not sponsor them. Most students live on or very near the campus, and the most common social activity is going to the Paradox Café for coffee and then more coffee. The library is open from 8 A.M. to 2:30 A.M., and most students spend far more time at the library than anyplace else on campus. Seniors get their own desks in the library, and seniors in the sciences get access to their own lab space. The Reed Student Union is open twenty-four hours a day, and is the only building in the country that is 100 percent under student control by explicit writ in the constitution of the college.

Reed is its own little self-contained island in an affluent suburb of Portland. Surrounded by tree-lined streets with elegant homes, it's across the street from one of Portland's famous botanical gardens, and next to a golf course. The campus itself is a wildlife refuge, but tame ducks looked like the main "wild" life. Portland is one of the nicest small cities in the United States, with a good public transportation system. (A car is not needed at Reed.) Although Portland is in the Pacific Northwest, the annual rainfall is only 37 inches. That's less than New York City (44") and Pittsburgh (38"), and way less than Miami (56") and New Orleans (65").

Reed has a ski cabin on Mt. Hood, where, at least in theory, you can ski twelve months of the year. Any currently enrolled student can stay there at any time, for free. The Pacific Ocean is a couple of hours away, with Cannon Beach, Haystack Rock, and an elaborate system of tide pools being the top attractions.

DOWNSIDE: Reed was once called the "Parris Island of prep schools," after Parris Island, South Carolina, the famed boot camp for the United States Marine Corps.

REED SCHOLARS WIN HONORS

National Science Foundation (73)	Fulbright (43)	Goldwater (11)	Danforth (2)
Watson (55)	Rhodes (30)	Marshall (2)	Carnegie (2)
	Mellon (18)	American Association of University Women (2)	Churchill (1)

Although Reed glories in its reputation as a tough place, it has significantly beefed up student support services in recent years. Still, some students are going to prefer an easier place to spend four years. Students who thrive at Reed are often a little more mature, a little better able to take care of themselves, and dedicated to their studies. Students who fail at Reed often fail because they can't handle the social freedom or they lack the self-discipline to keep performing when external motivators are withdrawn. For example, faculty don't assign busy work to see if students are keeping up with the class assignments. Many classes are graded on two papers or two exams per semester, and that allows a student to get *way* behind before anyone else will notice.

One student told me that she felt the faculty fawned over those students who were going on to graduate school, especially the ones who planned to become college professors themselves. [Just to be fair, this is a common complaint at all institutions of

> ❝ **You could take from me everything I've learned at Reed, and I could get it back on my own. What they really teach you here is how to learn.** ❞
>
> —*Reed student*

EVERY REED SENIOR WRITES A THESIS

Here are a few examples, out of a few thousand:

Platonic Soul Theory in the Middle Dialogues: The Phaedo, The Republic, The Phaedrus

Deamidation of Glutamine and Asparagine Residues: An Approach to the Study of Protein Folding

Acetylcholine in the Barnacle Central Nervous System, Or, The Light That Never Did Shine

Olympia: The Plural Ideal, Modern Greek Spacetime & The Art of Mass Consumption

Acousto-optics and Real-Time Fourier Spectrum Analysis of Radio-Frequency Spectra

Jews Burn Too: The Development of Hell in Judaic Theology from the Exile through the Herodian Period

Cannibalism and Anticannibal Behavior in Bombina Orientalis: The Oriental Fire Bellied Toad

The Demolition of Zhejiangcun: A State Spectacle of Destruction in a Beijing Migrant Enclave

An Additive Synthesis of Jungian and Eliadian Archetypal Theory

Dueling Galaxies

Electron Relaxation in a Quantum Dot by Defect-Assisted Tunneling

The Dynamics of Flylines and Other Classical Strings

Energy Czars and Hot Boxes: Appropriate Energy Matching Using Second-Law Efficiency and Solar Dynamics

Death from Above: The Global Smiting of the Amphibian

Aplusia Californica: It's Not Just for Breakfast Anymore

Borders & Boundaries: Cowboys, Cactus & Cuervo in El Paso, Texas

Regeneration of Rear Derailleur Efficacy Following Chronic Exposure to Substantial Litterfall in Pacific Northwest Forests & Xenopus Laevis Splenocytes

higher learning.] She told me, "If you weren't one of their darlings, you just didn't get the same attention. A lot of Reedies are just after a good education, and then they plan to go to work, or they may not even know what they want to do after graduation. It would be nice if the school acknowledged that better."

Reed has an egalitarian flavor, with a complete range of socioeconomic backgrounds, and an increasingly diverse student body—approaching 25 percent students of color. But the college has no minority-focused scholarships. (On the other hand, if you do get into Reed you'll know it wasn't because of your race.)

Finally, Reed is so intense that students sometimes don't plan for the day after graduation. They are so focused on finishing their theses and passing their oral exams that they wait until June to even think about what to do after Reed. This is a minority of students, of course, but a noticeable phenomenon nonetheless. This doesn't seem to keep them from succeeding later, however.

MORE UPSIDE: Understanding that many of the most brilliant students are poorly served by the secondary education system in this country, Reed will sometimes take a chance on a student with great potential whom other schools would pass over. If you have evidence that you're brilliant, or even just unusually driven to succeed, Reed is probably going to be interested in you. Reed is the best school in the country that

CoOl WeB SiTe!

Check out the latest and past winners of the annual Bulwer-Lytton Fiction Contest for bad writing, named after Edward George Earl Bulwer-Lytton, who once began a novel, "It was a dark and stormy night . . ." Here's a recent winning entry for worst first sentence of an imaginary novel:

Through the gathering gloom of a late-October afternoon, along the greasy, cracked paving-stones slick from the sputum of the sky, Stanley Ruddlethorp wearily trudged up the hill from the cemetery where his wife, sister, brother, and three children were all buried, and forced open the door of his decaying house, blissfully unaware of the catastrophe that was soon to devastate his life.

Perhaps your entire freshman dorm would like to enter this year's contest. Check it out at www.bulwer-lytton.com.

While we're on this topic, a popular dorm activity at many colleges is to try to get a letter in Dear Abby or Miss Manners. Students invent all types of maladies, dilemmas, and pickles, and see if Abby or Judith will step forward with the solution. Handwritten letters work best. I believe the reigning champions for this are Yale students, but I am not sure who's keeping score. Oh, and one more tip: You can't all have the same postmark.

will consider a student with an imperfect background. The other top schools just won't, although many say they will.

You know Reed is doing things right when you talk to Reed alumni. They are almost cultlike in their devotion to this school. I met an alumnus who named his son after the college, and while reading student theses in the library, I came across this dedication, "To Reed College, with love." That's just not going to happen at most institutions. To Reed College, with love.

See for yourself.

Also, all the top schools that I have visited have different cultures; you might even call them atmospheres. Some of the schools full of the best and the brightest students have a leaden atmosphere, humorless, maybe even almost oppressive. But Reed has an undercurrent of irreverence and lightheartedness that offsets the seriousness of the academic workload. When I visited, there was a television buried face up in the middle of the lawn, showing Oprah reruns to the sky. Near it was a labyrinth laid out by hundreds of toothbrushes no doubt stolen from the dorms. Reed has an almost British acceptance of eccentricity. There's a Reed professor whose patents have done well, who has a Rolls-Royce with a uniformed driver wait for him outside his classes. Somewhere else this might be odd. Not at Reed.

Finally, because of all the communicating, orally and in writing, that Reed students have to do, they become highly effective and productive scholars later. Reed students win Fulbright, Rhodes, Mellon, and Watson and other prestigious academic honors and fellowships in numbers all out of proportion to the size of the college.

CROSS APPS: If you're interested in the scholarly community aspect of Reed College, check out the University of Chicago, St. John's College, Swarthmore College, Oberlin College and to a greater and lesser degree, any of the better liberal arts colleges. See the list beginning on p. 87. Also, check out The University of the South (aka Sewanee), which is very different but oddly similar, and not well known.

If you're interested in the Great Books aspect of Reed College, see also St. John's,

> **I would not trade the thesis experience for anything. Being involved in a project of such length and scope has prepared me for future writing and work in ways I could have never imagined. It has taught me that I can do high quality, consistent work for a year on one question and learn about a subject to a depth that I didn't even realize existed, let alone existed within my grasp. Being a senior writing a thesis with every other senior creates a bond. And one day when I was feeling particularly discouraged, I went into the thesis tower and read the Beat poets' theses from the '50s. Being connected with them made me feel connected to the academy and, quite frankly, to the past and the world in a way I didn't think I could ever feel. The experience has been priceless.**
>
> *—Reed alumna*

Reed comprises one-third of a book by Burton R. Clark, *The Distinctive College* (Transaction Publishers), in which Clark explicates what makes Reed an unusual and distinctive institution. The other two schools covered in the book are Antioch and Swarthmore.

Reed actually does offer underwater basket weaving as an activity during winter break.

Thomas Aquinas, Shimer College, The Thomas More College of Liberal Arts, and the University of Chicago.

If you're interested in the senior thesis, see also Princeton University, New College of Florida, and Davidson. I want to stress that this is an incomplete list, and that many other schools also allow, and some may require, a capstone project. Pay attention to the details, however. Some schools' "capstone project" is little more than a scrapbook of "stuff I learned while I was in college," while other schools' senior research project results in a thesis that could be published as an academic book. By the way, at some of the schools I visited, the undergraduate theses were vastly superior to many of the graduate theses I've read in my day.

If you're interested in Reed's honor code, you should know that approximately twenty of the older liberal arts schools still have them. At some schools the honor code is still taken seriously, while at others it's a vestige of more quaint times. At Reed, it remains the law of student conduct. As an interesting trivia item, many of these honor codes were first compromised when Ronald Reagan decided that each school receiving federal funding should have "an alcohol and drug abuse policy." That codified policy compromised the intellectual tradition of having a moral code embodied in the students themselves, and at many schools was an invitation to trash the honor code system in favor of rules and regulations provided by the administration.

Reed College

3203 S.E. Woodstock Blvd.

Portland, OR 97202

503-771-1112

www.reed.edu

INTERESTED IN A CAREER IN HIGHER EDUCATION?

Whether you are interested in being a college professor or an administrator, start reading the *Chronicle of Higher Education* while you're an undergraduate. You can read it for free at any college library. It's hilarious—full of intrigue, sexual shenanigans, embezzlements, bold power plays, cheating, and lots of government conspiracies. In fact, it reads like a police blotter for the ivory tower set. Of course it also has scientific breakthroughs and such, but it is the soap opera aspect of it that I find fascinating. And you thought these people were stuffy and staid . . .

A SHORT HISTORY OF EDUCATIONAL REFORM

The second to the last big education reform movement came about because the Russians launched Sputnik, the Earth's first human-made satellite, in 1957. A few years later President John F. Kennedy and his advisors, a lot of Eastern-school academics commonly known as the "Brain Trust," belatedly decided this constituted a national emergency. They poured money and rhetoric into education like it mattered. This wave pretty much died out after we walked on the moon twelve years later and the Russians could only watch. Not long after that NASA laid off thousands of engineers and scientists.

The last big education reform movement, which is still reverberating, was sparked by "A Nation at Risk," a special report of the National Commission on Excellence in Education. It contained the famous comment that U.S. education was facing "a rising tide of mediocrity" and bemoaned that "secondary school curricula have been homogenized, diluted, and diffused to the point that they no longer have a central purpose. In effect, we have a cafeteria-style curriculum in which the appetizers and desserts can easily be mistaken for the main courses." The report also pointed out that 25 percent of high school student credits were in health and physical education or remedial classes. The same trend was afoot at universities, covered in a later study funded by the Carnegie Foundation for the Advancement of Teaching and reported in Ernest L. Boyer's *College: The Undergraduate Experience in America* (Carnegie Foundation for the Advancement of Teaching), a book frequently cited in this text. At the same time, Americans were told to fear the Japanese, that the Japanese were overtaking us in mathematics and the basic sciences, and something "needed to be done."

This spawned the call in state legislatures from coast to coast for a return to "basics" and "standards," which they believed, being legislators and lawyers, they were best suited to define. Academics, who spent their lives studying how students learn and what they might benefit from learning, were ignored. This trend is still in full swing, with calls for a national high school exam and more and harder teacher testing.

During this same time, say, the last twenty years, there has been a totally separate and countervailing trend to reinvestigate the notion of a canon. In short, the proponents of this trend wanted an answer to this question: Ought we to study the thoughts and writings of only dead, white, European males?

Some major universities with academic reputations of the first order, are busy diluting, homogenizing, and diffusing their curriculum "to the point that they no longer have a central purpose," caved in totally to this trend and threw the baby out with the bath

> And, as a final comment, I think 'priceless' is the best word to describe the quality of my Reed education. Priceless in the same way that an Egyptian artifact is priceless: you can put a monetary value on it, but the monetary value has nothing to do with the true value. Reed has changed my life for the better in ways I didn't know my life could be changed when I arrived here. It has put me in touch with an intellectual and ideological rigor without which I would not be the human being I am now. It has given me the insight and training which I think I need to be a healthy, happy, and productive human being. I will be eternally grateful and incapable of expressing how valuable the experience truly was.
> —*Reed alumna*

water. "All thought is equal," they capitulated, "and whatever students want to study is fine with us, so long as they pay the tuition." Without naming names, let us say these were some of the very best institutions. Some of these same institutions have also been suffering massive grade inflation, as the average grade went from a C+ to an A-, presumably without the student work improving so dramatically. Student reviews of faculty were also popularized in higher education during this time, and the locus of power in many institutions shifted from the faculty toward the students.

We have to ask ourselves, Is this entirely good?

Certainly, some of it *is* good. But there is a reason that we still concern ourselves with the Greco-Roman-European tradition, and there is a reason that that tradition survived and accrued for some twenty-five centuries to come to us virtually intact. You can learn many things at a smorgasbord school, but will it be, ultimately, a coherent education? The schools without a pandering faculty resisted abandoning the canon in favor of improving it. They saw that the students had a point in wanting to add female and minority voices and points of view to the canon, and wanting to learn more about other, separate-but-just-as-important traditions, such as the five thousand years of Chinese history. But they did not decide that any collection of courses stacked up to an education.

SO YOU THINK COLLEGE PRESIDENTS HAVE IT EASY?

Recently, college presidents have had to resign for plagiarizing a speech, for having a long-term affair with a family member's wife, for "misappropriating" $1.5 million, and for sexually harassing subordinates and downloading "sexual content" on college computers. And a trustee resigned in protest when a college president refused to resign after "misleading statements" were found on the resumé he used to get his appointment. Hmmmm. Looks like college presidents are "just folks" after all.

While we're on this topic, it is common practice for advising professors to list themselves as the primary author on work that is overwhelmingly, and sometimes entirely, done by graduate students. One professor at a "research university" was so in the habit of this that it is unclear when he last did any research of his own. One of the papers he so appropriated turned out to have been plagiarized by the student in the first place. What a dilemma! Beg off that he stole the work in the first place? Or fall on his sword as a plagiarist? Thief? Plagiarist? Tough call. He and his department just decided that he should retire early. Maybe there is a God.

The latest attempt at higher education reform comes from President George W. Bush's federal Commission on the Future of Higher Education. The commission, pushing for accountability and measurement of learning, stopped just short of demanding a national, standardized exit examination for graduating seniors. It is important to note that George W. Bush is famous for saying, "Rarely is the question asked: Is our children learning?" Stay tuned for updates; this debate is surely not over.

CoOl Web SiTe!

Check out www.collegiatechoice.com for a selection of college tour videotapes made by independent college counselors, as in, not affiliated with the school covered in the videotape. They vary in quality, but the interest factor and the honesty are astounding.

> **Nearly all men can stand adversity, but if you want to test a man's character, give him power.**
>
> —*Abraham Lincoln*

CoOl BoOk AlErT!

The Fiske Guide to Colleges by Edward B. Fiske (Times Books)

There are dozens of college guides, many of which are very good at getting the basic statistics out about a college. There are none that I would censure. However, there is a special place in my heart for the *Fiske Guide*. Edward B. Fiske has spent almost two decades publishing his guide, which goes beyond the statistics to give you an idea of the flavor of a place. He respects the student who might be interested in something a little different, and does the best job of describing the schools that are not cookie-cutter copies of the norm. Also, and this matters, he actually *likes* colleges. He writes about them as if they might be great places to go and learn, and in this, he is right. Check it out. Want to know the best way to check out a guide? See if the schools are organized nationally or by state. If by state, the guide was not written for the student interested in a nationally significant institution.

SWARTHMORE COLLEGE

a very impressive student body • **academically demanding** • *well funded* • **tough grading** • *school of engineering* • **tradition**

Swarthmore is the quintessential liberal arts college. It is both academically excellent and just the right amount of insular, creating a scholarly community virtually free of distractions. It is located on a campus of green lawns and tree-studded rolling hills in a suburb of Philadelphia. In fact, the entire campus is a nationally registered arboretum. It snows in the winter. You can take a train from the edge of campus to downtown Philadelphia, and with one transfer you can be in New York City. When you see the college experience in old movies, this is what they were trying to re-create. Except at Swarthmore, it's not a movie; it's the real thing.

Swarthmore has long had a preference for valedictorians, and has at times claimed the highest percentage of valedictorians of any institution in the United States. Although not every student is a valedictorian by any stretch of the imagination, their presence permeates the campus as a whole. Valedictorians set very high standards for themselves, and tend to be good citizens as well as good students. The student body at Swarthmore is respected by the faculty, and there is an understanding here that students will conduct themselves with professionalism and decorum.

In fact, student housing is mixed in with faculty offices and classrooms. Nowhere else would the administration be crazy enough to put students and their stereos so close to classrooms and professors' offices, but at Swarthmore this has not created many problems. The school is committed to the practice. The value of mingling faculty, student life, and teaching spaces is seen as more than worth an occasional disruption.

"Class" as a discrete activity that happens within four walls and fifty minutes is a misnomer at Swarthmore, where learning spills over into all hours and all places.

Swarthmore is very intentionally a culturally diverse community. The school goes to great lengths to recruit minority and international students with outstanding academic preparation. Originally started by Quakers, Swarthmore continues to have an activist tradition. The students and the institution itself are more involved in global affairs than would be the case at many liberal arts colleges.

The students work hard, some would say very hard, but mostly they compete with their own expectations. Like Reed and Harvey Mudd, Swarthmore has very tough grading. A popular campus T-shirt used to be, "Anywhere else it would have been an 'A.'" Making Bs is often shocking to students who were valedictorians at their high schools, but the grading system lets everyone know there is always room for improvement.

Swarthmore is organized like a mini-university, with Black studies, engineering,

GRADE INFLATION

Swarthmore is one of four colleges with virtually no grade inflation. (Harvey Mudd, Reed, and Sewanee are the others.) Students who have never made a B learn how at Swarthmore. At any of these schools, a B is an indication of extreme effort *and* talent, and an A still means "outstanding." An A is, in fact, extraordinary in the literal meaning of the term.

Grade inflation originated in response to certain U.S. military draft policies of the Vietnam War era. For a time, young men could get a draft deferral by being full-time college students. Faculty members became reluctant to give young men failing grades, as they could be sentencing those young men to tours of duty in Vietnam. So students who should have flunked out received a C, and students who were legitimately earning a C now "deserved" a B, and students earning a B got an A. The "Gentleman's C," originally a weak effort that nonetheless complied with all course requirements, became a solid B. Eventually, a C became something it had not been before then: shameful. Grade inflation has been exacerbated in recent years by student aid policies with minimum GPA requirements ("Prof. Wilson, if you give me a B I'll lose my scholarship!") and the continuing devolution of higher education into a pander bear for students as consumers (grade harshly and watch your student reviews drop like a rock). So today students who come to class and comply with the minimum course requirements strongly believe that they "deserve" an A.

This problem is continuing to worsen. It starts in high school, where students with a pulse expect to make an A. This is one reason that admissions deans are spending more time on activities, evidence of focus and strength of character, and SATs and ACTs. There are so many young men and women with nearly perfect GPAs that it is just not that useful to use the GPA as an admissions decision-making tool.

CoOl BoOk AlErT!

Colleges That Change Lives by Loren Pope, Director of the College Placement Bureau and former education editor for the *New York Times* (Penguin USA)

Loren Pope is no fan of large research universities, which he proves "cheat undergraduates" using an array of statistical, rhetorical, and anecdotal presentations. Graduates of small colleges are overrepresented in the faculty of major research universities. The faculty of major research universities are more, not less, likely to send their own children to small colleges. An analysis of *Who's Who,* Nobel, and other national and international honor listings shows that graduates of small colleges are overrepresented, statistically. A small college can turn an indifferent high school student into a lifelong scholar. And on and on. Pope identifies and describes forty colleges that "change lives." This is a fantastic book for any student, teacher, or counselor. Here are Pope's forty schools, in reverse alphabetical order:

Whitman College, Walla Walla, Washington

Wheaton College, Wheaton, Illinois

Western Maryland College, Westminster, Maryland

Wabash College, Crawfordsville, Indiana

Ursinus College, Collegeville, Pennsylvania

Southwestern University, Georgetown, Texas

St. Olaf College, Northfield, Minnesota

St. John's College, Annapolis, Maryland, and
   Santa Fe, New Mexico

St. Andrews Presbyterian College, Laurinburg,
   North Carolina

Rhodes College, Memphis, Tennessee

Reed College, Portland, Oregon

Ohio Wesleyan University, Delaware, Ohio

Millsaps College, Jackson, Mississippi

Marlboro College, Marlboro, Vermont

Lynchburg College, Lynchburg, Virginia

Lawrence University, Appleton, Wisconsin

Knox College, Galesburg, Illinois

Kalamazoo College, Kalamazoo, Michigan

Juniata College, Huntingdon, Pennsylvania

Hope College, Holland, Michigan

Hiram College, Hiram, Ohio

Hendrix College, Conway, Arkansas

Hampshire College, Amherst, Massachusetts

Guilford College, Greensboro, North Carolina

Goucher College, Towson, Maryland

Evergreen State College, Olympia, Washington

Emory and Henry College, Emory, Virginia

Eckerd College, St. Petersburg, Florida

Earlham College, Richmond, Indiana

Denison University, Granville, Ohio

Cornell College, Mount Vernon, Iowa

College of Wooster, Wooster, Ohio

Clark University, Worcester, Massachusetts

Centre College, Danville, Kentucky

Birmingham-Southern College, Birmingham, Alabama

Beloit College, Beloit, Wisconsin

Austin College, Sherman, Texas

Antioch College, Yellow Springs, Ohio

Allegheny College, Meadville, Pennsylvania

Agnes Scott College, Decatur, Georgia

Also see Cool Book Alert! on p. 48 for Pope's *Looking Beyond the Ivy League.*

computer science, and other emphases that are not common at liberal arts colleges. It also has one of the most vigorous career planning and placement offices available at any college, with 265 companies recruiting Swarthmore students every year. (In case you don't realize it, this is *very* unusual at a liberal arts college.) Basically, Swarthmore packs a major punch in a little package.

The college offers an honors option that is similar to Reed's senior thesis project, leading to oral examinations. A Swarthmore degree, with or without the honors option, is a valuable ticket to life. Swarthmore graduates are all over the world, but they are particularly well represented in the Northeast. Once you are a member of this family, you are well connected.

Most of the socializing at Swarthmore seems to focus on small group gatherings, many of them impromptu. The college puts Adirondack chairs on the lawn in front of Parrish Hall, and students can be found reading in them even in inclement winter. (They call it "Parrish Beach.") The Greek and varsity athletic systems are typical, but definitely take a back seat to academics.

DOWNSIDE: It is quite difficult to get into Swarthmore. They reject three out of four applicants. I found Swarthmore administrators to be very friendly and approachable, in spite of this. Some schools that I won't name have absolutely arrogant administrators, but Swarthmore seems to be staffed by conscientious administrators who seem genuinely delighted to get to work with this student body.

> **All my classes are taught by full professors. They earned their doctorates at the best graduate programs. When I get ready to go to graduate school, they can open a lot of doors for me. That's just not true as an undergraduate at a large university.**
>
> —*Swarthmore student*

" Swarthmore? Intense. In a word, intense. " —*Swarthmore student*

Swarthmore can be a big challenge. Students who are happy at Swarthmore like to study; they enjoy the work itself. Students who are unhappy at Swarthmore tend to be unhappy because of the workload and the unrelentingly high expectations. On the other hand, many of the students at Swarthmore exacerbate the workload by committing to a list of activities that would wear out a pair of identical twins pretending to be one person. The admissions materials coming out of Swarthmore today downplay the workload, but it is very real.

MORE UPSIDE: Swarthmore is always ranked at or near the top for liberal arts colleges in the United States by *U.S. News & World Report,* which means you don't have to explain your decision to go there to your parents or your friends. Swarthmore is in a very secure position, with good management and good funding, and is unlikely to fall very far from its lofty perch any time in the immediate future. It has deep pockets, which allow it to make competitive or superior financial aid offers. If you can get into Swarthmore, you'll probably survive it financially.

Finally, Swarthmore graduates seem universally grateful for the experience. I've interviewed a number of them, and they seem to have some *je ne sais* what, a kind of confidence that comes from substantial and real personal accomplishment. At the risk of being corny, they glow from within.

CROSS APPS: Swarthmore is not unlike many elite liberal arts schools; it just happens to do a very, very good job of being a liberal arts college. If you are attracted to Swarthmore, also consider the schools in the following section, or any good liberal arts school in the nation.

Swarthmore College
500 College Avenue
Swarthmore, PA 19081
610-328-8000
www.swarthmore.edu

For every accredited college and university in the U.S. and Canada go to www.donaldasher.com/colleges

CoOl ScHoLaRsHiP!

You've heard of the Rhodes and perhaps the Watson and the Fulbright and the Javits, but have you heard of the Wofford Presidential International Scholarship? Wofford College of Spartanburg, South Carolina, offers a fully supported year of international travel in the developing world to "the singular student best fitted to benefit humankind." Students submit travel and service plans in an open competition to win this scholarship. Wofford also publishes the first novels of select creative writing students under the Benjamin Wofford Prize. How's that for a college that honors and supports its own students? Check them out.

THE CONSORTIUM OF LIBERAL ARTS COLLEGES (CLAC)

The Consortium of Liberal Arts Colleges (CLAC) evolved from a series of meetings of college presidents at Oberlin College in the 1980s. The original concern was for the future of the liberal arts college as an educational institution with a clear vision of what it wanted to provide to undergraduate students. It has since evolved to focus on academic and administrative computing and related technologies, ways to create economies of scale by consortium, and so on. Basically, it serves as a forum for the exchange of ideas among its members. These are all excellent schools.

The present membership includes the following colleges and universities, in reverse alphabetical order:

Williams College, Williamstown, Massachusetts

Whittier College, Whittier, California

Whitman College, Walla Walla, Washington

Wheaton College, Wheaton, Illinois

Wheaton College, Norton, Massachusetts

Wesleyan University, Middletown, Connecticut

Wellesley College, Wellesley, Masschusetts

Washington and Lee University, Lexington, Virginia

Washington College, Chestertown, Maryland

Wabash College, Crawfordsville, Indiana

Vassar College, Poughkeepsie, New York

Union College, Schenectady, New York

Trinity University, San Antonio, Texas

Trinity College, Hartford, Connecticut

Swarthmore College, Swarthmore, Pennsylvania

St. Olaf College, Northfield, Minnesota

St. Lawrence University, Canton, New York

Smith College, Northampton, Massachusetts

Skidmore College, Saratoga Springs, New York

Sewanee - University of the South, Sewanee, Tennessee

Rhodes College, Memphis, Tennessee

Reed College, Portland, Oregon

Pomona College, Claremont, California

Ohio Wesleyan University, Delaware, Ohio

Occidental College, Los Angeles, California

Oberlin College, Oberlin, Ohio

Mount Holyoke College, South Hadley, Massachusetts

Mills College, Oakland, California

Middlebury College, Middlebury, Vermont

Manhattan College, Riverdale, New York

Macalester College, Saint Paul, Minnesota

Lawrence University, Appleton, Wisconsin

Lafayette College, Easton, Pennsylvania

Kenyon College, Gambier, Ohio

Kalamazoo College, Kalamazoo, Michigan

Hope College, Holland, Michigan

Haverford College, Haverford, Pennsylvania

Harvey Mudd College, Claremont, California

Hamilton College, Clinton, New York

Grinnell College, Grinnell, Iowa

CoOl BoOk AlErT!

College: The Undergraduate Experience in America by Ernest L. Boyer
(Carnegie Foundation for the Advancement of Teaching)

Ernest L. Boyer conducted a national review of undergraduate education as part of a grant from the Carnegie Foundation for the Advancement of Teaching. The result was *College: The Undergraduate Experience in America.* The book investigates the undergraduate educational process, what is done well and what is done poorly, and goes beyond a purely descriptive approach to attempt to be prescriptive. It is a bold book. It makes an argument for an integrated core of knowledge followed by a thoughtful accumulation of expertise in a major field of study; it rejects the smorgasbord approach to curricular offerings. It reveals the trials and tribulations of being a professor, or a student, at different types of institutions. Anyone involved in higher education, either as a student or a member of faculty or staff, should check it out. This will probably be the last book of its type, as higher education sinks into relativism, curricula become "student oriented," and grade inflation is the law of the land. For the latest research findings, go to SUNY Stony Brook's home page, www.sunysb.edu, and click on "Boyer Commission Report."

Gettysburg College, Gettysburg, Pennsylvania

Franklin and Marshall College, Lancaster, Pennsylvania

Earlham College, Richmond, Indiana

Dickinson College, Carlisle, Pennsylvania

DePauw University, Greencastle, Indiana

Denison University, Granville, Ohio

Davidson College, Davidson, North Carolina

Connecticut College, New London, Connecticut

Colorado College, Colorado Springs, Colorado

College of Wooster, Wooster, Ohio

College of the Holy Cross, Worcester, Massachusetts

Colgate University, Hamilton, New York

Colby College, Waterville, Maine

Carleton College, Northfield, Minnesota

Bucknell University, Lewisburg, Pennsylvania

Bryn Mawr College, Bryn Mawr, Pennsylvania

Bowdoin College, Brunswick, Maine

Beloit College, Beloit, Wisconsin

Bates College, Lewiston, Maine

Amherst College, Amherst, Massachusetts

Alma College, Alma, Michigan

Albion College, Albion, Michigan

THE HIGHEST PAID PROFESSORS IN AMERICA
(AVERAGE SALARY OF FULL PROFESSOR)

Harvard University $168,700

Princeton University $156,800

Stanford University $156,200

University of Chicago $155,100

Yale University $151,200

University of Pennsylvania $149,900

California Institute of Technology $147,900

Yeshiva University $144,200

New York University $144,000

(Source: The Chronicle of Higher Education)

Check out the CLAC Web site at www.liberalarts.org. Also, be sure to remember that there are at least two hundred other excellent liberal arts colleges that just don't happen to belong to this association.

What about Bryn Mawr?

Bryn Mawr is without a doubt one of the most intellectually-oriented colleges in the country. Scholarship is revered for its own sake, conversation is practically a religion, and the students have a shoulders-back confidence that is inspiring. The school is a prodigious producer of future Ph.D.s, especially in the humanities. The faculty are famously committed. The students are famously independent thinkers—and the students play as hard as they work—at least some of them do.

As a lecturer at college and university campuses all over the nation, I have developed an unusual campus ranking system: humor. At some campuses, students wouldn't get a joke if you explained it to them and provided diagrams and drawings. Most disappointing of all, at some campuses that are supposedly famous for their academic quality if you tell a joke the students just write it down! But at Bryn Mawr the students always get every joke, no matter how subtle. Bryn Mawr ranks number one in the nation according to my humor intelligence scale.

I would not give a beggar a crust of bread, but I would build him a library.

—*Andrew Carnegie*

UNIVERSITY OF CHICAGO

one of the world's great universities • **with a quirky student body who would rather study than . . . well, anything** **ranked dead last for social life, and proud of it** • *more Nobels than a Swedish phone book (70, to be exact)* • **3,900 undergraduates** • *8,550 graduate students*

The University of Chicago is like a Roman city, rising from the shores of Lake Michigan just south of downtown Chicago. It *feels* like a great university, with massive English gothic architecture framing expansive green lawns. Totally lopsided in favor of graduate studies, it nevertheless offers its undergraduates a chance to go to university with like-minded overly studious young scholars. Serious intellectualism is in here, and the type of career-minded lollygaggers you find at some of the Ivy League campuses is totally absent. Welcome to a study hall that never ends.

The University of Chicago is famous among the academic crowd for three things. First, it ranked dead last in a survey of social life at colleges and universities. Instead of bemoaning this fact, the students printed up T-shirts with this number on them, "300," a cryptic reference to being found 300th, dead last, in this ranking. ("No social life" generally means more or less sober students sitting around and discussing books and ideas.)

> **Chicago students continue to revel in the stereotype that they are library-shackled intellectuals.**
>
> *—Chronicle of Higher Education*

Professors at Chicago are not called "Dr." or "Professor," as this is thought to detract from the community-of-scholars concept. Also, for the same reason, freshmen are called "first-year students."

Second, Dr. Hanna Grey, a former University of Chicago president, told her students that they needed to get out more, go to the bars in Chicago, and get more of a social life going. This caused quite a stir. While other colleges and universities are fretting over excessive alcohol use by their students, Dr. Grey thought that what her students needed most was a good night out on the town. At least once a month or, if that was too distracting, once per semester. Recently, the students held a mock "Fun In" after the administration again focused on their lack of a social life.

Third, the University of Chicago asks the weirdest questions on its application essay. One example: "Given the probability that the federal tax code, nondairy creamer, Dennis Rodman and the art of mime all came from outer space, name something else that has extraterrestrial origins and defend your hypothesis." Another one invited the candidate to pitch a TV pilot involving Van Gogh's ear, a proton accelerator, and Muddy Waters guitar. Students are warned: "Remember that this is Chicago so it is better to err on the side of intellectual pretension than on the side of pure silliness." One thing is certain: The University of Chicago does not want your form essay.

Although usually mentioned in the company of Princeton and Yale, Chicago goes its own way. It is a very intentionally scholarly place, interested in truth and thought for its own sake, tolerant of all manner of quirkiness as long as it is accompanied by a razor-sharp mind. It once refused to give an honorary doctorate to Queen Elizabeth "because she hadn't made significant contributions to a field of study."

So, what do you learn at the University of Chicago? There is a core curriculum somewhat like Reed's and having a great deal in common with St. John's. It focuses on a Great Books sequence and mastery of a second language. After that, you can branch out in many directions at one of the great research universities in the world. Chicago claims, with no false humility, that "in the wake of the national hue and cry over the failings of higher education the College does not seek a 'return' to higher standards because it never left them."

DOWNSIDE: Chicago has no traditional collegiate social life. This is either a draw or a repulsion, but it would be a mistake to be neutral about it. Like Swarthmore,

---

Chicago is one of the few schools that is roughly gender balanced. It has approximately half men and half women. Women outnumber men in most schools except engineering specialty schools and some business programs. Where are all the men? Not in college, is what the sociologists say.

Chicago can certainly be relentless. Also, Chicago recently went through a period of turmoil, in which the core curriculum was cut by one-seventh amid great protest, eventually resulting in the ousting of the prior president of the university. Perhaps that will be old news by the time you arrive. Finally, Chicago really is a Class I research university (see the Carnegie Foundation system for classifying colleges and universities, this page). It has teaching assistants, bigger classes, and a more impersonal atmosphere. It's like its own town, with several newspapers and more than one culture. It's the only university strongly recommended in this book (if you don't count the *much* smaller Caltech or the overnamed University of the South). It's here for two reasons: one, it makes minimal use of teaching assistants, and two, the quality and particular nature of the program are too strong to overlook.

MORE UPSIDE: This is a quality education, certainly one of the very best available in the country for an internally driven and self-consciously intellectual person.

University of Chicago
5801 South Ellis Avenue
Chicago, IL 60637
773-702-1234
www.uchicago.edu

THE CARNEGIE FOUNDATION FOR THE ADVANCEMENT OF TEACHING CLASSIFICATION SYSTEM

There are two major classification systems for colleges and universities in the United States: the National College Athletic Association's Divisions I, II, and III, with subcategories that have to do with intercollegiate athletic competition, and the Carnegie Foundation for the Advancement of Teaching Classification System, which has to do with the missions of the institutions themselves. Academics everywhere refer to the Carnegie system, but rarely is it explicated. Here it is. Now when an academic intones to you, "This is a Class I research university," you'll know to respond, "What you mean is that educating bright young undergraduates is not really the central mission of this institution."

> I chose the University of Chicago because I wanted to be at a school that will call me a first-year instead of a freshman, teach me how to think, show me that facts aren't important, and arm me with the necessary knowledge to strike fear into the hearts of Ivy League graduates!
>
> —*University of Chicago student*

> **❝ I wanted to go to a place where it wouldn't be weird to spend Saturday night in the library, and indeed, all my friends would be there too. ❞**
>
> —*University of Chicago student*

Research Universities

RU/VH: Research Universities (very high research activity)

Formerly and still commonly known as a Class I research institution

RU/H: Research Universities (high research activity)

1. May have a full range of baccalaureate programs, *but...*

2. Committed to graduate education through the doctorate

3. Give high priority to research

4. Receive extensive external funding

5. Produce high volume of scholarly works (publications)

6. Labs, famous professors, etc., may not be accessible to undergrads

Doctoral Universities

DRU: Doctoral/Research Universities

1. May or may not have full range of baccalaureate programs

2. Committed to graduate education through the doctorate

3. Produce less research for external consumption

4. Award at least 20 doctoral degrees per year

Master's Universities and Colleges

1. Award at least 50 master's degrees per year

2. Divided into three categories by size: larger, medium, smaller

Baccalaureate Colleges

1. Award fewer than 50 master's degrees per year, fewer than 20 doctoral degrees per year, and at least 10 percent of undergraduate degrees are bachelor's degrees

2. Divided into categories by major academic foci, as follows:

3. Bac/A&S: baccalaureate colleges—arts and sciences*

4. Bac/Diverse: baccalaureate colleges—diverse fields

5. Bac/Assoc: baccalaureate/associate's colleges

Almost all liberal arts colleges fit this classification.

Associate's Colleges

1. All or almost all degrees are at the associate's level; bachelor's degrees account for less than 10 percent of undergraduate degrees

2. Divided into 14 categories by mission

Special Focus Institutions

1. Spec/Faith: theological seminaries, Bible colleges, and other faith-related institutions

2. Spec/Medical: medical schools and medical centers

3. Spec/Health: other health profession schools

4. Spec/Eng: schools of engineering

5. Spec/Tech: other technology-related schools

6. Spec/Bus: schools of business and management

7. Spec/Arts: schools of art, music, and design

8. Spec/Law: schools of law

9. Spec/Other: other special-focus institutions

Tribal Colleges

1. Members of the American Indian Higher Education Consortium

It is important to note that these are not rankings, and should in no way be considered or construed as rankings. This was never the intent of the Carnegie Foundation for the Advancement of Teaching. This is a system for categorizing institutions by their missions, i.e., that which they strive to be best at. One problem is that an institution might very well meet some of the criteria in one category, and some in another. The criteria for classification are complex.

(Source: The Carnegie Foundation for the Advancement of Teaching, www.carnegiefoundation.org)

> **A great many people think they are thinking when they are really rearranging their prejudices.**
>
> *—Edward R. Murrow*

A NOTE ABOUT URBAN DANGER

The University of Chicago keeps showing up in national articles as a "dangerous" school. This is based on crime statistics from a nearby neighborhood that has almost nothing to do with the campus itself. Chicago students are as safe as any urban institution's students as long as they don't hang around on street corners in that particular neighborhood. Columbia and the University of Pennsylvania are also in challenging urban environments, yet they have somehow avoided the undue attention that the University of Chicago has had to endure. Visit the campus and you'll see that it's really a matter of zip code boundaries, not safety.

TOP TEN MOST INNOVATIVE AND/OR UNORTHODOX COLLEGES

Reed College

Antioch College

Marlboro College

University of California, Santa Cruz

Pitzer College

Sarah Lawrence College

Eugene Lange College of the New

School for Social Research

Bard College

Cornell College

Deep Springs College

(Source: The Insider's Guide to the Colleges, 25th ed., St. Martin's Griffin, 1998)

FOR POORER?

When it comes to school admissions, according to a Mellon Foundation study, athletes enjoy a 30 percent preference over otherwise identical students, racial minorities have a 28 percent advantage, and children of alumni warrant a 20 percent preference. Socioeconomically disadvantaged (which means "poor") students enjoyed no preference of any kind and, indeed, even those colleges and universities that admit students from low-income backgrounds often don't provide enough financial aid to allow the possibility of acceptance to become a reality.

(Source: Chronicle of Higher Education)

CoOl BoOk AlErT!

The Innovative Campus: Nurturing the Distinctive Learning Environment by Joy Rosenzweig Kliewer (Oryx Press)

The Innovative Campus investigates many of the same institutions listed in this guide, but unlike the book in your hands, it has a defensible academic methodology. For example, Ms. Kliewer defines "innovative college," which you have to admire. She also does an admirable job of providing a context for the genesis of many of the innovative colleges, describing the history of their launch, the motivations of the founders, and the twists and turns of their evolution, and even their prognosis for future success. This is a great book for the innovating educator, the serious college counselor, and the more serious high school student, and for the parent who wants to know more about the innovative college her son or daughter wants to attend. She gives full-chapter profiles to these colleges:

Pitzer College, Claremont, California

New College of Florida, Sarasota

Hampshire College, Amherst, Massachusetts

The University of Wisconsin-Green Bay

University of California, Santa Cruz

The Evergreen State College, Olympia, Washington

Definitely worth a read.

SEWANEE – UNIVERSITY OF THE SOUTH

a world unto itself • **a liberal arts university on a mountaintop** • *an old-fashioned gentility* • **a 10,000-acre campus** • *Is it a small university? Or is it a large college?*

The University of the South is one of those institutions that defies categorization. It is partially like a university, with sororities and fraternities and football, and partially like a small and quirky liberal arts college, with an academic tradition based on the British model. It's not particularly unusual in some respects, but it is very unusual in others.

With that said, here's what's important to know about Sewanee:

First of all, Sewanee was the Indian name for the mountain the school is situated on. The 10,000-acre campus is called "The Domain." It's off the beaten path, and no one comes here by accident. The campus is Gothic-ed to the max, but they do have a hewn log cabin, too.

The honor code here is sacrosanct. When students go through orientation, they ceremoniously sign the honor code in a massive ledger, containing the signatures of all the students who have so sworn before them. Students also sign their work, from tests to papers, with the simple word, "Pledged." That means they've done the work in com-

The University of Virginia, founded by Thomas Jefferson, does not have freshmen. They have first-year, second-year, third-year, and fourth-year students. Jefferson thought that since learning should be a lifelong endeavor, no student should ever claim the status of "senior."

pliance with the academic honor code. This has the gravitas of the sharia. When I was on tour I noticed a faculty member's office door was open. The light was off, she was gone, and the door stood open. I asked the guide about it and he said, "Someone might want to leave her a note."

Academic performance here is revered, and scholars have special status. At so many universities, special privileges are showered on athletes. Football players leave early, skip class, arrange to take exams at home and with help. Here, scholarship is

"Even brilliant students find it difficult to make the As they're used to."

the focus. This is evidenced by the fact that students who maintain honors status and are indoctrinated into the Order of the Gownsmen *wear academic robes on campus*. This is a symbol of their accomplishment, and they are to be honored and respected by others as exemplifying what the institution is all about.

Many of the men choose to wear a coat and tie to class, and many of the women wear skirts or dresses.

Most professors hold selected classes in their homes. Students frequently dine with faculty.

Sewanee's outcomes are impressive:

25 Rhodes scholars

34 Watson fellows

HAMPDEN-SYDNEY COLLEGE

At all-male Hampden-Sydney College, until recently young men could still be found wearing dinner jackets for evening conversation in the dorms. Although dress is certainly more relaxed now, it remains one of the last semi-aristocratic institutions in the United States.

Hampden-Sydney College • College Road • Hampden-Sydney, VA 23943 • 804-223-6000 • www.hsc.edu

26 NCAA Postgraduate schools

70 percent pursue graduate study

95 percent of graduates applying to law school are accepted

89 percent of graduates applying to medical, dental and veterinary school are accepted.

Students take comprehensive examinations in their majors, called comps, which they must pass to graduate, no matter what their GPA or other accomplishments are. Sewanee. Told you it defied classification.

Sewanee - University of the South

735 University Avenue

Sewanee, TN 37383

800-522-2234 or 931-598-1238

Free video: 800-255-0384

www.sewanee.edu

The Equestrian Center at Sewanee

Sewanee recently built a huge equestrian center and launched its own equestrian team, a member of the Intercollegiate Show Horse Association. The equestrian center has 32 stalls for college-owned horses and a boarder barn for students with their own horses. The college stresses that instruction and coaching are available for riders at all levels, from a beginner seeking to become proficient for pleasure riding to serious, national competitors. Riding is also available as a PE credit. The center has a show arena, adjacent pastures, and paddocks. Most impressive is its location on one of the largest campuses in the country. The 10,000-acre mountain-top home of the University of the South has trail access directly from its barns.

> **No greater glory, no greater honor, is the lot of man departing than a feeling possessed deep in his heart that the world is a better place for his having lived.**
>
> —*Robert Abbott, founder, Chicago Defender*

For every accredited college and university in the U.S. and Canada go to **www.donaldasher.com/colleges**

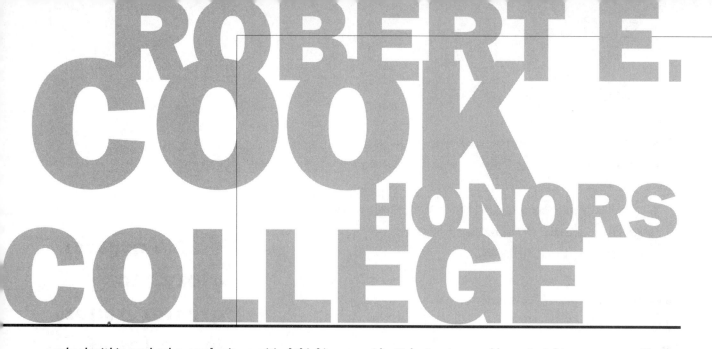

ROBERT E. COOK HONORS COLLEGE

a school within a school • **emphasis on critical thinking** • *residential retreat, a world apart, right on campus* • **like the rich uncle you never had** • *an intellectual family of peers* • **every possible advantage, at your fingertips**

Suppose you were to take truly bright kids who grew up in modest or perhaps challenging circumstances, and ship them off to a rich uncle's mansion. Further suppose that this uncle were wealthy, wise, and caring, and took it upon himself to be sure that his young charges would learn about philosophy and history and language and art and music and culture and the ways of the world. Wouldn't that be an educator's fantasy? Wouldn't that be the best way to actualize the potential of these bright young people?

The Robert E. Cook Honors College is exactly that rich uncle, and it takes exactly such kids, bright as all heck but not necessarily worldly, and gives them every advantage that education can bestow on those thirsty for the benefit. Conveniently located in the middle of nowhere in western Pennsylvania, The Robert E. Cook Honors College is part of the Indiana University of Pennsylvania (IUP) in Indiana, Pennsylvania. It is the brainchild of Robert Cook, "the rich uncle" and an alumnus of IUP, and Janet Goebel, "the governess" and IUP faculty member who is now director of the Honors College.

The thing to realize about the Cook Honors College is that it is designed, right down to the magazines on the tables and the wallpaper on the walls, to foster a life of intellectualism and culture. Many colleges have "honors classes" or an "honors program." Don't mistake an "honors program" for the Cook Honors College. First of all, this is a residential immersion program. All freshmen and most sophomores live in the dorm, which is a world apart from the rest of IUP and its remote surroundings. Paintings cover every wall, well-stocked bookshelves line every common room, sculptures and antiques and tapestries are just everywhere, and most amazing of all is it's all available for you to touch, pick up, admire, inspect, or rearrange for a different silhouette. The classrooms, the dorm, the great hall, and the administrative offices are all mixed together in the same building. The college has two kitchens, and the students often make meals

You can't be anonymous here.

here family style (as well as partake of the university's dining hall across the street). There are many study salons, where students can study and gather to talk.

While I was on tour, I noted that on a single coffee table were *The Congressional Record No. 114-Part II, The New York Times Review of Books, The Economist, Opportunities for the Academic Year Abroad, The Tunnel* by William H. Gass, and *Infinite Jest* by David Foster Wallace. At the reception desk was a three-foot tall stack of the current day's *New York Times,* one for each and every student in the college. Two students

THE REAL TRUTH ABOUT COOK HONORS COLLEGE

Q. What should a prospective student know about your program?

A. That this is an extremely nurturing place, where people will find out who you really are and help you to become the best person you can be. We try to spoil our students. We work at it. We demand a lot from them, but then we're going to take care of them in return. We took some students to Vienna last year, and through personal connections we were able to have some of our musicians play on one of Beethoven's pianos. Imagine that. These are the kind of life experiences that we strive to provide. This goes way beyond the curriculum or the reading list. And what we're *not* looking for are cynics or nihilists. We're looking for kids who are hungry, who will see what we're trying to offer here, and go for it. This is not a school with a parking lot full of BMWs, where the students run off to the Caribbean for spring break, and where your roommate is spending more to board her horses than your parents make. This is, however, a place where you can be a scholar in a community of scholars, where the people you go to class with are the ones you hang out with, where the professors have high expectations, where we listen to your input on how this place is run. If this sounds right to you, then we'd love to hear from you.

Q. Who would be unhappy here?

A. Someone who doesn't want to work. Someone who likes things really clean cut. Someone who brings a full set of opinions with them, but doesn't want to put them on the table. A whiner.

were in the great hall playing chess next to a Roman bust, while another walked by with a tray of cookies he'd just made in the kitchen. All three were barefoot, since this was also their dorm.

In the women's restroom I counted thirty-four different paintings, all images of women. (The men's room wasn't nearly as interesting, with some moody art shots of staircases.) There is a lightheartedness to the decor and the program, as well, which makes it seem inviting and fun and unintimidating. For example, one classroom is decorated with sixty-three paintings all related to the Arthurian legends. It's absolutely lyrical. In another classroom, a little knight in armor guards the door. One gets the impression that all this is not to be taken too seriously.

So, maybe by now you're saying to yourself, "Enough with the interior decorating, already. What's the curriculum like?"

The Cook Honors College has an innovative core curriculum. The core courses bring an integrated, cross-disciplinary approach to "Great Questions." The program is designed to hone critical thinking skills while providing a survey of the important writings in several disciplines. And, in a rather old-fashioned way, the curriculum means to impart a moral education, one of the goals of the college experience for hundreds of years before the "training school" and "smorgasbord" trends took root. (It is not at all designed to tell you your moral obligations, but is designed to get you to discover and develop your own thinking on such matters.)

The core courses are designed to create both critical thinking skills and content knowledge:

Unit A: "What do we know? What do we believe? What, therefore, should I do?"

Unit B: "What is good? What is evil? What, therefore, should I do?"

Unit C: "What is art? What, therefore, should I do?"

Unit D: "What is history? What, therefore, should I do?"

The most interesting thing the director said to me at the Robert E. Cook Honors College of IUP: "Anyone could do this. Dorms are remodeled every year at any university. Professors would be teaching classes anyway." "What about the decor?," I asked. "Surely it cost a fortune." "No way," she said. "We did all this on the cheap. All the paintings are prints, everything else is a reproduction, and the students hung the wallpaper." I guess you just have to know which reproductions to get, which professors to select, and which innovative curriculum to develop. Somehow I think there's a little more to it than just hijacking a dorm.

Unit E: "Why does science matter? What, therefore, should I do?"

Unit F: "What does it mean to be human?"

Unit G: "How do we understand the sacred?"

Unit H: "Must the need for social order conflict with personal liberty?"

Unit I: "What are the obligations of the educated citizen?"

Each semester, students write a major paper that is peer-reviewed through four revisions. This fosters close interaction, critical thinking, communication skills, mastery of the English language, and cooperation rather than competition among the students. This is, without a doubt, one of the most cutting-edge curricula in North America.

One good thing about the Cook program is that it is attached to a university. You can be in the honors program and pursue any major the university offers, from business to art to anthropology. One bad thing about the Cook program is that it is attached to a university. Once you get used to being an involved and engaged student, it can be

TRUMAN STATE UNIVERSITY

How important is visionary leadership in an academic setting? When Charles J. McClain became president of Northeast Missouri State University, it was just another state university in Missouri. In fact, they joked about it being so obscure it wasn't just a directional university—generally not a sign of a distinguished institution—it was a *bi*directional university! But President McClain had the vision and the power and the persuasiveness and the stamina to create something special. So he installed what he called "outcome objectives," actual measurements of pedagogical performance, which he captured and analyzed by department. In plain English, he decided to "measure if learning was really going on here." Then he sold it to the faculty, which was the first miracle. Then he decided there was no honor in being all things to all people, and got NEMSU's mission changed to "the liberal arts school in the Missouri state system." That was the second miracle. Then he went up and down the state telling anyone who would listen that NEMSU was the best place for the brightest and most inquisitive young people. He preached something like this: "Those other state schools are just fine for the engineers and whatnot, but the best and the brightest belong at NEMSU." (I feel the need to point out that there was no statistical evidence for this position whatsoever.) And by the power of his persuasion, the people of that entire region of the country began to believe that NEMSU was the best school for the brightest and most well prepared. "We don't need to send our children to distant and expensive schools! Dr. McClain and his dedicated teaching faculty are doing a great job right here in our own backyard," people began to say. So, Northeast Missouri State University became, in fact, what President McClain had envisioned: the place for the best and the brightest. In 1995 it was renamed Truman State University, and as a frequent visitor I can vouch that the students and the faculty there are doing some impressive work. Jack Magruder is president now, and he is continuing to build on the legacy of Charles J. McClain, a person with a vision and the leadership ability to actualize it.

rather discouraging to sit in lecture classes where the professor is not accustomed to being challenged, and where the other students only want to know what's going to be on the test.

DOWNSIDE: Although the HC students are always bonded to their core class brethren, some majors dominate student schedules in the upperclass years, which draws students away from the community at the Honors College building. Also, since the dorm is a virtual mansion right in the middle of a university campus, security is tight. If residents can pick up everything in the building, so could thieves. And, once again, it is important to remember that students cannot take all their classes at the Honors College, so it is important to be sure that you like the rest of the community, including the curriculum, the professors, the students, and the infrastructure.

MORE UPSIDE: This was the most genuine, unpretentious place I visited. The students were friendly, the staff was gracious, the building was beautiful, the whole thing was like a television show from the fifties. This is not a perfect program or a perfect school, but it is certainly one that is trying to be. And that's worth a lot, all by itself.

Also, check out the essay, "The Big Meeting," on p. 175, by a Cook student.

WARNING: Over two hundred universities claim to have honors colleges or honors programs, but most of them are not like this at all. They are not residential. They do not have an innovative, coherent, sequenced curriculum. They do not have a cultural component. They may or may not have caring staff interested in you as a whole per-

WHAT GRAD SCHOOL ADMISSIONS OFFICERS LOVE TO SEE ON YOUR APPLICATION

- Research or teaching assistant to professor (paid or unpaid)
- Departmental or subject tutor (college or high school levels)
- Writing center tutor/counselor/coach (especially if you really learned how to do it)
- A *completed* independent study class (incompleted counts less than zero)
- Residence hall advisor/peer counselor (shows maturity, plus you passed screening and training)
- Any extended research project (especially if you write a thesis or capstone paper, and doubly especially if you do a good job)

NOTE: For more on planning now to get into grad school later, read the sections on strategies to gain admission to highly competitive graduate programs in my book, *Graduate Admissions Essays: How to Write Your Way into the Graduate Program of Your Choice* (Ten Speed Press).

son. They may not have handpicked professors. They won't help you pick a semester overseas that you can afford. So what do they have? Slightly more demanding workload and a chance to study in a class with other students more like yourself than the average. In short, they are nothing more nor less than the higher education equivalent of "tracking," placing the smarter kids together. That's not nothing, but it's not like the Cook program at all.

That being said, you can visit the National Collegiate Honors Council at www.runet.edu/~nchc, and click on "Member Institutions," to explore other options. There *are* some good programs out there, working hard to offer elite educational opportunities at bargain prices. While you're at the NCHC Web site, check out the "Characteristics of a Fully-Developed Honors Program," which is interesting in its banality, if nothing else. The single most important factor to look for in a program would be the residential component. Without that, you're really just headed for another anonymous university experience.

Robert E. Cook Honors College at Indiana University of Pennsylvania

290 Pratt Street

Indiana, PA 15705

724-357-4971

800-487-9122

www.iup.edu/honors

INTERVIEW WITH ROBERT E. COOK

founding benefactor of Cook Honors College at Indiana University of Pennsylvania (IUP)

Q: "Bob, I've long been an admirer of the Cook Honors College. I am convinced there is no place like it in the United States at this time. The critical thinking pedagogy that takes place at Cook is superior to what takes place at some of the most famous programs in the nation. It harkens back to a prior age in American education when there was concern for the concepts of citizenry and education to benefit the soul. At the same time, there is a very practical outcome for the students in terms of career readiness. It is a unique institution. How did you decide on this direction for your philanthropy?"

A: "I grew up in western Pennsylvania, and I went to IUP. I had a job as a welder, and my father encouraged me to go to college. There I met Glen Olsen, a professor, who took a personal interest in me. He encouraged me to believe in myself. Working-class kids often tend to live up to other people's low expectations. He encouraged me to see my potential. That was a turning point in my life, and I'm returning the favor."

Q: "You're one of what the Wall Street Journal calls 'the new philanthropists,' not content just to give money but wanting to stay actively involved in how that money is used. How do you stay involved? How do you see your role now?"

A: "Well, I stay involved in the business side of the program. I make sure we're getting return on our expenditures. I make no comments whatsoever on the curriculum now that it's working so well. Here's what I think: No one thinks it's unusual to give a scholarship to a student who can jump higher, hit harder, and run faster. I think a student who can master Rousseau deserves a scholarship, too. It doesn't matter what he does when he graduates. If you can master Rousseau or Locke or Plato, you'll be a better businessperson, a better artist, or a better bureaucrat, for that matter. And we're investing in these kids beyond what happens within the curriculum. We're going to expand on what we're doing. We now have the Achievement Program that might fund a student for a term abroad, an unpaid internship in the summer, or travel-related expenses for their studies. We spend money on things like this, and I pay attention to all of it. We want our kids to be streetable, to be able to compete with anybody when it comes to an interview for a job or for a [graduate school] scholarship. I'm trying to get young people to think about being a star competitor for a job at twenty-six or thirty, not just that first job at twenty-two."

Q: "How's it working?"

A: "Great! Unbelievable! We sent a student to the British consulate in New York, and the first one was so good they asked for another, sight unseen. We're creating well-rounded college juniors and seniors who can compete. That's a good measure of whether you're efficacious. We just had a dean at Oxford tell us we sent him one of the best American students he'd ever had but, in fact, we didn't. We just sent him a good American student who could learn the way they teach at Oxford. So our system is working."

What do employers think of Cook graduates? This is part of a letter from an employer to Cook administrators:

"I want to compliment you all and the CHC faculty for doing an outstanding job at creating a culture that fosters motivation and critical thinking. I have truly found your students to possess both motivation and the metacognitive skills that are lacking in most college graduates. The fact that we can task undergraduate students like Tina [who succeeded on a million-dollar assignment] with serious projects is a testament to the success of the mission at CHC. What you are doing and have accomplished is unquestionably unique. You should be very proud.

"In fact, without mentioning the program, your undergraduate students have far outperformed MBA students who have worked with us in the past. Your students have now displaced that program's students as our main source for quality interns."

A COLLEGE OFFICER WRITES ABOUT DISTINCTIVENESS AT A COLLEGE

You are correct that it is extremely difficult to "pin down" the concept of distinctiveness in a college. That is precisely why the mass-market college guides resort to common quantifiable formulae in order to rank colleges. There are some colleges which seem always to leap to mind whenever terms such as "special" or "distinctive" are bandied about, but it is difficult to explain exactly why this is the case. Many of these colleges appear on the list you have supplied.

The problem you have bought with this project is that even faculty and staff who have extensive experience at these institutions sometimes have difficulty explaining what it is that makes their institutions distinctive. I will describe common characteristics which I believe these institutions should share:

A DOMINANT ETHOS: There is an old "professor's tale" in higher education about a distinguished German visitor to an American university. After the visitor was taken on a tour of all the buildings, the laboratories, the classrooms, and after he spoke to many of the students and faculty, the visitor said, "You have shown me all your facilities, and you have allowed me to speak with many of your students and faculty. And I have enjoyed wandering on your lovely grounds. But where is the spirit of your university?"

When you arrive at a campus with a dominant ethos, you can sense it because permeates every aspect of campus life and goes beyond the physical features of the campus. It can be described as a defining culture, and the very self-descriptive language of the college carries the ethos in its semiotic content. You can see it in the way the students, faculty, and staff speak of the institution, and even when they are complaining about the institution, they somehow do not doubt this ethos but rather the way the ethos is being used or abused. It is a self-defining niche in the grand scheme of higher education. It is the lack of this ethos which is palpable at many of the "diploma mills" which dot our landscape.

A SENSE OF HISTORICAL CONTEXT: A distinctive institution must have a sense of its own place in the history of our culture and in higher education. This does *not* mean that an institution must be old in order to be distinctive. This sense of historical place is precisely what some of the newer colleges on your list are attempting to capture when they design a curriculum focused on the great works or when a predominantly black college designs programs to refocus on its African-American heritage. Without a sense of historical place a college has an incomplete identity.

A REFLECTIVE PHYSICAL PLANT: By this I mean that the physical plant of a college should reflect its ethos and historical place. I was recently at [a large university in the Southwest] and was struck by an interesting paradox along these lines. My tour guide proudly showed me two structures. One was a magnificent fine arts center designed by [a famous architect]. The building itself was remarkable, and yet when I pressed the guide on how the building fit into the heritage of the school, he was unable to make any meaningful connection. Then, only two minutes later, I was shown the new library which was built mostly underground. As part of the guide's automatic spiel, I was told how the architecture emulated a desert arroyo and how the landscaping and materials were reflective of the desert Southwest heritage. This is what I mean by a reflective physical plant. When asked to think of great examples of this, we readily think of the Cloisters at Mr. Jefferson's University of Virginia or the eating clubs at Princeton. I, of course, immediately think of the neo-Gothic architecture of my own institution.

AN APPROPRIATE CURRICULUM: The college curriculum must reflect the ethos and historical place of the institution. In other words, the curriculum must "fit" the institution. What would St. John's at Annapolis be without its Great Books curriculum or West Point without its vocationally oriented technological curriculum and its cocurricular military programs, or Antioch without its humanistic/revisionist curriculum? The day Princeton or Harvard injects remedial education into their curricula is the day they cease to be Princeton or Harvard.

These comments are not comprehensive but do include criteria I feel are necessary for a college to be considered distinctive. The proof is in the living, not in the telling.

ON COLLEGE COUNSELING FOR THE INTELLECTUAL STUDENT

by Laura J. Clark

College Counseling Office

Ethical Culture Fieldston School

Bronx, New York

This is the text of a talk delivered at an annual convention of the National Association for College Admission Counseling (NACAC). It was intended for those inside the profession who work with high school students on a daily basis and are passionately concerned with placing them in suitable institutions of higher learning, but it also may be of great interest to parents and students who are interested in how these particular students are matched to (we hope) the right institutions.

Often intellectually advanced students are not recognized as a challenge by counseling professionals in the college placement process, either because they are self-sufficient and not well known or because they will get in wherever they apply. This is a mistake, since for these students an appropriate match, both academically and socially, is extremely important.

The first step is identifying the young intellectual, the student for whom the life of the mind is of paramount importance. Though grades and scores indicate some ability, sometimes the most "intellectual" students do not have a perfect numerical record. Frequently high school academics bore them and they can feel disconnected from their peers so they don't "show" in traditional measures. Often they have been traumatized by high school social life and their best talents may well emerge in what they do on their own, outside the curriculum. They may not be student leaders or star performers in other areas. This can be a problem as well for counselors, parents, and sometimes the students themselves, who may not feel intellectually gifted. I have tried to adopt an approach with all students that will foster trust and help me to identify the student for whom the life of the mind is of paramount importance.

To this end, in a first meeting with the family I ask students who their friends are, what they do for fun, and what they don't like about high school. (The parents are always *very* interested in this—I am sure to ask the students again later, without the parents, so they can tell me what they left out the first time.) I also ask to see artwork if they have made any, and an academic paper they are proud of. Sometimes art, theater, and music programs become a safe haven for intellectuals, since the students interested in these pursuits are often more socially tolerant of students who may not fit in.

Parental input also helps to form a clearer picture of the student. I ask them to write a letter specifically describing how their child learns best. In some cases, however, this letter tells me more about the parents. The therapist who talks about the "five salient personality traits" and the mother who writes in thirty-five different ways "I love my son" on flowered stationery give me insight into the student's support network at home, and thus into the student.

I also ask the teachers of the junior class for a list of their most interesting students and for information on how these students learn best to discover which students think originally in the classroom and on paper. The college match for these highly motivated students is crucial. Most importantly, high selectivity at the college level does not necessarily indicate an appropriate match for a bright student. It may indicate a reasonably bright student body, but selectivity does not predict social comfort, an intellectual atmosphere, an appropriate curriculum or professor availability.

I remember one student who was always trying to create independent study projects, with any teacher who would support him, on everything from Asian frogs to jazz in the thirties. No surprise that he loved his time at Hampshire College. I had another extremely bright student who was so shy that during one college interview he rolled his T-shirt up until it was collected under his arms and then used it to mop his brow. He found academic heaven in the large lecture halls of a big state university's math department, where no one called on him, ever, and he was free to think without fear of interruption.

It is important to be able to predict this sort of thing. Questions to ask both teachers and students might be:

- Is the teacher's personality and a small class imperative?
- Does she need a core curriculum to structure her study?
- Is this a student who can tolerate a fraternity/sorority system, or are other social options a better idea?

Through this process the student begins to know him or herself and the parents begin to see who their child is. If these discussions are exhaustive it helps a great deal later on when trying to get past some of the stereotypes about "intellectual" environments that rankings and the media in general produce.

The problems which emerge as students research college choices are obvious to all of us. Students are inundated with newspaper articles, brochures and documents, most of which don't speak to them and some of which actually mislead them. Many commercially published general guidebooks encourage misleading stereotypical judgements about campus life. Some colleges have "no social life," are "party schools," or "encourage hallucinogens." Try convincing even the hippest parent that one of your favorite small colleges for brilliant students is a great place for her child after that comes out in print!

Rankings are clearly influential and often lead even very bright students to conclusions that have far more to do with prestige than academic aspects related to their own learning styles. A breath of fresh air came for me last week when one of my best students asked me what could have changed enough in one year for a college to move from #42 to #12 in the *U.S. News and World Report* rankings.

Most printed information seems to encourage students to stereotype colleges based on small "bites" that have no texture. It is the counselor's job to cut through this and help the student find the truth. Counselors also must be careful, by the way, not to stereotype the students in the same way: "He's a real (fill in the college name) type." Our brightest students need to do a special type of research and we, as educators, have to make sure that they do it. All colleges are not right for all students and we are not doing our jobs if we become merely distributors of leaflets, keepers of records, and spin-doctors.

I keep a list of former students willing to host on Friday and Saturday nights; my most intellectual students need to look at social life to find out what there is to do and talk about when much of the college population is drinking beer. I have another list of students at college who will take visiting students to class with them and talk to prospectives on the telephone. Students should visit courses in the disciplines that interest them. I remember one science student who visited small humanities classes recommended by admissions at one university and loved them enough to enroll. When he began to attend his freshman science and math courses, he was shocked to find they were 200- to 400-student lecture classes.

I also have accumulated the names of a number of professors who like to talk to prospective students. I'll never forget when I was still in admissions taking one of my favorite physics recruits interested in astronomy down to meet the expert in string theory at Princeton. I watched them "talk" to each other in numbers on blackboards for forty-five minutes. The student's comment when we left: "That was great." I had had no idea what was going on at the time.

It is also important to make sure the Nobel laureates and Pulitzer novelists so attractive to voracious readers and researchers really teach undergraduates. The young intellectual may also want graduate courses as a junior or senior, independent research with professors, and special programs that link courses like the Structured Liberal Education program at Stanford, the Honors College at Michigan, and Saint John's entire curriculum. Some students need special major programs, like one unusual environmental expert who wanted a major in waste management. It is also worth considering that a student like this may have "focused" her interests in high school to feel socially secure, to give herself an area of expertise that no one can assail. We need to be sure she realizes what else is out there, too.

My students taught me something about bashing stereotypes and breaking the media code—it is difficult! Last year one of my students methodically visited only colleges with "poor social life" ratings in the college guides. His list grew to include seven of them when he found "no social life" tended to mean sitting around talking about books and listening to music. Public relations efforts can mystify rather than clarify as students try to cut through to the truth. In a fervor to lure more attractive applicants, colleges represent themselves as both more selective than they are, and as having all things for all students.

That student and his girlfriend also worried, when an article came out in the *New York Times* about University of Chicago being in short, "a fun place after all," that maybe it was not in fact as intellectual as it seemed, or that the administration was trying to change its focus on academic life in some way. Another student asked me if the huge number of brochures that arrived from [a major university] meant that the college was having trouble filling its freshman class, or was not so strong academically as it once had been.

The word "pressure" in guidebooks, usually seen as a negative, can mean "stimulation" for students with certain learning styles. One of my students asked for a place where kids "cared enough to compete."

As an aside, admissions work is an exhausting job, demanding passionate dedication, long hours of isolation on the road and reading files for relatively low pay; no wonder admissions offices have trouble keeping experienced and knowledgeable personnel for any length of time. In-depth knowledge of an institution—both the college and the high school—takes time; if they go to high schools, most admissions officers visit four to six a day, for forty or fifty minutes each. This sort of presentation encourages the sound bite. Because time constrains both class periods and their own schedules, it is near impossible for them to address individual questions in depth, give a deep and individualized picture of their institution, or get to know the students in their audience.

There is also the danger of the students equating the personality of the admissions representative with the personality of the college, misleading at best. Last year the Haverford College representative to our school was so charismatic that every student who attended his presentation wanted to apply because they liked him. Probably not the most sensible reason to choose a college, though Haverford is a fine institution. Some admissions personnel use these trips to get to know the school instead, and educate me so I can pass on the information to the appropriate students. This seems to work well. Of course, many high schools are not on the "visiting trail" for one reason or another, and colleges are beginning to doubt the efficacy of this use of personnel, since Web pages and brochures can do much of what these whirlwind tours can.

Some colleges seem to have mastered the way to approach the young intellectual. These colleges know themselves and are not afraid not to be all things to all people. In a survey I handed out to my "intellectual" students attending college, they chose, among others, Colgate, Harvard, Hampshire, Macalester, University of California at Santa Cruz, Bard, Kenyon, University of Chicago, Johns Hopkins, Oberlin, Union, McGill, and the University of Wisconsin at Madison as some of the colleges who "were most honest" in their public relations. Altogether these represent an eclectic list. Students told me that these places had put them in touch with professors to talk to and sent them to a wide variety of classes. They had been honest about the social life and intellectual rigor in their mailings, and sent them selected brochures about special programs that showed they had looked carefully at the students' applications.

In several cases, the students had spoken to or e-mailed admissions personnel and received real and thought-provoking answers to their questions rather than what they felt was standard public relations. One admission officer admitted to a student during a recruiting function that his college probably did not have the best academic program for that student. The student was grateful and considered attending that college simply because the admission officer was so honest.

There is nothing more liberating than when a really bright student can find her element. One student I worried desperately about in high school because he had no friends, though he was fiercely interested and interesting, e-mailed me last week. "I'm popular here," he said. "I can't believe it. People here like me. No one thought it was weird when my roommate and I spent all night making an alarm clock out of the contents of the hallway trash can!"

A few words about presenting students to a college. I tell my students that admissions officers are not the IRS or the House Judiciary Committee. I tell them the application should be fun and interesting to fill out, that they should feel they risked something, and that it could make them laugh. I tell them to list *all* the ways they spend their time, including reading books, going to films, etc., and say how long they spend doing each activity. Many of my most intellectual students don't have lots of organized activities. It isn't necessary to have them, but they need to say what they *do* do with their time.

I also tell them if there is something the application doesn't ask for that they want to say, put it in. I spend time with our teachers talking about being clear on paper about our brightest kids, I try to do it myself, and I try to let admissions know in one way or another, who the special ones are. Many teachers, particularly in math and science, think that grades tell the whole story, and spend their letters telling what a nice person the student is, or, how the student seems "nerdy" and cut off from his/her peers. I remember a discussion I had with a science teacher who told me how one of her students had drawn a completely original conclusion from an experiment. She later showed me her college letter, which detailed only the student's extracurricular activities.

I try to review the student's entire file, if I can, to see if it gives a complete picture. If it does not, I may ask for an extra letter of reference, enclose an English paper I have seen, or ask the student to document something else.

Content of student essays is so important for these particular students, far more, I think, than grammatical accuracy. One of the best essays I ever read I saw when I was at Princeton in admissions—a one-sentence stream of consciousness piece on race relations in Los Angeles. I could tell from the rest of the application that the student was traditionally articulate, but it was this risky piece that packed the intellectual punch.

There are also a few brilliant students I have worked with who have represented a "hunch" for the admissions dean who accepted them. These successes have been the result of searingly honest phone conversations with people who have been kind enough to trust me about kids who didn't show their stuff in traditional ways. This is not the norm, but many of these kids are the ones I was most excited about and for whom the rewards of an intellectual environment were immense. It may seem obvious, but developing relationships with admissions colleagues around these issues teaches us what is available and can, occasionally, really help us place our students intelligently. It has also helped me immensely in these conversations to be a classroom teacher. I often have seen these kids in action and it keeps me thinking about what college professors need.

There is often a huge gap between what counselors and admissions professionals know and even the best-educated world assumes. For a little while my teaching and my admissions career overlapped at the same institution. I remember vividly a faculty meeting where a professor was ranting on about his two favorite students, two he assumed had high verbal scores on the SAT, since they were so articulate and such good writers. I went back and looked at our files and found that the two students in question had low 600 verbals and that one of the "passive" learners he was complaining about had an 800. He was, of course, blaming admissions for their lack of consistent rigor and was astounded when I set the record straight. Not surprisingly, the two he loved had been admitted primarily based on their grades, essays, and the strength of teacher support. One had had a fabulous creative writing portfolio.

One of my worries is that in a world where rankings determine numbers of applicants and perceived quality, increasing emphasis on testing and grade point averages close doors at some of the places most challenging to young intellectuals. By quantifying and oversimplifying the process of research and of academic evaluation, the media forces colleges to collude with it in order to "sell spaces." Colleges may find themselves compelled to bypass students admissions officers know to be intellectually interesting and dynamic to admit more conventional students who spent time on test preparation, and hounded their teachers for grades.

These students help the rankings and please trustees and college presidents who don't have to teach them. Granted, often the really intellectual student has managed to master the conventional approach as well without really thinking about it, but I find more and more that my most interesting students rebel against the time, money, and energy it takes to prep for SATs and maintain the perfect record. They would rather be reading philosophy, grinding the perfect telescope lens, or taking the intellectual risk that may not get them the A.

The way to get past these problems is to find more accurate and creative means, first, to teach the students about their academic options, then to evaluate those students. Clearly this means a more individualized approach, which in turn means more personnel and more money in an age where great faith has been placed on the computer statistics and mass mailings to deal with an ever-expanding population.

Most high schools don't have the luxury of one counselor for each 50 to 70 students, and most admissions staffs have huge turnover, making the close relationships between counselors and colleges difficult. There are lots of us on both sides struggling to make a difference in this area, but to serve our most intellectual students we need to retrench and redirect some funds to come up with new tactics. In the meantime, students need to take more responsibility for their own destinies, researching more deeply, challenging the process with harder, more thought-provoking questions and applications that represent who they really are, rather than some prepackaged idea of what the colleges want. They need to use both their intuition and common sense to see past rankings, prestige, and empty publicity to analyze what kind of education they will actually receive at the college of their choice. In turn, the colleges need to work to see through to the real student in whatever creative ways are available, rather than relying on statistics and standardized measures.

ADVICE FROM A DISTINGUISHED COLLEGE PROFESSOR

We have three daughters, and while one would think that two parents who are both college professors would have been experts in the college selection process, we made our share of mistakes along the way. My advice to the many students and parents who come to visit us is shared here.

Some people approach college selection as if looking for a good vacation spot. A relative has said something about a particular school or perhaps a friend is planning to go there. Maybe a school has name recognition because of its football team or because it has been featured in a movie. The glossy brochures have attractive pictures and it sounds good. This was the thinking that led our oldest daughter to commit herself to what turned out to be over five years at Big State University in the Southwest. She had never even been to the state, but her best friend from high school was there and that snowy February it must have sounded very romantic to be in the desert. She was adamant, and we let her have her way. This turned into quite a disaster academically. Her classes were huge, and in the first two years not a single one of them was taught by a real professor—all were graduate students focused on their own degree requirements. She was just a number and unable to find the help she needed in classes or in planning for her future. She made it through, but without anyone ever sitting her down to talk about doing an internship or linking her academic interests to a career plan. She is happily married, but still has no clear direction for a career and thinks of her undergraduate years as "a mistake."

Another approach to college selection is the "buying a car" model. You pull out the guide books and look at the rankings and prices. The average student there has a certain SAT score and the library has a certain number of books, therefore this is a top-ranked school. You look at the student-faculty ratio and make the mistake of concluding that this means classes will be small (at some schools with graduate programs and many professors doing research, the ratio is low but the introductory classes still have 150 to 300 students in them). Then you head for the "showroom." You visit the school during summer vacation and note that the buildings appear in order and the staff sound friendly. They tell you about the great things their alumni are doing, and you are sold. You are approaching the school as a product which appears to guarantee that for the money you invest, you will get "the best" school in return.

We used this "product" approach with our second daughter. We agreed that with some sacrifice we could afford private college tuition for a real quality education. A "first tier" school was in order. We visited in summer and found, as the guidebook claimed "a campus like Eden." When the acceptance letter came, we all rejoiced. Her future was now in the bag if only we could scrape up the money. We should have known on move-in day to expect problems. As we arrived in our Honda Accord to unload boxes in a sea of Mercedes and BMWs, we realized that the peer group here was of a significantly different income level. When we returned six weeks later for parents weekend, we found our daughter quite miserable. The other girls wore pearls to class and the dining hall; their values and world view were almost as uniform. One mother asked me if I realized that the school had a place to board horses and was my daughter going to Europe over spring break. I felt underdressed and uncomfortable, and I could tell that the problem here was social not academic. There was nothing wrong with the school. Our daughter just didn't fit in and wanted to leave. Plus she was now interested in graphic design, and there was only one course in that field at this small college. We had looked at the school as a product without thinking about our daughter's unique personality and how she would interact with the school, socially as well as academically. (We realized too late that this might have been a great school for our eldest daughter!)

The product approach neglects the role of the student in his or her own education, but it is rampant and underlies many of the guidebooks and advice to parents one finds in magazines. Americans talk about "shopping for colleges" and/or being "informed consumers" in the process. We see this in the kinds of questions we are asked as educators. One high-school student, the child of a distant acquaintance, called to inquire: "If I go to your school, can you guarantee I will get a job on Wall Street?" Of course we couldn't! No one could. We can provide quality instruction, advice, many opportunities for internships and other career-enhancing experiences. Will a student take advantage of all of this and succeed brilliantly? Will the kind of instruction we offer fit this young man's learning style so that he is challenged to excel? Will he find friends and social roles to expand his leadership skills? That depends on him or her.

The approach I recommend for parents and students seeking a college is to think of it like searching for a mate. That may sound a little dramatic, but I think it holds up to scrutiny. Does it bring out the best in you? Does it fit with your personality and learning style? Are the qualities it possesses those that you value or even love? A new experience is going to take some getting used to, but will you feel comfortable enough there eventually to take the risks you need to take to challenge yourself and succeed? When you are there without your family and friends, without the identity you had in your high school and hometown communities, will it be an exciting transition or a frightening one? If you commit to this mate, will the two of you working together be able to turn your dreams into aspirations, then into realizable goals?

The school where you receive your undergraduate degree is with you for a lifetime— it launches you into your future and stays with you in the form of friends, faculty who will write recommendations for you, and the foundation it gives you. There is not a "best" school or even an "excellent" school; there are only "best" schools for individuals because they are a good match.

So no school is right for everyone. Yes, visit in summer, but make sure you return during the academic year so you can see what it's really like. Students should sit in on classes. They should spend the night in the residence hall and see what students are like outside of class, away from tour guides and authority figures. They should ask a thousand questions, but also just listen.

And what should the parents' role be in this extended visit? Come along if you can, see what the school is like, and share your impressions. But remember that, finally, it is the student who must make the relationship work. We've had a few students over the years who really didn't want to be at our school, but were coerced into it by parents who liked it very much. They all found ways to leave. Some of those ways damaged their futures.

The college's job in hosting students and in the final admission decision we make is not to find the "best" students, but to find students whom we believe will thrive in the unique environment we provide. When we do it right, we don't try to "sell" our program, but to describe it. Both our school and our students are served best when we are honest with each other. If students can't be accepted as they really are, they will probably not be happy. We find the interview is an excellent way for us to get to know each other better.

One final tidbit: The absolute worst reason ever for choosing a school is because a boyfriend or girlfriend is going there. I've been teaching college freshmen for twenty years and known most of my students well enough to learn a little about their personal lives. Of the hundreds of relationships in high school that were transplanted to college, I have known only a few that made it through the first semester. The college choice will certainly last much longer than that.

For every accredited college and university in the U.S. and Canada go to **www.donaldasher.com/colleges**

C o O l   B o O k   A l E r T !

The Templeton Guide: Colleges That Encourage Character Development edited by the John Templeton Foundation
(Templeton Foundation Press)

The John Templeton Foundation was established in 1987 with the purpose of supporting higher educational programs and institutions that encourage character development by inspiring "students to lead ethical and civil-minded lives." Mr. Templeton felt that previous to the college years, the student is shaped by his or her parents and school experiences, but once in college that development can either continue or stagnate depending on what type of support and guidance is provided in the higher educational environment. Our society tends to focus on the younger years as those being important for shaping the personality and character, when in reality it is also the college years that are "critical to forming a strong and steady character."

The Templeton Guide is a collection of approximately 550 programs and institutions found by The Templeton Foundation to encourage character development through volunteering, community service projects, substance abuse prevention programs, superb guidance and mentoring throughout the college years, a curriculum dealing with ethical and character issues, and programs supportive of spiritual development. The book is a good resource for students looking for an educational experience that goes beyond just the books. Full of detailed program descriptions, the guide will give the reader a very good idea of which institutions will provide the right environment for the type of growth they are interested in.

BRAINS AND BRAWN

Stanford University and the University of California, Berkeley have a longstanding athletic rivalry, which is odd for two schools whose primary mission is, without question, academics. This rivalry has led to stolen mascots and icons, pranks, and sharp verbal exchanges, some of it demonstrating a sharp wit. For example, on Saturday, February 19, 2000, the men's basketball team at the University of California, Berkeley (known the world over as "Cal") lost to Stanford, 101-50, the worst point-spread loss in the history of Cal basketball. The next week at Cal the *Daily Californian* carried this headline: "The Cal men's basketball team makes history at Stanford." That oughta show 'em!

"Our lives begin to end the day we become silent about things that matter."

—*Dr. Martin Luther King*

MIT'S CHARM SCHOOL

During winter session, MIT has a charm school for its famously eggheaded scientists and engineers, covering such subjects as "Walking," "Table Manners," and the all-important "Buttering Up Big Shots." The busiest lobbies on campus are set up like a carnival. Bright yellow banners reading, "Please," "Thank You," and "You're Welcome," are hung from the rafters, while red and white streamers and bows mark off the "Ballroom Dance" instruction area. The Beaver (MIT's mascot), wearing top hat and tails over his costume and carrying a cane, mingles with the crowd throughout the day.

Students entering Charm School choose the booths they wish to attend. A yellow coupon is given to each student who participates in a Charm School "class." If students attend at least six classes, they receive a Charm School Bachelor's Degree. If they attend eight, they receive a Master's and if they attend twelve, they receive a Charm School Ph.D. Charm School is fun, with the Fashion Police giving out neon orange "fashion violations" for such improprieties as being a "walking jewelry store," or "using both straps on a backpack."

Charm School has its own commencement ceremony, and recent guests of honor have included Judith Martin (better known as "Miss Manners"), and Dan Zevin, reporter for *Rolling Stone* and author of the book *Entry-Level Life: A Complete Guide to Masquerading as a Member of the Real World* (Bantam). The event is accompanied by the music of The Chorallaries, playing Pomp and Circumstance on kazoo.

The event is intended to be humorous, but it has a serious side, too. Every future techie millionaire needs to know "How to Be the Perfect Host," and "How to Deliver News Someone Really Doesn't Want to Hear."

Chapter Four

THE GREAT BOOKS PROGRAMS

Once upon a time all colleges had "Great Books" programs. In other words, scholars everywhere believed that great thought from the past was useful for understanding the present. In the latter half of the last century this fell out of favor, as students clamored for vocational training and more pluralistic points of view. The Great Books programs are dedicated to the theory that great thought, thought that has survived the centuries, is quite relevant to life today. Many of these programs have revised their curricula to allow pluralistic points of view by finding them in the past, not by turning to whatever was written in the paper last week. These programs provide a classical education that will illuminate any life, even a very modern one.

ST. JOHN'S COLLEGE

"the freedom of no choice" • **the curriculum is exactly the same for everybody** • *professors teach across the curriculum* • **profs are called "tutors"** • *professors demonstrate continued learning themselves* • **the most intelligent and the most contrary** • *a Great Books program where intellectualism is the norm—all day, every day* • **one in the East, one in the West**

St. John's College is the Rock of Gibraltar in higher education. It is an institution that ignores every trend, as if it existed on a separate plane altogether. Perhaps it is its own universe, even. St. John's harkens back to the origins of higher education in this country, when faculty set the curriculum and directed students to get to it. St. John's has a pure Great Books program, all the way through. This is not some core curriculum that students get through before they go on to specialize, this is *the entire curriculum.* Students read original works starting with Homer. They learn Greek and French. They re-create the great experiments from the history of science. They produce Shakespearean plays without updating the language. They study the great problems of math through the minds of the mathematicians who were there.

Not only is the curriculum an anachronism, the students and the faculty and the very atmosphere of the place are as well. For example, the students dress almost neatly, and they are very civil to one another. Broadsides in the student newspaper read like a transcription of a Senate debate, wherein anything might be said but only in the most overly polite manner. Students are taught the art of civility, conversation, and rational discourse in class, and carry this over to their everyday interactions. The main activity here, night and day, is conversation. All students used to learn to waltz, and although that tradition has faded in recent years, it tells a lot about the community's

> ❝ **What is the number one characteristic of innovative schools? We give students a voice. We offer students a seat at the table** ❞
>
> —*St. John's admissions publication*

expectations of its members and the extremely high premium placed on social grace.

St. John's College has no busy work and no pop quizzes. St. John's students are simply expected to do their work for the intrinsic interest of learning from it. There are oral exams, and many papers to write, but few tests. A student here will never see a multiple choice test or learn what a Scantron is. There is no such thing as cheating at St. John's, for the only person to cheat would be oneself.

The faculty are expected to teach across the curriculum, which means that whatever their expertise was when they were hired, they have to learn everything in the curriculum eventually. Faculty study groups are common, both to advance mastery of the curriculum, and to pursue outside interests. This is truly an intellectual community, with the camaraderie of shared experience virtually universal.

In addition to all of the above, each student writes a lengthy senior essay that is reviewed by a faculty committee and then defended in a public oral examination. The examination also serves as a comp, and St. John's students can be asked a question from any part of their four-year education.

St. John's is famous among academics and virtually unknown elsewhere. In academic circles, a St. John's graduate is a known quantity, and a degree from here is well respected at the best graduate schools. On the other hand, your parents' nosy neighbor may be clueless about what you're up to.

Although St. John's is the third oldest college in the nation (after Harvard and

> **An education at St. John's provides students the opportunity first to learn to think well, second, to learn to learn, and third, to learn to apply what they learn to any situation.**
>
> —*St. John's admissions publication*

> # I recommend biting off more than you can chew—to anyone.
>
> —*Alanis Morissette*

William and Mary), the lockstep Great Books curriculum only dates back to 1937. It was the trough of the Depression, and the college was one step away from closing its doors. Several benefactors convinced the college to reject a watered-down curriculum in favor of becoming a very distinctive academic community. Thus this great institution was reborn as a survival measure. It is secure today, and has been for decades. Although different, it is not really, anymore, experimental.

You also need to know that St. John's is not after perfect students, but the most

THE READING LIST FOR FRESHMAN YEAR (PARTIAL)

Aeschylus	Cannizzaro	Herodotus	Nicomachus	Sophocles
Archimedes	Euclid	Homer	Plato	Thucydides
Aristophanes	Euripides	Lavoisier	Plutarch	Virchow
Aristotle	Fahrenheit	Lucretius	Proust	

THE READING LIST FOR SOPHOMORE YEAR (PARTIAL)

Apollonius	Beethoven	Epictetus	Pascal	Shakespeare
Aquinas	Chaucer	Haydn	Plotinus	St. Anselm
Aristotle	Copernicus	Luther	Plutarch	Stravinsky
Augustine	Dante	Machiavelli	Ptolemy	Tacitus
Bach	Descartes	Montaigne	Rabelais	Viète
Bacon	Donne	Mozart	Schubert	Virgil

THE READING LIST FOR JUNIOR YEAR (PARTIAL)

Adam Smith	Eliot	Kepler	Molière	Spinoza
Austen	Galileo	La Fontaine	Mozart	Swift
Bernoulli	Hobbes	La Rochefoucauld	Newton	
Cervantes	Hume	Leibniz	Pascal	
Dedekind	Huygens	Locke	Racine	
Descartes	Kant	Milton	Rousseau	

THE READING LIST FOR SENIOR YEAR (PARTIAL)

Ampère	Einstein	Jay, Hamilton, and	Millikan	Valéry
Baudelaire	Faraday	Madison	Nietzsche	Wagner
Bohr	Faulkner	Kierkegaard	O'Connor	William James
Booker T. Washington	Freud	Lincoln	Rimbaud	Yeats
Conrad	Hardy	Lobachevsky	T. S. Eliot	
Darwin	Hegel	Marx	Tocqueville	
Dostoevsky	Heidegger	Melville	Tolstoy	
DuBois	Heisenberg	Mendel	Twain	

interested students. It will take a chance on students with As and Cs, if they have the curiosity and the eagerness that are hallmarks of a St. John's student. And unlike so many of the colleges we've discussed so far in this book, the workload is not quite so oppressive here. I am sure that some students and faculty at St. John's will vigorously protest this statement, but it is my impression that there is more time for discussion, more time to reflect, than at so many of the schools that we've covered so far. Since the assignments are the same for everybody, there's always someone nearby to discuss whether beauty has utility and whether society has purpose. This is the perfect place for the student who is interested in ideas for their own sake, and for whom the title intellectual is the opposite of scary.

St. John's has two campuses with exactly the same curriculum: one in Annapolis, Maryland, and one in Santa Fe, New Mexico. Technically, they are separate institutions, but they function seamlessly as one. Students and faculty interchange between the East and the West, gaining the flavor of both places. However, you should know that the great croquet game with the United States Naval Academy is only available in Annapolis.

CROSS APPS: If you are interested in the Great Books concept, check out Shimer and, especially but not only if you are Catholic, Thomas Aquinas College in pastoral Ojai, California, (see p. 220) and The Thomas More College of Liberal Arts in Merrimack, New Hampshire. The University of Chicago and Reed College offer core curricula based on the Great Books concept. If you want to read the books yourself (without the benefit of honing the meaning through lively discourse), *Encyclopaedia Britannica* has compiled a list in *Great Books of the Western World* edited by Mortimer J. Adler (Encyclopedia Brittanica).

DOWNSIDE: The students at St. John's gain mastery of an intellectual tradition that goes back several thousand years, but they may not know the latest in teenage street fashion or other aspects of contemporary culture. However, the students I spoke with didn't care. Basically, the students who are drawn to this curriculum seem not to find any fault with it.

> **If one asks the chief executive officers of business corporations and nonprofit organizations what they prize most in an employee, the list resembles the mission statement of a liberal arts college—critical thinking, oral and written communication abilities, conceptual application of quantitative skills, a commitment to lifelong learning, and the like.**
>
> *—Paul Neely, trustee, Williams College*

DOES ST. JOHN'S EVER CHANGE?

St. John's curriculum does in fact evolve, just not very fast. It changes on the time scale of a glacier, or perhaps the evolution of a species.

> ❝ **The fixed curriculum of the colonial era is as much an anachronism today as the stocks in the village square.** ❞
>
> —*Ernest L. Boyer,* College: The Undergraduate Experience in America (*Carnegie Foundation for the Advancement of Teaching*)

St. John's College

P.O. Box 2800

Annapolis, MD 21404

410-626-2522

800-727-9238

www.stjohnscollege.edu

St. John's College

1160 Camino Cruz Blanca

Santa Fe, NM 87505

505-984-6060

800-331-5232

www.stjohnscollege.edu

admissions@sjcsf.edu

THOMAS MORE COLLEGE OF LIBERAL ARTS

Located in Merrimack, New Hampshire, this school provides a rigorous curriculum in the humanities. This is one of the smallest colleges in the country with only ninety-five students, almost exactly half women and half men. Students read the great texts of West civilization in their entirety, organized around cultural context rather than strictly chronologically. The school is affiliated with the Catholic faith, but claims to be "dedicated to providing a Catholic education for students of all faiths." All students learn Greek or Latin so they can read texts in their original language. All students study in Rome at the college's Roman campus. All students—freshmen, sophomores, juniors, and seniors—read the same texts at the same time in the core humanities program, even when upperclassmen have chosen a major. All students belong to one of the most intense academic communities in the country. To learn more, call Joanne Geiger, director of admissions, at 603-880-8308. She will be happy to discuss in detail all that the school has to offer. Website: www.thomasmorecollege.edu.

Also check out the College of Saint Thomas More in Ft. Worth, Texas, www.cstm.edu.

This college feels like a much bigger school than it is because there's no difference, really, between being in class or not in class. The whole place is a class. The buzz: "You might be questioning, as a lot of people do here as the workload sets in, 'Why did I come to this school? I have a thousand pages to read before the end of the week!' Then you'll find yourself on the back porch engrossed in a conversation, and you realize there's nowhere else you can go and have a conversation like this. There's nowhere else."

Thomas More College of Liberal Arts

Six Manchester Street

Merrimack, NH 03054

603-880-8308

www.thomasmorecollege.edu

"Become thyself."
—Nietzsche

SHIMER COLLEGE

Shimer College is one of the least-known jewels in higher education today. About two thirds of classes are in the core curriculum where students work strictly and only from original classical texts. The other third are electives. Shimer makes scholars out of all who are willing to be so molded. Shimer doesn't care as much about your high-school grades and scores as they care about your intellect and intent. Shimer proves that the curriculum and the faculty make the college, not outstanding grades for incoming freshmen. Shimer usually admits around 90 percent of those who apply, but they counsel candidates closely to reduce frivolous applications. They'll actually take the time to talk to you to see if you are motivated and intelligent. All who are admitted will become scholars. The school's admissions documents say, "Once a student has encountered original sources—works often thought to be too difficult for the undergraduate—that student knows that no material is too complex, no subject too arcane to be approached and mastered."

> **Books, like proverbs, receive their chief value from the stamp and esteem of ages through which they have passed.**
>
> —*Sir William Temple*

Located on the campus of the Illinois Institute of Technology, the school offers access to this campus's electives (in addition to their own electives), as well as everything that Chicago has to offer. Shimer classes are limited to twelve students or fewer, working directly with a curriculum designed to give students a strong background in the humanities, social sciences, and natural sciences. With a diploma from Shimer, students know they have an education. There would be no doubt about it.

Shimer College
3424 South State Street
Chicago, IL 60616
312-235-3500
www.shimer.edu

For every accredited college and university in the U.S. and Canada go to www.donaldasher.com/colleges

---

RECENT PILOT GREAT BOOKS PROGRAMS

There is a revival of interest in the Great Books canon, as evidenced by new programs at the following institutions:

Wilbur Wright College of the City Colleges of Chicago

University of Wisconsin, Milwaukee, Wisconsin

University of Montevallo, Montevallo, Alabama

Middle Tennessee State University, Murfreesboro, Tennessee

Louisiana State University, Shreveport, Louisiana

Indiana University of Pennsylvania, Indiana, Pennsylvania

Gardner-Webb University, Boiling Springs, North Carolina

Delta State University, Cleveland, Mississippi

Clemson University, Clemson, South Carolina

California Polytechnic State University (Cal Poly), San Luis Obispo, California

Bethel College, St. Paul, Minnesota

Austin Peay State University, Clarksville, Tennessee

(Source: Chronicle of Higher Education)

Just for the record, a DWEM is a dead, white, European male.

Chapter Five

ECO SCHOOLS

Eco schools were once a fringe element in higher education, places to study small-scale farming and better technologies for composting. But that was a long time ago. As the environmental movement has matured and become more mainstream, so have the institutions concentrating on environmental studies and their related sciences. You may, indeed, study composting at one of these schools, but today you are likely to be using state-of-the-art biochemistry and developing methods of scaling production up to the small-nation level to create a renewable energy source. Global interconnectedness and concepts of sustainability are in, and back-to-the-farm isolationism is passé. The future of our planet and the survival of the human species may depend on the activists and scientists currently being trained in these schools.

COLLEGE OF THE ATLANTIC

only one major: human ecology • **interdisciplinary approach** • *students design courses* • **tons of experiential learning and field studies** • *can be a future scientist or artist or activist or journalist or whatever* • **students involved in college governance** • *major capstone project in senior year* • **motto: the graduate school for undergraduates**

College of the Atlantic is the quintessential green school. In fact, human ecology is the only major offered, and every graduate gets a bachelor of arts in human ecology. You can approach human ecology from any angle, but the health and well being of the planet itself—and the future of humans on this planet—is the focus of all scholarship.

Of course you can study ecology and environmental sciences at many schools, but it changes the equation when *everybody* at a college has the same mission. This school has become an incubator for cutting-edge environmental thought, a place where big ideas are born and tested. There is a lot of cross-fertilization here. A future scientist influences a future politician, a future artist influences a future medical doctor, and all of them may design a research project and work as a team.

The school is small, about 300 students and 30 faculty, but the curriculum is the opposite of small. Laboratory and field sciences are strong, as you would expect, but there's much more to the story, academically, at COA. Despite offering only one major, courses may have widely varying content: from literature and creative writing, to education leading to a teaching certificate, to art and architecture, to entrepreneurship and green business practices, to economics and public policy, to you name it. It's just that the focus of all of these classes will be on human welfare, the environment, and ecological concerns.

Students have major input into the syllabi for most classes, and many classes are designed by individual students or groups of students. Independent study with a mentor is a popular option. Even within the well-established classes, independent study is expected. This allows COA students to create an infinite number of special interests within the structure of the curriculum. Two people can take the same class and go in very divergent directions at the same time.

All students are *required* to complete an academically related internship and design a major senior project, thus the college's unofficial motto: The Graduate School for Undergraduates (a whopping 65 percent go on to graduate school within five years). Senior projects might involve co-authoring a research paper submitted for publication, writing a senior thesis, making a film, or creating a presentation for the entire college community and taking questions from faculty, students, and invited guests.

Bar Harbor, where College of the Atlantic is nestled, is one of the most delightful little towns on the coast of Maine. You can walk from one end of the village to the other. Dorms, classrooms, and administration buildings are located on adjacent family estates in real mansions repurposed to academic service. The ocean waters actually temper the Maine winters, but you can expect a winter blanket of snow and certainly some storms.

COA students get around. You're just as likely to find them in the mountains of Peru and in the waters of the Great Barrier Reef as on campus in Bar Harbor, Maine. Here are some recent internships:

Mount Desert Island Marathon, Bar Harbor, Maine

Environmental Film Festival, Washington, D.C.

Bicycle Tricycle Conversion Project, Patriensa, Ghana

Madhya Paschimanchal Grameen Bikas Bank, Banke, Nepal

The Byre Recording Studio, Kiltarlity, Scotland

Marlborough Sounds Dolphin Project, Picton, New Zealand

Kelmscott Rare Breeds Farm, Lincolnville, Maine

Klamath Forest Alliance, Etna, California

Hubbell & Hubbell Architecture Studio, San Diego, California

COA is not a dogmatic place. While I was on campus, the student newspaper covered how to harvest and butcher road-kill deer with photographs and a recipe for venison ribs! There is a sense of creativity and irreverence on campus. So this is *not* a place inculcating students to a particular agenda. Students conduct research and

There's no such thing as bad weather, only bad clothing choices.
—*COA faculty*

inquiry with an open mind. There are Republicans here and no knee-jerk anti-business indoctrination. In fact, one administrator told me, concerning global warming, "People may be the problem, but they're also the *only* solution, and business will be the biggest part of that solution. We face a huge challenge but also a huge opportunity to be involved on the ground floor of the next industrial revolution." Indeed, green entrepreneurship is a primary student interest.

The college has very cleverly built alliances with other universities and organizations to allow student access to research projects and facilities. For example, COA collaborates with Mt. Desert Island Biological Laboratory, the Jackson Laboratory, the University of Maine, and Bates, Bowdoin, and Colby Colleges to participate in the Idea Network for Biomedical Research Excellence. The college has dozens of such affiliations, thus its small size is a non-issue in terms of opportunities for scholarship.

COA grads are an independent lot. Many COA alumni launch businesses, research projects, restoration efforts, or crusades of one type or another. Their career paths are way more diverse than you would think. Meet some grads:

Software Security and Data Mining Entrepreneur

Scientist, NOAA (National Oceanic and Atmospheric Administration)

Research Attorney, Marine Affairs Institute

Director of a Buddhist Center

Family Nurse Practitioner

K-12 Science Education Curriculum Design Specialist

Photographer

Physician of Emergency Medicine

Biodiesel Entrepreneur

Editor of Environmental Journal

Scuba Diving Instructor

Program Director for Sustainable Farming Initiative

Q: Who does well at College of the Atlantic?

A: Self-starters. Definitely. Self-motivated, smart, and engaged students. And it helps to be an extrovert, I think. You have to initiate so much, both at the college and in the "real world" as part of your education here.

Q: What kind of student simply doesn't make it at COA?

A: Overly introverted students who can't help themselves. There're resources here, plenty of them, but you have to reach out for them. You have to make everything happen for yourself, which is hard for some personalities. And there's a philosophy behind this place that's well thought out. You can't just build a kayak and go out and band birds and not come back and enter into intellectual discourse about it. Students who think there's no structure here are going to run into trouble.

Q: What was the biggest surprise for you about COA?

A: I was surprised that this was not just another hippy college. We are training professional advocates for our environment and society. Many of the people here are incredibly brilliant, and people work hard because they are passionate about their interests. And there is such a sense of community, a sense of shared purpose. It is impossible to describe this. It's like a force, or a vibration.

DOWNSIDE: This is a small school doing many, many things on a limited budget. Although there are good labs, and students can get 24-hour access to them, if you want access to multimillion-dollar equipment you're probably going to have to find a way to get involved with a research project based elsewhere. And as at other schools where students are responsible for providing so much of the structure and content of their educations, many eighteen-year-olds are simply not going to be ready to step up and take full advantage. Finally, this is a place with a lot of team projects and close interaction. People have to get along here, year after year. So anyone who holds grudges and nurses wounds should just stay away.

MORE UPSIDE: College of the Atlantic has a feeling of light and abundance. The generosity of spirit among the faculty, administrators, and students is no doubt part of the reason for this—and the campus, a combination of grand old estates, is another contributor—but there is more to it than that. This campus is clean, well-cared for, and loved. There is a real optimism here. The success of graduates in terms of both career and graduate school outcomes is proof that this school delivers the goods. The physical area is gorgeous: the Atlantic Ocean forming one border of the campus, a New England village next door, a national park down the road, ski and hiking trails all over. After all, the school's address is Eden Street.

CROSS APPS: Prescott College in Prescott, Arizona, is also an ecologically committed institution. It is covered at length in the next college profile. Evergreen State College in Olympia, Washington, has a lot to offer in terms of being "like" COA. Evergreen has self-directed coursework, an eco-ethic, a strong sense of community, and similarly minded students. Hampshire in Amherst, Massachusetts, claims no particular eco emphasis but has similar educational structure, including self-designed study and close interaction with faculty in small classes. And the schools in the Eco League may be of interest (see sidebar).

College of the Atlantic
105 Eden Street
Bar Harbor, ME 04609
800-528-0025
207-228-5015
www.coa.edu
inquiry@ecology.coa.edu

THE ECO LEAGUE

The Eco League is a consortium of colleges and universities that share a commitment to environmental learning. They have a student exchange agreement allowing students to spend a semester at any of the member schools or even to design a program of study involving attendance at a mix of member campuses.

Alaska Pacific University, Anchorage, Alaska

Antioch College, Yellow Springs, Ohio

College of the Atlantic, Bar Harbor, Maine

Green Mountain College, Poultney, Vermont

Northland College, Ashland, Wisconsin

Prescott College, Prescott, Arizona

All of these schools deserve attention from the eco-minded student. For more info visit www.ecoleague.org. Other schools that might be of interest include Sterling College, Craftsbury Common, Vermont (not to be confused with Sterling College in Sterling Kansas, an "enthusiastically Christian" college with a very different mission). Sterling in Vermont is a work college (see Chapter 9, p. 216) promising "hard work" for enrollees and offering degrees in:

• Conservation Ecology

• Sustainable Agriculture

• Northern Studies

• Outdoor Education & Leadership

• Self-Designed Studies

Sterling College, www.sterlingcollege.edu

Audubon Expedition Institute

For a totally different eco-school experience, either for your entire bachelor's degree or as a term woven into a degree from one of these other fine environmentally focused programs, check out living on the bus with Lesley University's Audubon Expedition Institute. The bus is outdoor education, and it goes all over the country. The school says:

"The Audubon Expedition Institute at Lesley University is an academically rigorous alternative to traditional colleges and universities for undergraduate or graduate students pursuing a deeper ecological understanding of environmental education, leadership and advocacy. Our goal is to create experiential learning communities that inspire informed and compassionate ecological leadership."

Audubon Expedition Institute at Lesley University

29 Everett Street

Cambridge, MA 02138

888-LESLEY-U or 617-349-8300

www.lesley.edu

info@lesley.edu

Not all eco action has to be large scale. Green architecture is about making small, correct choices about how a building is designed and used. Green living is an ethic, as well as a science and a topic for academic inquiry. Check out the green buildings at Northland College in Ashland, Wisconsin. Northland is part of the Eco League, mentioned above. Also check out Carriage House, the green dorm at Mount Allison University, Sackville, New Brunswick, Canada. And the students at Grinnell bind all their printed-on-one-side white recyclable paper onto the back of beer box cardboard and sell it as notebooks. It's fascinating to read some of the material printed on the paper that falls into recycling boxes, and can spice up note taking in class in expected ways.

The College Board gave its first standardized test for college admissions in 1901, and the version that came to be known as the Standard Aptitude Test (SAT) was launched in 1926. That's over one hundred years of biting pencils and sweating nervously.

(Source: Business Week)

NEW COLLEGE OF FLORIDA

you get to design your education • **small classes** • *a committed teaching faculty* • **the Learning Contract—you negoti-**ate **your efforts in advance** • *a private school education at a public school price* • **only for the self-motivated and self-**directed • *no hand holding here, but all the help you need* • **no grades, but you'll hear what your profs really think** *what's this got to do with a circus magnate?* • **596 students: 323 women and 273 men**

> **Most colleges, whatever their roots, have become consumer-driven, offering something for everyone. It becomes difficult to distinguish between them. New College, in contrast, embodies very strong, definitive educational intent.**
>
> —*New College administrator*

New College was founded in 1960 by a small group of educators and civic leaders to address the dissatisfaction they felt with the Northeastern educational establishment, which they felt was promulgating "a collegiate culture that tolerated amateur academics while promoting professional sports."

They founded the college upon four principles, which still guide the college's every action today:

1. A student should be responsible for his or her own education.
2. The best education demands a joint search for learning by exciting teachers and able students.
3. Students' progress should be based on demonstrated competence and real mastery, rather than on the accumulation of grades and credits.
4. Students should have from the outset opportunities to explore in-depth areas of interest to them.

A distinctive feature of the New College program is the Learning Contract. Learning Contracts are agreements developed and negotiated individually between a student and a faculty member. The student decides which main and ancillary readings to pursue, how many papers to write, and what field or lab work to conduct. At this college, the faculty member's guidance usually consists of paring down the student's ambitions into a coherent project that can be completed sometime during the student's lifetime.

The school is strong in the sciences as well as all areas of the humanities, and just

People don't come here by accident. The first essay question is "Why New College?"

CoOl WeB SiTe!

Do you shake in your shoes about having to take all those "tests" that may determine your "eligibility" to get into college? You'll find that in the past several years there has been an ongoing discussion in the educational community about the usefulness of such tests, like the SAT, as a measurement of one's academic abilities. Whether you value the worthiness of these tests or think they are a disgrace of our system, you might want to check out the National Center for Fair and Open Testing (FairTest). They now have a Web site, www.fairtest.org, with news, resources and publications, advocacy support, and fact sheets addressing these issues.

There are currently a fair number of schools that either no longer require the SAT for admission or have limited these requirements to certain cases. Here are a few that do not insist on the SAT, according to FairTest.

Academy of Art College, San Francisco, California

Antioch College, Yellow Springs, Ohio

Bard College, Annandale-on-Hudson, New York

Bates College, Lewiston, Maine

Bowdoin College, Brunswick, Maine

City College of City University of New York (CUNY), Manhattan, New York

College of the Atlantic, Bar Harbor, Maine

Dickinson College, Carlisle, Pennsylvania

Goddard College, Plainfield, Vermont

Golden Gate University, San Francisco, California

Hampshire College, Amherst, Massachusetts

Julliard School, New York, New York

Lewis & Clark College, Portland, Oregon

Muhlenberg College, Allentown, Pennsylvania

New England College, Henniker, New Hampshire

Prescott College, Prescott, Arizona

San Francisco State University, San Francisco, California

Shimer College, Waukegan, Illinois

St. John's College, Annapolis, Maryland

St. John's College, Santa Fe, New Mexico

Wheaton College, Norton, Massachusetts

If you'd like to take a look at the whole list (including schools that still require the scores but have reduced their role in the admissions decision), check out: www.fairtest.org/optinit.htm. Perhaps you won't have to go through a night of no sleep and three hours of sweating after all. But before you blow off the SAT completely, be sure to check with the admissions offices of those colleges you are applying to. Policies change annually, and you don't want to realize too late that you've overlooked a required piece of your application.

completed the addition of a major science building. As you would expect, students have access twenty-four hours a day, everyday.

Students here participate in regular seminar classes, but a big part of the New College education is designed and conducted by the student independent of the classroom workflow. Every student completes three significant independent study projects (one of

---

IS THE SAT REALLY FAIR?

AVERAGE SAT SCORES AS A FACTOR OF FAMILY INCOME:

Income	SAT verbal	SAT math	combined
More than $100,000	559	571	1,130
$80,000–$99,999	539	543	1,082
$70,000–$79,999	527	531	1,058
$60,000–$69,999	520	523	1,043
$50,000–$59,999	514	514	1,030
$40,000–$49,999	505	506	1,011
$30,000–$39,999	493	493	986
$20,000–$29,999	476	478	954
$10,000–$19,999	449	458	907
Less than $9,999	427	444	871

AVERAGE SAT SCORES AS A FACTOR OF RACE:

Race	SAT verbal	SAT math	combined
Asian, Asian-American	498	560	1,058
White	527	528	1,055
American Indian	484	481	965
Hispanic, Latino	463	464	927
Black	434	422	856

(Source: Educational Testing Service)

the undergraduate experiences that graduate schools favor the most). All students plan and conduct a yearlong research project leading to writing a thesis. They defend their theses in public oral baccalaureate examinations, at which no question is barred. (*The undergraduate experience that graduate schools favor most.*) The school offers twenty-one majors, which it calls disciplines, but the truth is you can design any major you want if you can find a faculty member to collaborate with you. The theses that I read here were some of the best I've ever seen by undergraduates. Many represented serious, original scholarship by undergraduates. Here are but a few titles:

Rigidity Theorems Involving Principal Curvature

Theory of Justice in Ancient Law Codes

The Significant Pleasures of Roland Barthes: From Structuralism to Post-Structuralism through Political Myths

The Eyes of Fishes: Ganglion Cell Densities in the Retina of the Teleost-Holocentrus Rufus

Comparison of Forest Floor and Canopy Humus in a Costa Rican Cloud Forest: Seasonal Fluctuations in Soil Moisture and Effects on Nitrogen Cycling

Sea Level Rise in Southwest Florida: An Economic Benefit-Cost Analysis of Policy Alternatives

Children's Eyewitness Testimony: The Effects of Narrative Style on Adult Perceptions of Credibility

No visit to the college would be complete without taking significant time to look at some of these theses in the library.

The college also offers competitive grants. Students without the financial means to pursue exotic interests can compete for grant money to fund their research.

> **Faculty serve as facilitators and mentors rather than as purveyors of information.**
>
> —*New College student*

How important is climate to you? Top students spend a lot of time in libraries and labs, and air conditioning and heating are pretty similar at all latitudes and elevations. You might really enjoy going to school where the weather is more than a casual conversation topic. For example, Michigan Tech in Houghton, Michigan, has its own ski run, the steepest in the Midwest, Mont Ripley Ski Hill. Students build giant snow and ice sculptures for Winter Carnival, and they last the rest of the winter. They also have sled dog races, with a twist: Teams of students pull dogs in sleds on a race course. Whether this is fascinating or horrifying to you, just remember, in the library it's 68 to 72 degrees Fahrenheit all over North America.

New College is well known among academics, though little known outside of academic circles. If New College students do a credible job on their classes and their theses, admission to graduate school should be a snap. Alumni have attended over sixty graduate programs from coast to coast, including virtually all of the A-list schools. New College has no grades, instead using a narrative evaluation that faculty give to each and every student they teach or advise. (For more schools that de-emphasize grades, see p. 151.)

The campus itself is a special added benefit. It is right on the shore of Sarasota Bay, on the grounds of the estate of Charles Ringling, the business manager brother of the Ringling Brothers, Barnum and Baily Circus. It has taken over several marble mansions that were built by monies from The Greatest Show on Earth. Next door is the John and Mabel Ringling Art Museum, an impressive collection.

Following is a sample narrative evaluation. The collection of these becomes, in fact, the student's transcript. When graduate schools receive these records, they have to take the time to actually look at the candidates. They cannot reduce them to a number and plug it into a formula. The real advantage, however, is to the students, who get feedback on what their strengths are and how they can improve as a scholar. Wouldn't you rather get one of these than an A? An A is a single letter, entered on some spreadsheet in a registrar's computer program by the stroke of a single key. Perhaps neither the professor—nor the registrar—nor even the student-thinks one minute about that grade. This, on the other hand, is a communication of real value and integrity.

Student: Nancy Adams

Project advisor: Dave L. Lawson

Title of the class: Three Works by Friedrich Dürrenmatt in the German Original

For this project Nancy read in the original German the following works by Friedrich Dürrenmatt: the dramas *Der Besuch der alten Dame* and *Die Physiker*, and the novel *Der Richter und sein Henker*. She also consulted relevant secondary sources and critical material contained in the Continuum translation of Dürrenmatt's works. As a final project Nancy submitted two medium-length essays in German, and one essay in English.

Nancy's first essay on *Die Physiker* showed a good appreciation of the play's comic and serious aspects. She focused on Dürrenmatt's use of thematic contrasts and the work's reflection of his dramaturgical principles. Her second essay on *Der Besuch der alten Dame* utilized Jean-Paul Sartre's *Huis clos* as a point of departure for an exploration of Dürrenmatt's representation of the character Ill's acknowledgment of his guilt and self-induced torment. Nancy correctly noted where Dürrenmatt and Sartre differ. Both these essays showed a good command of German stylistics for a student with Nancy's background of three semesters. She had clearly worked hard to locate good equivalents for abstract English expressions, and she avoided fundamental slips. To be sure, Nancy did not always locate the correct terms, and several errors in hypotactic structure and related mistakes did occur. But this is to be expected at this stage.

Nancy's English essay, "Objects of Concern: Dürrenmatt's Focus on Justice and Chance," linked *Der Besuch der alten Dame* with *Der Richter und sein Henker.* Her analysis of the role of chance in both works was quite effective, particularly with regard to the novel, where coincidence is a key concept. Nancy also brought up salient features of Dürrenmatt's treatment of justice. Here she noted the important Christian implications of Ill's suffering in *Der Besuch der alten Dame,* and she also traced the transformation in the town's position on Ill's "crime." On this point I would have liked to have seen more analysis of the process which the townspeople undergo as they abandon Ill and then "justify" his "execution" in the name of the very "Western values" they had invoked when they initially rejected Claire's offer of money in exchange for Ill's life. In her analysis of justice in *Der Richter und sein Henker,* Nancy recognized the ambiguity of Bärlach's moral position with respect to Gastmann and the legal form of justice the latter had successfully evaded. Her writing was clear and careful, and her argument was supported with relevant textual references.

Nancy's work for this project was very good. She learned a lot about Dürrenmatt and enhanced her active and passive command of German in the process.

DOWNSIDE: New College is quite small, and you have to make your opportunities. If you're looking for a sequence of classes you can pick out of a catalog, you're not going to like New College. Many of the students spend significant amounts of time working alone on projects unique to their own interests, which actually cuts down on the academic community aspect of the school, despite its small size. Since faculty members spend so much time in one-on-one academic "coaching," some of the seminar classes are actually surprisingly large for the size of the school. Finally, applicants must really ask themselves, "Am I self-motivated enough to run my own study programs?" The school warns: "We have found that students who attend college largely because all of their friends are doing so, or because no other alternatives seem open to them, lack the day-to-day motivation necessary to exploit learning opportunities available at New College." They are not kidding. Some students attracted to the experiential aspects of New College fail to realize that all learning here needs to be tied to a sound theoretical approach involving abstract and reflective thought. Activity without thought will result in failure at New College.

MORE UPSIDE: The faculty and staff that I have met at New College have all been completely engaged and committed. I can name no other place I visited where so much care was afforded the students by the faculty. Everyone here seems to realize that they're involved in a noble endeavor, something special, uncommon, and even precious.

CoOl BoOk AlErT!

This Way Out: A Guide to Alternatives to Traditional College Education in the United States, Europe, and the Third World
by John Coyne and Tom Hebert (Dutton)

This is a fascinating book, not only for the hundreds of colleges and programs that it describes but also as a period piece. It is one of a rash of irreverent, counterculture college guides that came out in the late '6os, early '7os. It's long out of print, but a cult favorite among college admissions deans and ex-hippie college counselors. I stole my copy from Audrey Smith at Hampshire College, swearing I would mail it back as soon as I read it. That was eight years ago. If you can find a copy, it's worth a trip to the copier machine. Sample: "Visually there is little difference between the freaks and the hippies, though at Goddard we noticed hostility between them. The freaks talked disparagingly about the hippies tinkling bells over brown rice, and dumped on the commune living. The freak is a private person who has taken from the hippie's counter-culture his dress, style of life, flexibility and is using the college to gain skills." Wow.

CROSS APPS: New College is pretty unusual, but one place like it is the Johnston Center for Integrative Studies at the University of Redlands in Redlands, California. If you're interested in writing a thesis, check out Reed, Davidson, and Princeton, among many others. You may be interested in Prescott College, which has learning contracts, narrative evaluations, and extensive self-designed study blocks (see p. 138). Prescott is a very different school, however, and a different type of student would be happy there than at New College. Hampshire College and The Evergreen State College use learning contracts as well. These comparisons conceal major differences between New College and all these referenced institutions, however, so investigate the differences as well as the similarities.

New College of Florida

5800 Bay Shore Road

Sarasota, Florida 34243

941-359-4269

admissions@ncf.edu

www.ncf.edu

For every accredited college and university in the U.S. and Canada go to www.donaldasher.com/colleges

C o O l   B o O k   A l E r T !

Major in Success: Make College Easier, Fire Up Your Dreams, and Get a Very Cool Job
by Patrick Combs (Ten Speed Press, 2007)

This is a book that actually answers the important questions about being a successful student. How do you figure out what career you'd truly love? How do you pick the best major for you? How do you get and stay motivated? What are some shortcuts to success? How do you get past the fears that hold you back? What will give you a competitive edge? With so much at stake during your college years—career, success, happiness, your future—you need this smart, savvy, and inspiring book to ensure you excel. The author, Patrick Combs, put himself through college by managing a rock band, then went on to land a great job with Levi Strauss & Company. Now he works as a professional speaker, award-winning Webmaster, and author.

HAMPSHIRE COLLEGE

the freedom to design your own program • **a liberal student body with a global perspective** • *saving the world is okay, even expected* • **being creative is okay, even expected** • *community service requirement* • **no grades per se, but narrative evaluations** • *learning contracts* • **extensive self-designed study blocks** • *it pays to be a self-starter* • **also welcomes nontraditional students who are ready to make a total commitment to their undergraduate education** • *1,350 students: 42% male, 58% female*

> **❝Nothing succeeds like excess. ❞**
>
> —Oscar Wilde

Hampshire College doesn't do anything halfway. I asked them to send me some basic information on their program, and I received an eight-inch stack of materials. That's how Hampshire works. If you are someone who has always had more ideas than time to do them, more energy than anyone you know, more creativity than was ever required by the situation, then Hampshire could be for you.

Hampshire is a college of action, for people of action. Its motto is *non satis scire*, which means "To know is not enough." If memorizing and passing tests are your gig, Hampshire is not. If you want to be engaged by integrating your studies with the world around you, Hampshire might be just right.

Hampshire used to be known as "that school in Amherst where you can get a degree in Frisbee." People thought you could go to Hampshire and just do whatever you pleased. But that's old news. The college is maturing, evolving, and improving. Hampshire has distribution requirements (required courses) and a coherent approach to learning across the curriculum. Students are required to complete a mix of basic studies (Division I) then pursue a concentration to the level of mastery satisfactory to their advisor (Division II), then complete advanced studies, which is a major self-designed project (Division III). "Each Hampshire student's intellectual or artistic vision culminates in a substantial independent project—an academic or research thesis, a scientific experiment, a film, an art exhibition, an original invention, or a project in theatre, music, or dance."

Students learn to initiate, plan, conduct, and finish projects in each class, as they prepare for greater personal responsibility for their own learning process. By the time students are doing Division III work, they are prepared. Hampshire doesn't have departments; it has schools: Cognitive Science; Humanities, Arts, and Cultural Studies; Interdisciplinary Arts; Natural Science; and Social Science. This reduces "compartmentalizing" of academic exploration, and allows students to approach any issue from multiple angles. There are no grades at Hampshire; students receive narrative evaluations on their performance in a class with suggestions on preparing for future academic objectives. At Hampshire, the faculty believe that giving students an A may keep them from doing their best work.

Hampshire students benefit from a consortium of Amherst-area schools, all allowing cross-registration for classes and open participation in many (but not all) student activities. The consortium consists of Hampshire, Amherst, Mount Holyoke, Smith, and the University of Massachusetts, allowing local access to 5,000 courses without paying extra. This is a key part of the Hampshire program as students pursue Division II concentrations. Amherst itself is a quintessential New England town, dominated by the colleges, with a coffee-house-and-poetry-reading flavor. Emily Dickinson is from here, and everyone goes by her house on their first visit to Amherst.

DOWNSIDE: Hampshire College is liberal, and if that doesn't appeal to you, you might need to think about that. Being gay is no problem, but cooking up a fat steak in the dorm or throwing away perfectly good recyclables may create a scene. Students are sometimes drawn to Hampshire because they want to escape the structure and control of their current learning environments, but escaping from is not a good enough reason to come to Hampshire. You must be *drawn to* the Hampshire program to find a genuine fit. The program is demanding in ways that are not at first obvious. You cannot just

> **Imagination is more important than knowledge.**
>
> —*Albert Einstein*

Hampshire has a student club called Basic Character Flaws. And another called Stage Combat. And another one called Mixed Nuts.

go through the motions and turn in a certain volume of work. Your work must improve in quality over your time at Hampshire or you will not be allowed to advance to Division III and complete the program. Students who are unhappy at Hampshire are the ones who don't listen when the school says it expects a lot from its students. Finally, as at New College, students are applying themselves to so many different projects that the academic community tends to diverge in the final year. The best way to beat that is to keep living on campus.

MORE UPSIDE: Hampshire College is a good horse to bet on. Almost any Hampshire student can identify with Mark Twain's boast, "I never let schooling get in the way of my education." Hampshire alumni become powerful academic citizens. For example, Hampshire alumni have started no fewer than twenty-six graduate programs at other institutions. Hampshire College will not get in the way of your education.

CROSS APPS: If you're interested in the capstone project, check out Kalamazoo College in Kalamazoo, Michigan, as well as New College, Davidson, and Reed, and Prescott College, which is covered later in this chapter. Prescott and Evergreen are in many ways the most similar colleges to Hampshire, but they are, you guessed it, very, very different. They all have narrative evaluations, student-planned learning, and no grades, but the atmospheres at these colleges are very different. Visit the school, and you will know if it appeals to you. If you are interested in the liberal student body and social involvement aspects of Hampshire, consider Earlham in Richmond, Indiana. Students who apply to Hampshire might also apply to Bard, Sarah Lawrence, Pitzer, and Marlboro.

Hampshire College
893 West Street
Amherst, MA 01002
413-549-4600
www.hampshire.edu

Hampshire College has a working farm. Students can study sustainable agricultural practices on a micromodel basis. The School-to-Farm program brings K-12 students on campus for education in organic farming, global agricultural issues, and sustainable agricultural practices.

WHAT IS INTELLIGENCE?

by Ruby A. Ausbrooks, Ed.D., master teacher and secondary education consultant

Did you ever wonder why everybody thinks the person with an "A" in math is smart, but no one seems to be much impressed with another person's "A" in music or art? Why not? Doesn't achievement in those fields—music or art—require as much attention, evaluation, synthesis, and work as math demands?

What *is* intelligence? What do we mean by *smart*?

The astronomer Carl Sagan believed a long pass by a quarterback to the end zone is an example of a fantastic combination of fine motor skills and applied physics. While maneuvering through a field of shifting obstacles, a quarterback must adjust his throw for direction, speed, distance, and wind vectors. If people can do this extremely well, sports journalists call them brilliant.

There is more than one way of being smart. On some level we always have understood this. We've used descriptive words that illustrated this understanding, phrases such as "talented musician," "wise investor," "witty humorist," or "gifted chess player." British writers seem to have favored "quick" as a necessary criterion of intelligence.

Is intelligence, then, a concept dependent on its context?

Yes. What if we lived in a less technical culture? What if there were no stock markets for the investor, no laboratories for the scientist, no machines for the engineer? Would a chess player have high status in a society of hunters and gatherers? Valuing and nurturing intelligence depends on context.

And no. Outstanding persons would seek other outlets or create new ones. Mathematicians and astronomers looked to the stars. Naturalists became herbalists and healers. Someone in an ancient community built a toy steam engine.

Pacific island navigators have demonstrated ability to cross a trackless ocean, guided by celestial features, currents, and color of the water. Writers have claimed that Columbus carried a spatial awareness inside his head, locating himself by those same celestial features, currents, direction, and sailing time (although, this seems unlikely if he believed he had reached Asia). Columbus and the islanders possessed skills derived from the same kind of intelligence.

If a superior intelligence means better ability to learn, solve problems, make logical judgments, and direct one's actions, we see immediately the problem with such a definition. Examples are all around. What are they thinking, we wonder, the millionaire athlete who murders his girlfriend, or the respected physicist who knowingly risks global annihilation?

The implication is that a person can be smart and dim-witted at the same time. Jimmy Carter is generally rated as one of the most intelligent presidents the U.S. ever had, but he was ineffective as a chief executive. Ronald Reagan is considered by many historians to be one of the great leaders of the last century, but he was certainly near average in classical intelligence.

The concept of intelligence as something to define and measure wasn't even around before 1900. Alfred Binet created for Parisian administrators a test that attempted to measure ability in children. Americans seized the idea of measuring intelligence, and within a few years a test score and a chronological age became the familiar IQ, intelligence quotient.

Few are in agreement about what IQ tests actually measure, except that it probably isn't intelligence. IQ tests have been misused widely. Officials used fear of diluting our national pool of intelligence, whatever that is, to promote restrictive immigration laws. IQ scores became part of personnel files, affecting promotion in business and industry. Schools separated students into college preparatory and vocational tracks.

More recently, the author of a best-selling book offered IQ scores as proof that some racial and ethnic groups are superior to others. One of those superior groups, Asians, was also one of the groups most feared eighty years earlier because they might dilute the national IQ.

Howard Gardner grappled with some of these same problems when he was developing the theory of multiple intelligences which he presented in the book *Frames of Mind: The Theory of Multiple Intelligences* (Basic Books, 1993). Educators greeted Gardner's book with a nation-wide, "Aha!" It was the kind of response that occurs when someone organizes intuitive knowledge and states it in understandable terms.

Like theories on cell biology that appeared before anyone saw inside a mitochondrion, the theory of multiple intelligences was a working model that could be used to understand the present and to investigate the future.

If there is more than one way of being smart, and common sense tells us there is, how does one isolate an intelligence? Neurobiology offers little help; the brain uses many different sites and millions of neurons to process information from one sensory perception.

Gardner drew on biological and anthropological research to answer the question of what intelligence is. He developed several criteria; among the more specific are the following essential characteristics:

An intelligence can exist in the absence of other abilities. Gardner cited instances where brain injury or birth defects damaged other mental capacities while leaving intact outstanding ability in one area, a savant, for example.

If an intelligence is distinct, there will be persons who demonstrate exemplary performance in that intelligence, such as a musical prodigy or a mathematical theorist.

A set of core information-processing functions can be identified with an intelligence.

An intelligence can be destroyed, even though other abilities remain (a condition opposite of that in the first statement; again, true instances were cited).

Gardner initially described seven distinct intelligences:

1. Logical-Mathematical—involves deductive reasoning, detecting patterns, analytical thinking. Persons who exhibit exemplary ability likely will be mathematical theorists or scientists.

2. Linguistic—mastery of language and nuances in the use of words, uses language to interpret and process information. This is the intelligence domain of novelists and poets.

3. Spatial—the ability to create and manipulate images and shapes and to orient objects in space. This is the special intelligence of architects, artists, as well as some explorers.

4. Musical—involves recognition and understanding of pitches, tones, and rhythms; a dominant musical intelligence interprets the world in these terms, exemplified in great musicians and composers.

5. Bodily-Kinesthetic—mastery of fine motor skills and utilizing physical skills to maximize mental abilities. Outstanding examples are superior athletes and dancers.

6. and 7. Personal—combines two separate intelligences, understanding ourselves (Intrapersonal) and how we relate to others (Interpersonal). Philosophers and essayists, Henry Thoreau, for example, have exceptional ability in intrapersonal intelligence. Charismatic religious leaders, teachers, and politicians may be gifted in interpersonal intelligence.

Gardner expected more distinct intelligences to be identified.

He soon added more distinctions. Gardner's eighth intelligence is the naturalist. This is intelligence which notes differences and similarities in plants and animals and the environment, and which appears to recognize interconnections in the natural world. Charles Darwin demonstrated outstanding ability, although it is said that as a young man his mental ability wasn't particularly memorable. Other achievers in this intelligence are the persons admired in colloquial terms as the man or woman with a "green thumb."

Other psychologists, notably, Peter Salovey, a Yale psychologist, Reuven BarOn, an Israeli researcher, and Daniel Goleman, author of *Emotional Intelligence* (Bantam Books, 1997), incorporated part of Gardner's theory of multiple intelligences and placed greater emphasis on emotional development.

Goleman expanded Gardner's idea of a personal intelligence into a sweeping concept—the command of ourselves and how we relate with others make up the set of skills that determines whether or not we succeed in workplace, home, or personal satisfaction.

No intelligence functions alone in a healthy person, and accordingly, Goleman links emotional intelligence closely with kinesthetic intelligence and sensory processing, music, and artistic awareness. In Goleman's view, emotional development is the key to making sound judgements and to nurturing the development of all mental abilities.

It appears now, looking at implications for schools and education, that we have completed a circle—returning to the importance of school climate, attention to emotional development, and a goodness of fit for the student who lives outside the middle of the Bell curve.

CoOl BoOk AlErT!

How College Affects Students by Ernest Pascarella and Patrick Terenzini (Jossey-Bass)

This is not a book for high school students, but at 894 pages it is an exhaustive review of what we know about what college does to young people. If you are looking for original research on any education-related topic, whatsoever, this guide can be priceless. And high-school students can get some curious ammunition if they are willing to lift the cover of this weighty tome. For example, B students everywhere can rejoice in this comment on the body of research concerning GPA and income: "These reviews are quite consistent in concluding that the average correlation between college grades and earnings is statistically significant and positive, *but quite modest in magnitude.*" So, take that, grade grubbers.

SCHOOLS THAT DE-EMPHASIZE GRADES

New College of Florida has no grades at all. In place of grades, students receive very personal narrative evaluations (see sample on p. 127). The small size of the college, combined with the close interaction with faculty, allows this system to flourish. Faculty and students alike love it. The Johnston Center for Integrative Studies at University of Redlands has a similar system, as does Hampshire College, covered in the previous profile. Prescott College also works very similarly with a narrative evaluation system. Prescott is covered in the next profile. Alverno also has no grades and uses an evaluation process. Brown University, certainly one of the best small universities in the world, has grades but students can opt to take a significant number of classes on a credit/no credit basis. Brown students strive to excel in those classes for the sake of learning, not for a grade. (Interestingly, Brown also has no distribution requirements. They trust their students to select a mix of classes appropriate for their aspirations. Amherst and Grinnell also have no distribution requirements.) Reed College has regular grades, recorded in the registrar's office, but not distributed to students. Reed students need to make an appointment with a faculty advisor or the dean of students to discover their grades. Most don't. How do Reed students get feedback? Faculty members write narrative remarks on papers and labs that are then returned to the students. Sarah Lawrence has a similar system. Sarah Lawrence and Reed have the same philosophy as Brown, i.e., students should pursue learning for its own sake and not worry about earning a grade. At the University of California, Santa Cruz, students have a class-by-class option to choose a grade or evaluations.

> **Chemistry is a class you take in high school or college, where you figure out two plus two is 10, or something.**
>
> —*Dennis Rodman*

CoOl BoOk AlErT!

Pledged: The Secret Life of Sororities by Alexandra Robbins (Hyperion)

Ever wonder what really goes on in Greek life? This insider's guide is quite the thriller, which has landed it in the top five campus bestseller-lists nationwide. A better anthropology study would be hard to find, as the author follows a group of sorority sisters over the course of a college year. It's a little hard to understand how these women graduate, what with all the parties, drinking, and, well, you can just imagine. If you attend a school with an active Greek scene, you may find this book illuminating as far as understanding some of your fellow students. Fraternities and sororities bill themselves as institutions that foster leadership and instill a sense of service in their members, but many fall woefully short of such ideals. By the way, one school that does have a healthy Greek scene is University of South, aka Sewanee.

PRESCOTT COLLEGE

the coolest way to learn: outside • **heart, hands, head** • *experiential eco-school* • **the environment, the Great Southwest, and the liberal arts** • *every day is Earth Day* • **where students really matter** • *block system* • **things go way too fast to get bored** • *510 students* • **very small class size** • *50% male, 50% female* • **students come from all over the nation only 6% are from the Southwest**

Prescott College is an "experiential education" school, which means that students learn by doing, going, seeing, hearing, tasting, experimenting, working, thinking, reflecting, and touching as much as they learn from reading and being lectured at. High quality research and scholarship happens at Prescott, but it happens in a very different way than at most other schools.

Although there is a regular core of classes, the point of Prescott is to master self-directed learning. Students design the direction and the methodology of their overall degree program, in close collaboration with their advisors. They enter into contracts of learning, as at New College, and must prove mastery of subject matter to advance. Tests are relatively rare, and multiple choice tests almost unheard of, but papers and direct oral examinations are common. Students receive narrative evaluations of their performance, and letter grades are only entered on the transcript if a student specifically requests it.

The locals pronounce "Prescott" with the same cadence as "biscuit," not with a two-beat "Press Scott," as most outsiders say.

The school uses a novel "block and quarter" trimester. A block is an intensive, four-week long course dedicated to only one subject, and a quarter is an eleven-week period when students can take several classes simultaneously. During block periods, students are expected to be 100 percent available and dedicated to the class. Many courses have strong field components, and some are conducted entirely in the field, with on-site programs throughout the American Southwest, Mexico, Africa, Europe, Central and South America, the Caribbean, and the world. With this calendar every class moves along at warp speed, and students are expected to keep up with the academic side of their assignments as they travel, camp, relocate, mesh with local communities, conduct field studies, and otherwise pursue the "experiential" side of their educations.

Prescott is a good place to be an eco-vegetarian. Many students are veggie, and the environment is the point of this college. Prescott College was an early adherent of the outdoor education and adventure education movements, that is, they believe that being in, surviving, exploring, and paying very close attention to the outdoors is educational and character forming in and of itself. All new students spend three weeks in the Wilderness Orientation Program, a program intended to be an acclimation to the ecology of their new

> **All genuine learning is active, not passive. It involves the use of the mind, not just the memory. It is a process of discovery in which the student is the main agent, not the teacher.**
>
> —*Mortimer J. Adler,*
> *The Paideia Proposal:*
> *An Educational Manifesto*

The World Is Our Classroom.

home as much as to the institution that they have joined.

Many incoming students are transfers from other institutions, where they may have become disillusioned by an educational process that favored learning meaningless and isolated facts over understanding a world of interlinked systems. Prescott definitely favors the meta-level in everything: the meta-cognitive approach to education, and the meta-view of subject matter. If you come here, you'll never view a fact in isolation again, even when seemingly confronted by one.

The faculty-student interaction at Prescott is different from classroom-based programs. Faculty and students travel and study and research and write and work more

A Prescott professor of environmental studies has spent twenty years leading safaris in Africa, and Prescott students frequently accompany him on these educational and research-oriented treks.

closely together than at any other institution in this book. Students are involved in every aspect of running the college, and their opinions matter. This is an academic community unlike others, perhaps less bookish than others but with more emphasis on community.

How academic is it? As academic as you want to make it. Prescott grads have advanced to graduate study at Cornell, Stanford, Tulane University Law School, Tufts University School of Medicine, Union College, University of Oregon, University of Arizona, Loyola University, and Antioch College, among many others. They have also gone on to thrive in roles as educators, ecologists, conservationists, field biologists, botanists, public policy consultants, museum docents, social workers, authors, storytellers, outdoor guides, kayak instructors, emergency medical technicians, financial consultants, recording engineers, journalists, poets, psychologists, and activists, to name just a few examples.

Throughout the student's Prescott career, he or she builds a learning journal, or portfolio, and students cap their time at Prescott by designing and conducting a major project as a senior. These projects also become the high point in their portfolios. The learning journal is intended to help students tie all their learning experiences together as they occur, to make coherence out of their program as it actually develops. Most courses also require their own portfolio, which is then subsumed into the student's larger collection. The content and nature of portfolios vary widely, according to the college, but may contain course portfolios, personal journals, statements of learning goals and objectives, essays, exams, photographs, maps, drawings, letters, and awards.

Here are some sample senior and independent study projects by Prescott College students:

Sacred Earth, Sacred Self: Implementing a National Ecopsychology Conference

Verde Basalt: A Climber's Guide

Socio-Political Survey of Ecuador

Wolf Conservation

Girls' Wilderness Therapy

Nature Conservation in Japan

Native Alaskan Cultural Studies

Siberian Exploratory River Expedition

Storytelling

Health Care in Central America

Interdisciplinary Synthesis: Connecting Photography and Science

Economics of Sustainability

Straw Bale House Design and Construction

Orchard Planning, Design, and Implementation

Embodying the Dream World

Avalanche Forecasting and Snow Dispersal

Prescott College is also home to a NASA-funded Sustainability and Global Change Program, an attempt to use educational outreach to link local community practices to global environmental impacts. The program focuses on such topics as, for example, local causes of global warming and sea-level rise. NASA hopes the program will help disseminate information about the Earth as an interlocked ecosystem.

Prescott is one of the top five sources of baccalaureate degrees for Native Americans. Prescott students frequently travel to Arizona reservations to gain understanding of Native American spiritual and ecological traditions, and while "on the res" they are expected to assist with farm and herd chores just like everyone else. The college also hosts the Center for Indian Bilingual Teacher Education, an innovative program to develop community teachers with local ties and traditional cultural knowledge to earn the Arizona teaching credential. All Prescott students are eligible to pursue an Arizona teaching credential, either concurrent with their undergraduate studies or after their baccalaureate degree is complete.

The students who are happiest at Prescott are those who revere the out-of-doors but never forget they are at college. Those who don't make it are those who forget that

THE PRESCOTT COLLEGE MISSION

The mission of Prescott College is to educate students of diverse ages and backgrounds to understand, thrive in, and enhance our world community and the environment. We regard learning as a continuing process and strive to provide an education that will enable students to live productive lives of self-fulfillment and service to others. Students are encouraged to think critically and act ethically with sensitivity to both the human community and the biosphere. Our philosophy stresses experiential learning and self-direction within an interdisciplinary curriculum.

the papers have to be written and the projects finished. This is not a four-year vacation, as students soon find out. The fast pace of Prescott's calendar makes it easy for students to get behind, and those who catch the last bus out of town, so to speak, are usually carrying a load of incompletes.

DOWNSIDE: Prescott is not long on infrastructure. They've recently inaugurated a magnificent new campus center designed top to bottom as a green building. But if you've got to have big Tudor halls around a quad to feel that you're at college, Prescott may not be for you. Also, Prescott requires a level of self-motivation that is, to put it frankly, lacking in most new high-school graduates. Before starting here at age eighteen, I'd take a long hard look in the mirror. On the other hand, this might be the perfect school for a student who's a little bit older and a little bit more mature to finish an education that lacked meaning and focus at a prior institution.

MORE UPSIDE: This is not your everyday college. The commitment to ecology, sustainability, and global activism is real and universal. At many campuses you can find a club with these interests, but at Prescott these concerns infuse *everything* and *everybody* at the institution.

CROSS APPS: If you're interested in other schools where you can design your own curriculum and pursue opportunities for independent study, see Hampshire, Marlboro, and New College.

If you're interested in the small size of Prescott, see Marlboro, New College, and College of the Atlantic, among others. Also see the list of "Smaller Colleges and Universities," p. 22.

If you're interested in Prescott as an eco-school, also check out College of the Atlantic, Green Mountain College, Berry, Unity, and Evergreen.

MAHATMA GANDHI'S SEVEN SINS

Wealth without work

Pleasure without conscience

Knowledge without character

Commerce without morality

Science without humanity

Worship without sacrifice

Politics without principle

If you are attracted to building a portfolio of your college experiences, check out Kalamazoo College in Kalamazoo, Michigan, and Wheaton College in Norton, Massachusetts.

Prescott College

220 Grove Avenue

Prescott, AZ 86301

520-778-2090

www.prescott.edu

WHY KIDS AREN'T HAPPY IN TRADITIONAL SCHOOL

by Ruby A. Ausbrooks, Ed.D., master teacher and secondary education consultant

Why does one person sail through schooling while a sister or brother suffers through the grade structure as if each year were a jail sentence?

Why do so many smart people flounder through public school like fish caught in a net? Or accumulate a record of detentions and instant recognition by the principal responsible for discipline?

Even those who discover or create a niche for themselves often hate school. One young woman, now a college junior and who was almost a stereotypical cheerleader and member of the *in* crowd, says her high school years were wasted. She got through it by concentrating on the social life and taking a course load that got her out in three years.

Recent research on individual differences and how we learn allows us to speculate on part of the answers.

Some people have different learning clocks. A student may be ready to read, say, at eight years instead of six—so she spends three years feeling stupid—or she's ready to tackle algebra at ten, but she has to sit through years of stupefying boredom.

Some students have a dominant sense for learning, just as important for dealing with daily life as being right- or left-handed, that doesn't fit the popular mold. We no longer force left-handed people to write with their right hands, but we think nothing of forcing auditory learners, who learn by listening, or kinesthetic persons, who learn by doing, to sit silently for hours with books their only source of instruction.

I think the reward for conformity is everyone likes you but yourself.

—*Rita Mae Brown*

If we're doing some things wrong, we've been doing them wrong a long, long time. Egyptian papyri bear the copying work of school children: letter forming exercises, lists of nations, phrases of moral instruction. In the archives of Duke University there is a bit of papyrus with margin notes that mention Argos, Troy, and Helen.

An educator friend, whose experience includes both upstate New York and Nevada, points out schools have used many of the same methods for centuries because these methods work. There have been always, he says, students who don't like or fit the system; that's the way people are.

A former high school principal and superintendent of schools in Illinois, Bill Hayes, had this comment, "Schools are very narrow minded and short tempered in dealing with someone who disagrees with the way they have their system set up."

Sometimes, the people who don't like the way things are effect changes when they get their chances. Sometimes, they give up.

For a number of years, I was a teacher, director, and curriculum coordinator in a cooperative high school that served five separate school districts. The students who came to our school were creative, talented, and bright. Some of them were angry. Most had one thing in common—they didn't fit the stereotypes.

Our school had a number of young men and women who suffered from a lack of goodness of fit. When I remember some of them, their individualities stand out like sapphires sparkling in a fuzzy web.

Angela wanted to be an auto mechanic after she graduated, and she was already working through an apprenticeship despite a ton of pressure from her family and friends who insisted that girls didn't repair cars.

Our school had an unusually large number of musicians, so large that for my own satisfaction I did the numbers. According to the statistical software I used, the probability was less than .0005 that, strictly by chance, one school would have so many young men whose tests indicated music as the primary interest in their lives.

People who are born musicians hear music and rhythms in everything around them, the sound of air brakes on a truck, the beat of tires hitting pavement grooves, voices blending in a crowded hallway. These students might thrive in a school where there is as much emphasis on music as there is on sports in the traditional secondary schools. History can be learned through studying and listening to the changes in musical tastes over decades as well as through memorizing data. Playing in a band is the usual compromise.

Stephanie appeared, at first, to fit the stereotype our culture constructs for young women. She was thin to the point that I wanted to grab her and start spoon-feeding her chicken soup. Her long blond hair shined and waved around a thin face that was expertly made up. Her clothes bore the approved labels.

One of the most fascinating things about Stephanie was that through the influence of a former boyfriend she had developed a hobby. She raised goats for showing in competition. Trophies and award ribbons adorned her room at home. This was what consumed her interests and time.

Steve was a talented mechanic who was left in the charge of two older brothers while his parents, both truck drivers, made long-distance runs from ocean to ocean. The brothers, serious burly men who would tolerate no problems from their younger sibling, were the guardians who came to parent conferences. They looked overpowering, tall, scowling, and obviously able to lift tall buildings. I hesitated to say anything that might be used against Steve once the family returned home.

Steve, however, was a real pain in the neck. He hated schools, teachers, "busy work" assignments, persons in authority, a lot of his fellow classmates ("these dumb jerks"), and who knows what else. Steve invented a device that simplified unloading large trucks. A trucking company purchased Steve's invention for a good sum, which Steve used to set himself up in business after he got out of school, and today he is a successful businessman. I doubt that he ever learned to tolerate busy work.

Except for a few magnet or theme schools sprinkled sparingly like exotic spice, traditional high schools are designed to fit no one, although many students do fit well enough that they prosper.

Goodness of fit is a real-world phenomenon that really does matter. There exists somewhere a public high school for performing arts, a school of science and mathematics, a school for creative writers and artists, a school of applied sciences. Somewhere. As yet, none except that for applied sciences is in my neighborhood.

Adults choose, if they can, to work and live among people of similar lifestyles and interests. It makes nights more interesting, mornings more worth getting up for. Artists like access to galleries, musicians to concerts and opportunities to make music with other musicians. Golfers prefer neighborhoods with golf courses. Hikers look for open countryside. Athletes want handy gyms, handball and basketball courts.

Selecting a college is the first opportunity most of us have to find a goodness of fit. College is the single most important leap, outside choosing a life partner, in creating the kind of life we really want. Somewhere is the college that fits our learning styles, personalities, and interests, where there never again need be more square pegs pounded into round holes.

BETTER LATE THAN NEVER

Many (certainly not all) liberal arts colleges will entertain late applications, especially if the student identifies a close fit with the ethos at that school, or discovered the school after the applications deadline, or just spoke with an alumnus or alumna and learned how good a match it could be. Also, if your first semester at a college or university is a total train wreck, you can try to transfer into these institutions with a personal appeal like this: "Help! Help! I think I've made a terrible mistake!" It's absolutely worth a try rather than enduring four (or more) years of misery.

"The whole aim of practical politics is to keep the populace alarmed (and hence clamorous to be led to safety) by menacing it with an endless series of hobgoblins, all of them imaginary." —H.L. Menken

CoOl BoOk AlErT!

College Unranked: Ending the College Admissions Frenzy by Lloyd Thacker (Harvard University Press)

Lloyd Thacker has ignited a storm of controversy with this collection of essays and observations on the college admissions process. More important than that, he seems to be the catalyst for many college presidents and deans of admission to reconsider the frenzy that the admissions game has become. In addition to creating this book—a must read for educators nationwide—he founded Education Conservancy which organizes retreats and symposia on college admissions. This book is a fun read, with chapter titles like "Faked Figures Make Fools of Us" and "As If Learning Mattered." Mr. Thacker is a crusader for a just cause! Maybe your high school should invite him speak to parents?

MARLBORO COLLEGE

self-directed study • **on an isolated mountaintop** • *a real community, in the sense of a Swiss village* • **direct democracy** *a strong writing curriculum* • **the opportunity to do a major research project, but you have to be self-directed and self-motivated** • *special invitation to home-schooled students*

Marlboro College is a very small academic community perched on a mountaintop. The entire community—faculty, staff, and students—totals only 370 people. The whole place gets snowed in every winter, sometimes several times. This institution offers an extraordinary college experience.

The first two years of the program are writing intensive. The student works closely with faculty to explore the curriculum with an emphasis on bringing the student's writing up to a high standard. The college offers an impressive array of classes for so small an institution, from organic chemistry to early Soviet cinema to Irish history to "Zap! Hands-on Electricity & Magnetism." Check out the course list at www.marlboro.edu/academics/courselist2000spring.html.

By the end of the freshman year, students must pass the writing requirement, and those who do not are asked to withdraw. From that point on, all writing is expected to meet publishable-level standards. At the beginning of the junior year, students

Q. What do you like most about Marlboro?
A. It's really small.

Q. What do you like least about Marlboro?
A. It's really small.

embark on a two-year endeavor to garner and demonstrate mastery of a subject matter, usually using a multidisciplinary approach. In collaboration with faculty advisors, students develop reading lists and study plans that they will, predominantly, pursue on their own. The library is the center of this campus, and reading is the central activity. The library is open twenty-four hours, and students check out their own books, on the honor system.

The faculty and the students become colleagues and peers during the process, with rapport similar to that at the best graduate programs. The faculty at Marlboro cannot rely on yellowed lecture notes, but are charged to keep up with student interests that are ever changing. As one said to me, "No two students have done anything the same."

Students complete the research project by writing a thesis, and must defend their thesis before an orals board of two professors plus an outside examiner. The outside examiner sets the grade. Marlboro is extremely well thought of in academic circles, and has no trouble getting experts from all over New England to come up on their mountain. Rarely, the student and both faculty members will travel to the outside evaluator's turf.

Marlboro tends to appeal to more mature students, who know what they want. It draws a lot of transfers, in some years as much as one-third of the incoming class. Nontraditional and home-schooled students are welcome. If you visit, be sure to read some of the theses by past students.

A lot of schools claim that they are small and intimate. At Marlboro you will know *everybody* in the community.

The governance aspect of Marlboro is very exciting, reminiscent of Deep Springs. Students are involved in every aspect of college operations, but Marlboro goes beyond that. The college is run like a Swiss village democracy, since the entire community regularly assembles to discuss and decide on community issues en masse. Students hold a majority on Community Court, which "has the power to fine any community member and suspend or expel students who violate community rules or violate state or federal law."

DOWNSIDE: Being at Marlboro is like being at home, smack in the center of a 400-acre lawn. If you went to a high school with two thousand students, as more and more students do, this could be an attractive adventure. However, there is nowhere to hide in a school this small. If you don't do your work, your professor will know, and so will everyone else. Most eighteen-year-old students who have been coasting through high school would find it difficult to succeed at Marlboro, unless they are uncommonly mature and self-motivated. It helps to hit the ground running here, and if you don't keep moving along you won't finish on schedule.

MORE UPSIDE: You'll have friends for the rest of your life, as close as siblings. You'll be more than ready for graduate school. You'll know how to write much better than I. The cornerstone of the program is one-on-one faculty attention, and you can't beat that anywhere. My favorite admissions booklet: "After Marlboro: One Hundred Marlboro Graduates and Where They Are Today." Finally, the Internet has been a real boon to places like Marlboro. If you want to learn something, you can do it just as easily on a mountaintop in Vermont as in Manhattan. Probably easier, because there're a lot fewer distractions.

Marlboro College
South Road
Marlboro, Vermont 05344
800-343-0049 or 802-257-4333
www.marlboro.edu

For every accredited college and university in the U.S. and Canada go to **www.donaldasher.com/colleges**

> **We do not offer institutional research projects, major collegiate sports, extensive social endeavors, or any of the other activities which are 'sold' in various ways at universities or large colleges. We offer learning.**
>
> *—Marlboro administrator*

SUICIDE AND THE SMALLER COLLEGE

The national suicide rate for Americans age fifteen to twenty-four is 1.1 per 10,000 per annum. So, for any seven liberal arts colleges with 1,500 students each, it would be absolutely normal for one of them to have a suicide in any given year. However, on the specific campus that has the suicide, the event has magnified impact due to the small size of the institution. Parents may wonder if the school is providing a nurturing and protective environment. Student peers may wonder if they missed the warning signs that could have saved their friend. And the administration may worry about getting an undeserved reputation while they also worry about liability. Besides, being enrolled in college may actually prevent suicide. Enrolled students are half as likely to be suicides as young people of the same age who are not attending college.

THE BLOCK PLAN SCHOOLS

concentrate on one class, full-time • **moves really fast** • *students are available to go on-site, all of them, anywhere, even out of the country* • **it's focused and intense**

COLORADO COLLEGE

Colorado College has an unusual schedule. Students study one course at a time, full time. Classes last three and a half weeks, then students get four days off, and then the next block begins. "The class bells never ring at Colorado College." Students concentrate on one class with no interruptions and no distractions from other classes. This has unique advantages over most schedules. It allows professors to take their classes out of town, or schedule events at night, or overnight. They can coordinate with the schedules of cultural events, even in distant cities. At Colorado College in Colorado Springs, Colorado, students may take a two-week trip to the Grand Canyon to do hands-on research, something that simply isn't possible with a traditional semester or quarter system. Says a professor, "We tend to draw students who are obsessive about their studies, and they like the block plan." One problem: You absolutely must keep up with your work, *every day,* or you'll be in serious trouble fast.

Colorado College
14 East Cache la Poudre Street
Colorado Springs, CO 80903
719-389-6000
www.coloradocollege.edu

CORNELL COLLEGE

Cornell College in Mount Vernon, Iowa, also has the block plan, which it calls "One-Course-At-A-Time," a phrase that it went to the trouble to protect with a trademark.

Cornell College

600 First Street, West

Mount Vernon, IA 52314

800-747-1112 or 319-895-4000

www.cornell-iowa.edu

" Education is the sleeping pill that makes dreams happen. "

—*Peggy Hill, King of the Hill*

TUSCULUM COLLEGE

Tusculum College in Greeneville, Tennessee, is also using this innovative schedule.

Tusculum College

60 Shiloh Road

Greeneville, TN 37743

423-636-7300

www.tusculum.edu

Also note that Prescott College (p. 152) uses a modified block plan schedule.

If you are "a little bit obsessive" the block plan schedule could be of interest to you.

BLOWING SMOKE

A convicted cop killer is not disqualified from receiving federal student aid, but a young person who has the misfortune to be arrested for smoking even one puff of marijuana is going to lose her federal student aid for one year for a first offense, two additional years for a second offense, and forever for a third offense. Murder? No problem. Marijuana? Now that's a threat to society.

THE CO-OP SCHOOLS

go to school, go to work, go to school • **real world integrated with the ivory tower** • *the most employable graduates in the world* • **very diverse choices in programs**

UNIVERSITY OF CINCINNATI

Co-op education was pioneered by the University of Cincinnati, launched in 1906 by Herman Schneider, dean of the University of Cincinnati college of engineering. Dean Schneider thought it would be useful for students to alternate between classroom learning and learning on the job. His idea was an instant success, and thus was "co-op" born.

The University of Cincinnati today has the largest co-op program of any post-secondary school in the United States, with four thousand students participating in a variety of fields from engineering to business to French. Co-op is "a key component of the institution's overall mission."

University of Cincinnati
2624 Clifton Avenue
Cincinnati, OH 45221
513-556-2201
www.uc.edu

The #1 indicator of the first full-time job you'll hold after college is the last full-time job you held before you graduated.

ANTIOCH COLLEGE

Perhaps co-op's best known adherent is Antioch College in Yellow Springs, Ohio. This is a small liberal arts college with a big reputation. The thing to understand about the co-op program at Antioch is that it is about education, not vocation. "Our educational philosophy is driven not by the three Rs, but by the three Cs: classroom, co-op, and community."

This is a school for activists and would-be activists. The college's home page unabashedly asks, "Do you want to change the world?" If the answer is yes, then maybe Antioch is for you.

Antioch students alternate between classroom and co-op sessions, stretching the college term to five years. Students are independent and self-reliant by the time they graduate, because they've moved five or ten times and gotten the equivalent of five jobs. Co-op experiences are valued for numerous and in some ways divergent reasons: They offer a student a chance to make a difference in this world, to serve a community, or to work on a social problem. They provide the student with an opportunity to test out career options (and many find that it is just as important to find out what you don't like as it is to find out what you do like). Many earn money during co-op sessions that can be used to offset the cost of their educations. And finally, as a student nears graduation, the co-op can be used to create a smooth launch into the career world.

Antioch College

795 Livermore Street

Yellow Springs, OH 45387

937-767-7331

www.antioch-college.edu

Purdue University has a Rube Goldberg contest. Rube Goldberg was a cartoonist who drew pictures of elaborate machines that performed mundane tasks, like opening a window or making toast. Teams of engineering students from all over the country work all night for weeks in preparation for the event held on-site at Purdue University in West Lafayette, Indiana. Each machine must have at least twenty steps, operate mechanically, and take no further guidance from its maker after the "on" switch is triggered. Some of the machines operate for many minutes before completing a run. If you and your pals are interested in competing, contact the engineering department at Purdue, and start planning now.

NORTHEASTERN UNIVERSITY

Northeastern University is also a proponent of co-op education, but they have evolved a unique approach that they call "practice-oriented" education. By integrating professional education and the liberal arts and sciences with cooperative education, Northeastern hopes to maximize the impact of all three disciplines. Whether you study business or art, Northeastern wants you to experience the real world as part of your education.

Northeastern University

360 Huntington Avenue

Boston, MA 02115

617-373-2000

www.neu.edu

KETTERING UNIVERSITY

Kettering University is another exemplar of the co-op model of education, also with a four-and-a-half-year rotational program. Kettering was an engineering institute, owned by General Motors until 1982. It has evolved into a national university specializing in engineering, chemistry, biochemistry, physics, mathematics, computer science, and business. Kettering University is one of the top producers of mechanical engineering graduates and has the largest applied physics program with a co-op component in the country. Kettering also has the only undergraduate crash safety coursework with a lab component in the nation (think crash dummies!). Its students enjoy a near-100 percent placement rate, that is, nearly 100 percent of Kettering students have a job or are admitted to graduate school *before* they graduate from college. Kettering is the only university in the United States with two first days of school, as it staggers its classes to match the co-op rotations.

Kettering is an engineer's dream school. It's much more applied than Harvey Mudd or Rose-Hulman; it is loaded with labs and equipment, and students have lots of

As an odd piece of trivia, Kettering has tunnels connecting almost every building on campus. A student never has to step outside during the cold winter months. As a variation on this theme, Wartburg College in Waverly, Iowa, put in skyways between many of its buildings, providing the same utility with the added benefit of a good view.

access to the labs starting right from the freshman year. The school is "very aggressively recruiting women and minorities" and has a high minority retention rate as well, so it must be treating them right after it recruits them. Check it out.

Kettering University
1700 West Third Avenue
Flint, MI 48504
810-762-9500
www.kettering.edu

Keuka College
Another school that does a fantastic job of tying classroom experience to the real world is Keuka College in the beautiful Finger Lakes region of upstate New York. Keuka bills itself as "a national leader in experiential and hands-on learning" and has a holistic approach to make an intentional, coherent experience out of all of a student's classroom, activity, internship, and field experiences.

Keuka College
East Bluff Drive
Keuka Park, NY 14478
315-536-4411
www.keuka.edu

While we're on this topic, engineering students at LeTourneau University in Longview, Texas, are charged to walk on water. To pass Introduction to Engineering, they have to design and mount a water-walking device, and successfully traverse the campus pond. Dry.

"Success is to be measured not so much by the position that one has reached in life as by the obstacles which he has overcome while trying to succeed."

—*Booker T. Washington*

Chapter Six

ENTREPRENEURIAL STUDIES

Is a liberal arts education compatible with a strong interest in business? The short answer is yes, but there is more than one good answer to this question. Babson College is a unique liberal arts college dedicated to business in general, and entrepreneurial studies in particular. At Babson, students learn how Shakespeare might spice up a business meeting, among many other things. One thing that is clear from the direction of the economy: Only those who can learn quickly and continuously will survive. With this in mind, we've also covered the approach that many liberal arts colleges take to career development, in a series of "best practices" items collected from schools around the country, and we've included an essay from a student who describes using her liberal arts education to advantage. In a section we refer to as "career planning in two pages," we cover how to major in anything you want, from art to architecture, zoology to zymurgy, and succeed in your career.

BABSON COLLEGE

the world's best small college of and for business • **a leader in entrepreneurial studies** • *hands on* • **innovative competency model for curriculum** • *students run businesses while still students* • **business plan competition** • *a solid liberal arts core as well* • **a leader in every way** • *1,700 students from all over the world* • **60% men, 40% women**

> **Students are challenged in a curriculum that helps them become innovative problem solvers and future leaders in the world of business.**
>
> —*Babson admissions publication*

Babson College is a phenomenally successful small school founded in 1919 by Roger Ward Babson, an inventor, entrepreneur, and policy advisor to six U.S. presidents.

This school does not try to be all things to all people, but it does, with great self-confidence, say that it will prepare you for success in business and success in life. By combining business and liberal arts curriculum with a vigorous program of internships and "real life" learning activities, it promises to instill expertise in the student in seven general skill areas, which it calls "core competencies":

- Rhetoric
- Quantitative analysis
- Entrepreneurial and creative thinking
- Global and multicultural perspectives
- Ethics and social responsibility
- Leadership and teamwork
- Critical and integrative thinking

There are more *Wall Street Journals* delivered to Babson every day than there are students enrolled.

Classes are approximately 50 percent liberal arts and 50 percent business. All students participate in Foundations of Management and Entrepreneurship, including "launching, managing, and liquidating and actual for-profit venture." The profits from the business are plowed into a community service endeavor, which is an integral part of the assignment. In the upper classes, student internships and entrepreneurial endeavors are closely integrated with the on-campus curriculum.

The school sponsors a business plan competition, and the prize is a cash award to be used toward launching the proposed venture. Babson is extremely well connected with business leaders throughout the country, and Babson grads have the benefit of that network for the rest of their lives.

Located in Wellesley, Massachusetts, it draws students from across the United States and Canada, and sixty other countries. Babson reflects the business world of the future: global, multilingual, multicultural, entrepreneurial, and maybe even in-your-face. Eighty-five percent of Babson students live on campus, allowing students the type of close interaction and collaboration that a business incubator or a dot-com would offer. Babson graduates start their careers at places like:

Accenture	Harris Williams & Co.
American Express	IBM
Bear, Stearns & Co. Inc.	JPMorgan Chase & Co.
Boston Red Sox	KPMG
Cambridge Associates	Liz Claiborne
Cancer Treatment Centers of America	New England Consulting Group
Citigroup	Pepsi Bottling Group
Deloitte & Touche	PricewaterhouseCoopers LLP
EMC Corporation	TJX
Ernst & Young	Unilever
Estee Lauder	Plus some dot-coms and pre-IPOs you've
Fidelity Investments	never heard of
General Electric	

Babson ranked #1 in a survey of academics' choices for best undergraduate entrepreneurship programs, ahead of Wharton (Penn), Harvard, Stanford, Anderson (UCLA), USC, and Sloan (MIT).

At Illinois Wesleyan University in Bloomington, students taking an investment management class control IWU's Student-Managed Portfolio, now standing at more than $660,000. By investing real money, students studying business and economics can test out investment theories in a forum where the results matter. Profits are used for scholarships.

Students who are happy at Babson are entrepreneurial self-starters who can work well with others. Students who don't make it fall into two flavors: adenoid-grabbing-testosterone-driven-my-way-or-the-highway me-firsters, and those students who don't want to learn about anything *but* business. This is in many ways a liberal arts college, with a theatre and sports teams and a coffee shop where students discuss movies and art and literature, as well as business.

Most popular T-shirt on campus: Babson Means Business.

DOWNSIDE: If you major in business as an undergraduate, you may find an MBA later to be overkill. You'll already know a lot of what they'll throw at you in a graduate business program, so think that over before deciding to concentrate on business as an undergraduate. Also, in spite of its entrepreneurial bent, Babson is a little too cozy with big, old-line East Coast companies. Finally, if you change your mind about business and decide you want to pursue a career in peace and social justice, or studio art, or whatever, you are probably going to have to transfer.

MORE UPSIDE: In spite of the above, if you love business, and you're interested in a business-focused but still rounded undergraduate education, you can't beat Babson.

CROSS APPS: The most common alternative to Babson would be to major in business at a university with a good business school. However, most business schools focus on graduate students and none that I know of offers any business-only residential cluster, which makes the experience of being a business undergraduate entirely different from Babson. Two colleges sometimes mentioned with Babson are Bentley College in Waltham, Massachusetts, and Bryant College in Smithfield, Rhode Island, for business.

Graduates of Rockhurst University in Kansas City are remarkably accomplished. One in ten of them holds the title of CEO or president. Reed College in Portland, Oregon, also boasts an unusually high percentage of officers and entrepreneurs among its alumni, "nearly 10 percent have been or currently are founders, CEOs, or presidents of private companies," says Reed's public affairs office. These figures are eclipsed, however, by the independent-minded graduates of Hampshire College in Amherst, Massachusetts, an astounding one-quarter of whom have started their own businesses!

Babson College

231 Forest Street

Babson Park, MA 02157

800-488-3696 or 617-235-1200

www.babson.edu

A career trajectory that leads to six figures faster than any other is success in sales. Sales is seldom taught as an academic topic, even in some of the best business programs. Here are schools with programs in sales and salesmanship:

College of St. Catherine, St. Paul, Minnesota

Baylor University, Waco, Texas

Tuskegee University, Tuskegee, Alabama

University of Akron, Akron, Ohio

THE BIG MEETING

by Crystal Finkbeiner, Robert E. Cook Honors College

It was the first week of my internship. I realized the company went out on a limb to give me this position working side by side with one of the sportswear buyers. Somehow I even convinced them to pay me. I quickly became conscious that I was expected to do everything the assistant buyer did. After the first day, I was put in charge of some of the daily activities. If a sales report needed to be generated, I did it. If a purchase order needed to be created and faxed, I did it. Things were going smoothly as I adjusted into my new routine.

My buyer felt that I needed to experience all aspects of what goes on to keep the business up and running. This is why he invited me to sit in during a meeting to decide the collection for spring slacks. In order to maintain a consistent look throughout the stores, there needed to be an agreement between sportswear and formalwear. The meeting consisted of the buyer I was working with, the vice president, planner, and assistant buyer for the sportswear division along with the buyer, vice president, planner, and assistant buyer for the formalwear division. The two most important people in attendance were the general merchandise manager and the CEO of the company. Before any decision could be made, it had to go through these two gentlemen first.

> **❝ Never confuse brains with a bull market. ❞**
>
> —*Wall Street saying*

The University of Dayton also has an entrepreneur program. Students are divided into teams of four or five students, and the university hands them $3,000 to start a business. The fourth largest student-run business in the United States was started this way.

During the first two hours of the meeting, I felt we were going in circles. There were not any decisions made so far on which pants to purchase for the spring. The group went off on so many tangents that I thought for sure no decisions were going to be made during this meeting. By the look on everyone else's faces, I concluded this was their feeling too.

This is when one simple question changed the whole outlook of the meeting. Out of frustration, the CEO turned to me—I had been silent up until this point—and asked if I bought men's pants. I was taken back by this question and muttered a simple no. I knew I could have just sat there until he moved on, but I decided to seize the opportunity. I quickly mentioned that I had worked for one of the stores as a cashier for the past two years and witnessed many men buying pants. That did it, I caught his attention. I went on to explain the demographics of our customers. I explained how the accurate picture of what happens during the day cannot be determined solely on numbers, especially sale dollars. Honestly, I do not know much about men's pants. I do, however, know how to look at the bigger picture of a situation and use everything to form support for my ideas. During Honors Core, I learned that I could not just use something little to support my thoughts, unless it agreed with all the other information supplied. For example, the message of a whole book, with all of its reasoning and conclusions, is a much better source of support than one statistic from the book that may be deceptive.

Honors Core taught me that people will not only listen to me, but they will learn from me. I had nothing to lose when I was talking during that meeting. My internship was going to be over in four weeks and I didn't think I'd get fired for saying something wrong.

The conclusion of the meeting was better than I had hoped. Not only was the spring collection of pants decided upon, but I impressed everyone in attendance. Everyone shook my hand and personally thanked me, yes me, the new intern, for being an instrumental part of what they said was the most productive meeting ever. The realization that I can apply my critical thinking skills I acquired in college to the real world gives me confidence for when I enter the full-time work force.

Recognizing that Silicon Valley had a unique mix of business and engineering talent, and a 24-hour lifestyle, the University of Maryland, College Park, decided to put engineering, computer science, and business students into an intense, dorm-based residential entrepreneurship program: The Hinman Campus Entrepreneurship Opportunities (CEO) Program. One student already created a business with $300,000 revenues. Check it out. Stanford has a similar project, the Stanford Technology Ventures Program.

University of Maryland, College Park, Maryland
Stanford University, Stanford, California

ON CHOOSING A MAJOR AND LAUNCHING A LIFE

Today, it can take more than four years to graduate from college. Families may be dismayed that their offspring take more than four years, but on many campuses that is, in fact, the norm. Lighter loads taken by students who have to work while they are in school contribute to the problem, as does "difficulty in obtaining classes needed to graduate." If you change your major frequently, it will definitely add to your time in school. Take as many survey courses as you can as a freshman and sophomore. This increases your chances of choosing a major you'll actually like enough to keep through your upperclass years.

Remember, you can major in anything you want if you'll master these skills:

INTERPERSONAL SKILLS: If you will learn to work effectively with others on teams, it will help launch your career. If you can persuade others orally and in writing, you'll be ahead of your peers. If you learn in college to manage, supervise, and delegate effectively to others, your future career path will be accelerated.

How do you master interpersonal skills? By taking an interest in extracurricular activities, by learning how to work with others on team projects in class, and by taking seminar classes where you have to present your ideas before others. If you're on a team, try to be selected as the one who presents the team's work to the whole class. Even if you're shy, you need this practice. In fact, the more shy you are, the more you need it.

TECHNOLOGY SKILLS: If you will learn as much as you can about standard business applications, you can major in anything you want. Standard business applications are rather secretarial, really, but here they are:

> **Success is not the key to happiness. Happiness is the key to success. If you love what you are doing, you will be successful.**
>
> —*Dr. Albert Schweitzer*

Muhlenberg College in Allentown, Pennsylvania, offers entrepreneurial studies, and has a unique "Entrepreneur in Residence" to support the program. Finally, Rensselaer in Troy, New York, has its Incubator Program, which turned a student idea into a $60,000,000 company.

Word processing	Contact management
Spreadsheet	Visual presentation
Database	HTML and Web-page design
Project management	

Even if you major in business you may not gain much exposure to these applications, but they are as common as dirt in the real world. An internship is the best place to learn more about these programs, or just install them all on your college computer and teach yourself.

GENERAL BUSINESS CONCEPTS: How can data support decision making? Where does profit come from? How do workers create value? These concepts are relevant whether one wants to create peace and social justice or simply amass a personal fortune. (If you advance in the peace and social justice world, you will eventually face budgets that can be spent well or poorly, advancing or hindering your cause. Think about it.)

The best way to gain expertise in this area really is to take a sequence of two courses: microeconomics, and intro accounting or accounting for managers. You can pick this up on the job, if you want, but theoretical understanding makes it faster.

INDUSTRY-SPECIFIC KNOWLEDGE: This is generally picked up by having internships in a specific industry. This is not a classroom assignment at all. You need to know what jobs exist in any given industry. What are the entry-level jobs? What skills are needed to get those jobs? What jargon is needed to identify yourself as an insider? How does one advance after gaining one of the entry-level positions? What ensures continued success?

It helps if you discover your values, so that you can pick a career direction that aligns with those values. For example, if you have to help others or be creative in order to be happy, any career that lacks an element of helping others or exercising creativity

There have been complaints at Harvey Mudd, MIT, and several other institutions about student ideas being appropriated and patented either by professors, venture sponsors, or by the schools themselves. Think carefully about whether meager funding today warrants giving away all future benefit of your idea. Challenge, especially, those clauses that require you to turn over patents, etc., for a few thousand dollars. Some "honors" are better turned down in advance.

would be a poor choice. Also, try to learn your own abilities and limitations, and how to be honest and forthcoming. But that's about it.

So, if you'll take care of these career-readiness skills, you can major in whatever you want. Major in art or philosophy or business or calligraphy or hieroglyphics, it doesn't matter. It's generally best to major in what you love, because then you'll be an enthusiastic student. Your enthusiasm will carry you over the hurdles you will face. You'll be more creative in overcoming obstacles. You'll study more and harder without viewing it as a grind. You'll be happier. People will be drawn to you. You'll find the weather is consistently better.

There it is. Career planning on three pages, but the advice is sound.

Economics is considered the "business" major at most liberal arts colleges that don't have a school of business, which is, in fact, most of them. Most liberal arts schools are very weak in business, and most business schools are very weak in liberal arts. Babson is a business school that delivers liberal arts. As another take on this whole issue, Wheaton College in Norton, Massachusetts, is a liberal arts college that delivers on career planning and preparation, whatever your major, through a combination of curriculum, service learning, internships, reflection, and intensive one-on-one career counseling from *before* the first day of classes. Check this out; it's considered by many to be one of the best career center models in the nation.

THE FILENE CENTER FOR WORK AND LEARNING

Dr. Dan Golden, Dean for Work and Service Learning, Wheaton College, Norton, Massachusetts

"Study accounting and you'll become an accountant. I studied history and I run the company."

—Wheaton alumna, CEO of a Boulder, Colorado, software company

Well, it wasn't just studying history that paved the way for this liberal arts graduate's professional success, of course. She had plenty of translatable skills from other work and volunteer experiences, a keen sense of where her industry was going and, when coupled with the classic traits of the liberal arts—research, writing, creative problem-solving—her ascendancy to leadership was inevitable.

At Wheaton College, a relentlessly liberal arts school nestled between Providence, Rhode Island, and Boston, Massachusetts, our approach is to invite students to study fields about which they are passionate, not necessarily the ones they think will serve

Over 200,000,000 Chinese children are learning English, while only 24,000 American schoolchildren are learning Chinese.

—Chronicle of Higher Education

only to get them jobs, and simultaneously construct a professional development plan that begins from the day they're admitted to the institution.

Getting Them While They're Young

The Filene Center for Work & Learning is Wheaton's locus for student life planning and experiential learning. We like to say that we turn traditional career planning "upside down," in our obsession with helping younger students identify and pursue exploratory internships, field experiences and service, both domestic and offshore. Early is better, often is best.

Trying life on for size earlier than you think you're ready has tremendous upside benefits—you can identify and target your major areas of academic interest, you can clarify what it will take for you to succeed in a particular field in terms of skillsets and other relevant backgrounds, and, most important, you can avoid selecting a career path based on myths, presumptions, the expectations of others, and the often ludicrous portrayal of work as seen in the popular media.

As a life-planning office, we pursue new students in their First Year Seminars, in their sport and creative campus ventures, in their leadership activities—everywhere we can. And our approach is very "high touch" in that we want to ask every student by their first winter break, "What matters to you?" This starting phase of self-exploration and reflection leads to the next level of our obsession, which is tied to making the most of three collegiate summers.

Summertime for Learning and Earning:
The Indispensability of Interning

Add up three collegiate summers, and you have approximately a year's worth of practical time available to pursue internships—which have increasingly become expected components of any graduate's portfolio for post-grad study, fellowship application, and job searches. Some employers rank the relevant experiences one gets from internships even higher than academic grade point averages. We think you should get good grades, too, of course. But we know that if you graduate from college without relevant experiences, you may be hampered in your searches for a meaningful future and be forced to retrofit yourself with post-baccalaureate internships after you graduate, anyhow!

For the student who can clarify what his or her interests include, and who can research different career fields, finding an internship by April of every college year is a function of persistence, imagination (and, at Wheaton, of the partnership students forge with the Filene Center and our other advisement units, as well as a faculty that believes in the integration of study and field experience).

Since most internship experiences are unpaid and all college costs are on the rise, many students worry about losing time for earning necessary summer cash—and it's a fair worry. But at Wheaton, we are committed to replacing as much of that summer cash as we can. All students who receive Merit Scholarships upon admission are guaranteed one paid summer—and work with the Filene Center to invest that summer funding in a substantive internship experience.

Thanks to donations from loyal alumni (many of whom look back on their own life path and wish they'd been able to afford to intern), trustees, foundations and corporations, the Filene Center is able to award Wheaton and Davis Fellowships to fund summer interning, service, and research to the tune of nearly $300,000 per year. The goal of our Fellowship and the Merit Scholar programs is straightforward—we provide the earning, you do the learning.

If You're Going to Do It, Why Not Document It— Wheaton Style?

Ever since the Filene Center was created, a hallmark of our approach to career planning has been embodied in a quotation from the American poet Archibald MacLeish: "There is only one thing more painful than learning from experience and that is not learning from experience."

We don't want any students to be in pain, of course, but we also don't want them to miss the meaning behind their hands-on learning experiences, which is why we invented the Wheaton Work & Public Service Record from the beginning, our "second transcript" system. This portfolio is housed at the Filene Center, and every time a student reflects on the significance of a summer internship, job, campus leadership, service or other experience, an entry goes onto the "second transcript."

This portfolio becomes a useful self-advising tool as students review entries over the years, discern patterns in their own comments on prior activities, and get to read over their performance review from prior supervisors.

The portfolio also helps Wheaton students enter the chase for post-graduate options with a unique credential—they can copy out items for job, fellowship and graduate school searches, and our office can issue a composite letter of reference.

Does this unique credential attract attention? It must be providing a glimpse into the strengths and potentials of our graduates, as many of our students have used the second transcript as one of their supporting documents for national and international fellowship applications.

In the past five years, three Wheaton students have won Rhodes Scholarships, four have been designated Watson Fellows, thirty-three have won Fulbright Scholar awards of various kinds, nine have been named Truman Scholars, and the list goes on. Almost every one of these award recipients was an active user of the Filene portfolio system. Even when we didn't issue a composite reference letter, we're pretty sure their integrated perspectives on the link between academic masteries and experiential learning must have resonated to their selection committees.

Wheaton College believes in transforming students who, in turn, will change the world. We believe there's never been a better time to choose a liberal arts education—the kind of education that can help you grapple with the ambiguities and ironies and contradictions of life in the twenty-first century. An education that can help you remain ethically centered in the face of scandals that have rocked corporate, government, religious and sports settings.

You can't study "truth and beauty" alone—you need an education that melds top-flight academics with layers of experiential learning. You need to start early, plan wisely, invest your summers, and, perhaps most important, become a truly reflective learner, weighing the meaning of your hands-on and classroom learning so you can achieve a future that includes meaningful work, significant relationships, and a connection to community issues, local and global. That's the education we try to provide to every single student who chooses Wheaton.

OGLETHORPE UNIVERSITY'S CAREER EXPOSURE PROGRAMS:

OUr Atlanta, Urban Ecology, and Urban Leadership Program

Oglethorpe University takes full advantage of its location in Atlanta to get its students off campus and exploring career and service opportunities. OUr Atlanta begins for Oglethorpe students as freshmen during Fresh Focus, the university's comprehensively planned first-year experience. Oglethorpe's Urban Ecology Program and Urban

Leadership Program work in tandem with OUr Atlanta to teach students to engage with, explore, and serve their urban community.

These programs enhance the bond between the university and the city, and provide students with up-close-and-personal experiences in the city's cultural, athletic, business, research, and government settings. During students' four years at Oglethorpe, they will have access to multiple, in-depth excursions to Atlanta's premier institutions, often with intimate, behind-the-scenes tours and commentary from experts with the closest vantage point. As examples, students have toured the High Museum of Art at the Woodruff Arts Center hosted by the museum's director and chief curator; they have attended theatrical performances with backstage access and overview by the theatre directors; received an up-close-and-personal look at the art and science of managing the largest economy on Earth from the president and CEO of Atlanta's Federal Reserve Bank; attended an Atlanta Thrasher's hockey game in a skybox with executives from SunTrust; and toured Atlanta City Hall with the city council president.

Just as important as learning about their city is instilling the importance of giving back to it: A second component to OUr Atlanta is community service. Oglethorpe students are involved in human services and ecology projects throughout the area.

Immersing students in its city's offerings serves career exploration, and it stimulates thoughts of what the student may in turn offer the city. When Oglethorpe students graduate and establish their careers they leave college as engaged, enlivened, and contributing citizens.

Oglethorpe University
4484 Peachtree Road NE
Atlanta, GA 30319
404-364-8307
www.oglethorpe.edu

Would you still study just as hard if you were filthy rich? Many professors show up every day to teach who are exactly that. One professor at MIT is worth $2 billion, and shows up every day. Another at Cal Berkeley is worth $800 million. One-third of Stanford's computer science department are millionaires. A professor at Reed used to have a chauffeured Rolls wait for him outside class, yet he showed up every day. One would hope that you would, too. (*Source: Chronicle of Higher Education*)

Kansas State University Academic and Career Information Center's Peer Counselors

K-State uses undergraduate peer counselors to run every aspect of the career exploration process, as well as the center itself. (Please note that the ACIC is a support program to the career services center, and is housed separately.) Peer counselors are trained in the peer model, starting with process (e.g., how to ask nonthreatening, nonjudgmental questions) and continuing with content (e.g., how to administer computer- and paper-based assessment instruments). The students spend a good deal of their time in outreach and marketing. The development opportunity for the peer counselors themselves is explicitly a benefit of the program, enhancing their leadership and presentation skills and improving self-confidence. Students even get to teach a one-hour for-credit course, "Academic and Career Decisions."

The hiring process for peer counselors is complicated. The director says, "We don't just look for extroverts. We also look for quieter people, who may process information a little bit differently. We like to reflect the student body. We start advertising in January, and send nomination forms to advisors and student services administrators. Then, we use a group orientation session, stressing the paraprofessional aspect, that this is not just another student job. Then we hand out applications. Using a blind screening technique (names removed), we'll screen down to twenty applicants. Those twenty will go through interviews. We give them an "All about Me" form to fill out and bring into the meetings. Everybody goes through three meetings. We use the forms to generate nonintimidating talk in the first interview. Then, in meetings two and three, they face increasingly pointed questions. "Who have you admired and why?" plus some behavioral interviewing. Same questions of each applicant, in the same order. We strive to have qualitative and quantitative info in each weeding session. After meeting with the

In one of the only large, long-term studies of career outcomes for liberal arts graduates, AT&T's Bell System Management found that liberal arts graduates were more likely to be promoted into management than hires with business or technical majors. The study found that 43% of them advanced to senior management, compared to 32% of business graduates and 23% of engineering graduates. The researcher, Robert E. Beck, wrote, "The humanities/social sciences majors showed especially strong interpersonal skills and were similar to business majors in administrative skills and motivation for advancement."

(Source: Liberal Education and Careers Today by Howard Figler [Garrett Park Press])

interviewing committees, there will be about twelve final candidates left. All the final-ists will go through a structured thirty-minute interview with a hiring panel. We start with general questions, behavioral based, situational based, same questions, same order, for example, "Registration is here, you have two papers due, and your personal life is in turmoil. You come to work with a full day ahead of you. How do you deal with it?" Or, "You have a friend who's interested in a demanding career choice, but just failed biology, what do you do? What do you tell her?" Then, that clincher, "Why should we hire you over the other people we're meeting with today?" We extend an offer to those who best complete this round. We train in the spring, and in the fall they come in a day early for eight hours, plus one hour a week for staff meetings and in-service development.

Kansas State University

Seventeenth and Anderson Streets

Manhattan, KS 66506

785-532-6011

www.k-state.edu

COOLEST "JOBS" ON CAMPUS

Guest speakers committee: meet the phat and famous

Student activities committee: hire bands, poets, jugglers

Campus radio or CC TV god: on-air talent, or be a technician, producer, manager

Campus newspaper reporter or columnist: it may as well be you

Admissions tour guide: gain the most important business skill

Student government: rule today, rule tomorrow

NOTE: At the beginning of every school year there is usually an "activities" fair, where all the clubs and organizations seek new recruits. The larger organizations may hold their own open houses. Hot tip: Seek out the president, chief, czar, or direc-tor of any organization you're interested in *before* the open house or fair, so you can learn about the coolest assignments and pitch yourself for them ahead of the crowds.

Beloit College

Beloit College also uses peer counselors, which it sharply distinguishes from student clerical staff. They receive one-week in-service training (forty hours), plus a team-building retreat. Training covers role playing, explicit instruction on confidentiality and ethics, leadership development, all basic office skills, publicity design, and career content. The assistant director says one of the hidden benefits to the peer counselor model is increased student utilization of career center services.

Beloit College

700 College Street

Beloit, WI 53511

608-363-2000

www.beloit.edu

Principia College's Career Summit

Principia College hosts a paradigm Career Summit for some lucky departments. For example, the Biology/Environmental Science Seminar involves professors, students, alumni, and practicing professionals. They meet to discuss career options for people in fields related to this cluster of majors. This serves as a career development seminar and mini-

---

THE FIVE HIGHEST AND FIVE LOWEST PAYING MAJORS

THE FIVE HIGHEST PAYING MAJORS ARE:

Chemical Engineering

Aerospace Engineering

Computer Engineering

Physics

Electrical Engineering

THE FIVE LOWEST PAYING MAJORS ARE:

Special Education

Elementary Education

Home Economics

Music

Drama

(Source: The College Majors Handbook [JIST])

This does not mean, however, that you should start studying chemistry if you have no talent for it. It does mean, however, that if you would be equally happy as a chemical engineer or an elementary school teacher, you might remember that chemists earn, on average, 95 percent more than elementary school teachers. Every year.

reunion for department alumni as well. This collaboration between the faculty and the career services function seems to be the exact model that would ensure success.

Principia College

One Maybeck Place

Elsah, IL 62028

800-277-4648 or 618-374-2131

www.prin.edu

Junior Decision Programs: Santa Clara University and Washington University in St. Louis

Junior Decision Programs are career and graduate school planning days that, in both cases, started out as weeklong programs that were later shortened to one or two days. Regular classes are suspended during the event. Speakers are brought in to cover career planning, resumés, self-directed career launch, graduate school application essays, credit and financial management, and so on. Washington University in St. Louis charges students to participate and takes a no-nonsense approach. Santa Clara does not, and throws in business theater and corporate games-type experiences to keep attention. By the way, the official name of Washington U. is "Washington University in St. Louis," to keep it from being confused with more than a dozen other schools with a similar name.

Santa Clara University

500 El Camino Real

Santa Clara, CA 95053

408-554-4764

www.scu.edu

Studies of millionaires are pretty interesting. It turns out that the most important skill for someone to have, if interested in accumulating wealth, is not the ability to earn a lot but the ability to save a lot. If you're interested in accumulating wealth, read *The Millionaire Next Door* by Thomas Stanley and William Danko (Simon & Schuster) or *The Millionaire Mind* also by Thomas Stanley (Andrews McMeel).

Juniata College in Huntington, Pennsylvania, has a business plan competition and a venture fund sponsored by faculty, as do MIT in Cambridge, Massachusetts, and most of the well-established business schools.

Washington University in St. Louis

One Brookings Drive

St. Louis, MO 63130

314-935-5000

www.wustl.edu

Wellesley College's Management Basics

This is a sort of boot camp for liberal arts majors, an "intense crash course in business." The school brings in alumnae from all over the world to teach the course, all experts in such topics as accounting, finance, marketing, information technology, advertising, human resources, or manufacturing. Juniors and seniors have first crack at seats, limited to fifty per class, offered in the winter session. The fee is "several hundred dollars," but the experience is invaluable.

Wellesley College

106 Central Street

Wellesley, MA 02481

781-283-1000

www.wellesley.edu

For every accredited college and university in the U.S. and Canada go to www.donaldasher.com/colleges

Career counselors will tell you that success in life is fundamentally based on finding work that you enjoy. If you enjoy your work, you will succeed. If you don't, you won't. So make your choice of a major based on what you really enjoy, but do watch out for accumulating those skills mentioned on pages 162 through 164, mostly gained outside the classroom, during your college career. For more on this, see Patrick Comb's *Major in Success* (Ten Speed Press), profiled in the Cool Book Alert! on p. 143.

Chapter Seven

THE ENGINEERING SCHOOLS

While we're in this chapter, we'll consider where millionaires come from and take a look at some of the greatest schools of engineering in the world. Interested in science? Want to study at a school with the best opportunity to prepare you for a Ph.D., or set off your meteoric rise in a career in industry? Then you need to consider more than just who has the most Nobel Prize-winning scholars. You may read about a school's atom smasher or other "Big Science" project, but those are mostly reserved for grad students, even post-docs. As a prospective student you need to find out about access. The thing that engineers want more than anything is unfettered access to labs. In the schools in this section, undergraduate engineers and scientists have plenty of access to labs and equipment, in some cases twenty-four-hour access to their own labs and equipment. Be sure not to miss the fine engineering schools in the next chapter as well, "Flying, Sailing, and Militarizing." Oh, and what the heck is a jackalope? And why is it so hard to photograph?

There are numerous specialty engineering schools in the United States. Here are the ones I know the most about, followed by a list of the rest.

HARVEY MUDD COLLEGE

science and engineering plus liberal arts • **a team-based, real-world curriculum that is also steeped in theory** • *access to four other colleges that you'll be too busy to take advantage of* • **famously tough grading system** • *designed for versatile thinkers*

Harvey Mudd is one of those schools that everyone in higher education knows about and few not in higher education know about. It is an engineering college with a strong liberal arts component. Harvey Mudd puts out engineers who can think, write, and present their ideas before a group. They learn to work well in teams, not always part of the curriculum at other engineering schools. In the past their incoming class routinely had the highest average SATs in the nation, as they needed both analytical talent and verbal talent, thus hitting on all cylinders for the SAT. Every year they admit *several* freshmen with perfect SATs. They don't have any grade inflation at all and, along with Swarthmore and Reed, a B is a good grade and an A really is what it used to be: "Outstanding."

Harvey Mudd is a prep college, and most "Mudders" go on to graduate school, if not right away at least within a few years. HMC is number one in graduating students who go on to complete their engineering and science Ph.D.'s, according to *Chemical and Engineering News*. Harvey Mudd is the kind of place where the faculty and the students built their own supercomputer, from scratch, because they thought they needed one. They have their own cable TV show on technology developments.

Harvey Mudd is part of the Claremont Colleges, a five-college consortium with literally adjoining campuses. Although cross-registration is touted as a benefit of this arrangement, the Harvey Mudd curriculum is so intense and time consuming that a student pretty much needs to come in the door running and never slow down. Here are the consortium members:

Harvey Mudd College (strong in science and engineering)

Scripps (women's college; strong in humanities and arts)

Pomona (strong in liberal arts and humanities)

Claremont McKenna (strong in liberal arts and business and government)

Pitzer (strong in social and political sciences)

If you want to tease Harvey Mudd students, ask them about Harvey Mudd's nightlife. Not the college's. The founder's.

Harvey Mudd students have a sense of humor. They spend their time stealing Caltech's cannon. They also have a famous group unicycle run, so b sure to bring your unicycle.

Harvey Mudd College

301 East 12th Street

Claremont, CA 91711

909-621-8120

www.hmc.edu

> ❝❝ **They are ill discoverers that think there is no land, when they can see nothing but sea. ❞❞**
>
> —*Francis Bacon*

A "Mudder" recently won a grant to go around the world to study roller coaster design. "The goal," she says, "is scaring people to death."

The doctor who knows only disease is at a disadvantage alongside the doctor who knows at least as much about people as he does about pathological organisms. The lawyer who argues in court from a narrow legal base is no match for the lawyer who can connect legal precedents to historical experience and who employs wide-ranging intellectual resources. The business executive whose competence in general management is bolstered by an artistic ability to deal with people is of prime value to his company. For the technologist, the engineering of consent can be just as important as the engineering of moving parts.

—*Norman Cousins (in "How to Make People Smaller Than They Are," Saturday Review)*

CALIFORNIA INSTITUTE OF TECHNOLOGY (CALTECH)

one of the best technical institutes in the world • **more grad students than undergrads** • *no teaching assistants, just real professors* • **do real science, don't just read about it** • *focus on advanced skills at the undergraduate level*

Caltech is nerd central, and proud of it. The lucky undergraduates at Caltech do *not* get taught by graduate assistants; all classes are taught by full professors, who are, good news, among the best in the world. Undergraduates are coddled here. Caltech is currently ranked number one for spending per student by *U.S. News & World Report*. With only nine hundred undergraduates and about one thousand graduate students, Caltech is, like Harvey Mudd, a very small but globally important science and engineering school.

You can check Caltech's Web site for its latest list of inventions and awards and scientific breakthroughs, but what you really need to know about is "Ditch Day." Ditch

Major universities usually claim that they produce the greatest number of Ph.D.'s, but this is a blatantly misleading statistic. If you have forty thousand students, you're going to produce some Ph.D.'s by accident, if nothing else. Smaller colleges are actually much greater producers of Ph.D.'s relative to their size. Among all undergraduate institutions of any size whatsoever, Caltech, Harvey Mudd, and Reed rank as the top three *per capita* producers of Ph.D.'s. Considering only undergraduate colleges, Oberlin ranks number one for total numbers, but after the above schools on a per capita basis. Over the years, Oberlin has been a prodigious producer of future Ph.D.'s. If you're interested in more statistics, review the list on p. 64, read the academic journals in a specific discipline, check out the National Center for Education Statistics at http://nces.ed.gov, and check out *Educational Rankings Annual* (Gale Press). Don't be fooled by press releases from mega-universities.

Day is a day in the spring when all seniors at Caltech ditch classes and leave campus for fun and revelry. Since this is pretty much the only time the students go out for fun and revelry, the faculty tolerate this. The underclassmen, however, do not. If seniors are caught on campus on Ditch Day, they are summarily duct-taped to the nearest tree.

The actual date of Ditch Day is changed every year, and is a secret. To protect their rooms while they are away on Ditch Day, Caltech seniors use "stacks." Stacks are like locks, except that they may be physical locks, or they may be conceptual locks. They come in several flavors:

Brute Force Stack: This is when a senior will, for instance, pour a concrete slab in front of the door to her room. Underclassmen have been known to rent jack-hammers to remove Brute Force Stacks. This is not an exaggeration. (Obviously, seniors not using a Brute Force Stack are safe on the honor of the underclassmen not to use brute force to enter their rooms.)

Treasure Hunt Stack: The senior may, for example, leave a clue on his door. That clue leads to other clues. In a recent year, the final clue was a lap dance from an exotic dancer, after which the underclassman was presented with the key to the senior's room, by the dancer. Other Treasure Hunt Stacks have involved taking airplanes to distant places and looking behind pictures in certain bars in other cities, for example. Remember, all of this has to be done in one day.

Puzzle Stack: A senior may leave very difficult physics problems on her door. The underclassmen must solve the problems before entering. In a recent year, a Nobel laureate was unable to solve a student's problems, and his door remained unopened.

Finesse Stack: A senior may leave a series of Herculean tasks for the underclassmen to perform in order to advance to the magic "open sesame."

So what does an underclassman get for entering a senior's room? Usually booze, food, or candy, sometimes money. If the underclassmen feel that the prize was chintzy

---

The University of Alabama at Huntsville, established in 1950 at the urging of the famed rocket scientist, Wernher von Braun, is the only university in the country that regularly launches its own rockets. The campus draws the best and the brightest. This is one of the centers for missile defense system (Star Wars) research.

The University of Alabama in Huntsville • 301 Sparkman Drive
Huntsville, AL 35899 • 256-890-6120 • www.uah.edu

in proportion to the effort expended, they may trash the senior's room, or they may set their own stacks, which the senior is honor-bound to resolve before returning home. One perennially popular stunt: dismantling the senior's car and reassembling it in her room.

Caltech students begin planning their senior stacks from the moment they receive their acceptance letters, while still in high school.

California Institute of Technology (CalTech)

1200 East California Boulevard

Pasadena, CA 91125

626-395-6811

www.caltech.edu

For every accredited college and university in the U.S. and Canada go to www.donaldasher.com/colleges

ReAlLy CoOl ScIeNcE!

You don't have to go to a world-famous institution like Caltech or MIT to get to do really cool science. As mentioned elsewhere, the science departments at regular liberal arts colleges can be exciting, hands-on places. For example, Reed College is also known as the Reed Institute. Senior science majors get their own labs to do independent research, something that would never happen at major research universities where students almost always contribute to professors' research. Santa Clara University in the Silicon Valley seeks a mix of people in its engineering programs, and has increased enrollment of women by 25 percent. "Like in any other field, a diverse population means more creativity," said Terry Shoup, dean of Santa Clara's school of engineering. "So if we want to produce the best engineers, we've got to have more women." Six of their students recently designed three satellites with off-the-shelf parts and put them into orbit (*San Francisco Chronicle*). Here's the team: Maureen Breiling, aka Mars, project manager, VLF receiver; Dina Hadi, attitude control, antenna deployment; Corina Y. Hu, sensor subsystem, systems engineer; Theresa Kuhlman, materials, thermal and radiation analysis; Duncan Laurie, computer sciences and flight code; Amy Slaughterbeck, power subsystem; Adelia Valdez, communication systems.

FRANKLIN W. OLIN COLLEGE of ENGINEERING

a brand new school, very well funded • **aims to be the best** • *engineering is focus* • **everything is brand new** • *everything is focused on undergrad ed* • **lab access from the first day** • *only 300 students, with 35 faculty* • **55 % men, 45% women** • *encourages study abroad* • **cross register for classes at Babson, Wellesley, and Brandeis** • *oh, and it's free*

Olin College is one of the bright new stars in American higher education. It aims to be the best undergraduate engineering experience in the country. Perhaps even more important, it wants to change the way engineers are educated in this country, to make them better visionaries and global in reach from the day of graduation. The school is brand new; the first graduating class came out the doors in 2006. Which means all the labs and equipment are brand new, and they didn't have to retrofit any technology. You can major in electrical, computer, mechanical, or general engineering, with enough business and liberal arts to prepare students for long-term success. Olin specifically says it is seeking "socially adept" students who can master the curriculum and become global competitors.

Each entering student immediately receives a $130,000 full-tuition scholarship. They want the best and the brightest, and they're willing to make it an easy choice. Olin's admissions materials have this headline: "There's only one thing cooler than getting into Harvard, MIT, and Stanford... Turning them down to help build Olin College of Engineering!" They don't lack for confidence, either.

Classes are so small there is no way to fall through the cracks here. Expectations are high, the energy level is high, and this is definitely a unique college choice. The project-based curriculum puts students in the lab from the first semester to the last.

One more unusual thing about Olin is one-third of students have been studying abroad or pursuing a special opportunity at another institution. This is rare among engineering schools where the progression of classes is usually inflexible. This is part of Olin's initiative to instill a global perspective in their engineers.

Just to be technical, I need to point out that because Olin is so new, it is in the accreditation review process even as this book went to press. Everyone in higher education expects them to sail through, so check their website and ask their admissions representatives for an update.

Franklin W. Olin College of Engineering
1000 Olin Way
Needham, MA 02492
781-292-2300
info@olin.edu
www.olin.edu

Concerned that students have lost the art of presenting an idea well, some schools have begun to teach you know, like, "speaking," across the curriculum. Schools that were mentioned in articles about the new speaking-intensive curriculum include:

- Mary Washington College in Virginia
- Stanford University in California
- Smith College in Massachusetts
- University of Pennsylvania
- Mount Holyoke College in Massachusetts
- DePauw University in Indiana
- Butler University in Indiana
- College of William and Mary in Virginia

- University of Richmond in Virginia
- University of Utah
- Allegheny College in Pennsylvania
- Hamilton College in New York
- North Carolina State University
- Central College in Iowa
- Hamline University in Minnesota

I attended classes at one of the top large universities in the nation. The students were like sheep. They wrote down anything the professor said. They never asked questions, and they never, never, never challenged the professor. In the seminar format of some smaller colleges, you get "speaking" in every single class, even mathematics.

ROSE-HULMAN INSTITUTE OF TECHNOLOGY

outstanding in engineering, mathematics, and science education • **faculty dedicated to teaching, not just their own research** • *studying night and day here is just fine* • **rural campus allowing total focus** • *unfettered undergraduate access to labs and equipment*

Rose-Hulman is an outstanding engineering school. At the time this book went to press, it was ranked number one in the nation by *U.S. News & World Report*. However, you need to know that the president of the college made it an institutional goal to rise in the *U.S. News* rankings. In other words, the school was trying to rank highly, and it succeeded.

Rose-Hulman and Harvey Mudd are mainly different in that Rose-Hulman is in Terre Haute, Indiana, and Harvey Mudd is in suburban L.A. Harvey Mudd students are definitely quirkier. Rose-Hulman appears more conservative and more laid back, but the students actually work very hard here. If you want world-class engineering *plus* football, a healthy Greek system, and home-coming week, Rose Hulman has all that.

Rose-Hulman Institute of Technology

5500 Wabash Avenue

Terre Haute, IN 47803

800-248-7448 or 812-877-1511

www.rose-hulman.edu

After these four institutions of astounding quality, there are many very good engineering schools.

COLORADO SCHOOL OF MINES

The Colorado School of Mines favors a laboratory and hands-on approach to engineering training, and students are quite studious there. One told me, "People study on Saturday night. No one will think you're weird if you like to study here." That says a lot. Colorado School of Mines is *right next* to the Rockies. They literally come up to the edge of campus. They also have one of the only known pictures of the elusive jackalope. Ask to see it if you visit.

Colorado School of Mines

1500 Illinois Street

Golden, CO 80401

800-446-9488 or 303-273-3000

www.mines.edu

COOPER UNION FOR THE ADVANCEMENT OF SCIENCE AND ART

Cooper Union is a school of art, architecture, and engineering, and it is truly outstanding at all three. This is why it defies easy categorization. Oh, and by the way, it's tuition free. As Cooper Union says about itself, it is "the only full-scholarship School of Architecture, Art, and Engineering in the country."

Needless to say, it is extremely competitive to get into Cooper Union. It draws students nationally and internationally, because of its quality and the fact that it is tuition-free.

When rankings came to Sweden recently, educators were understandably upset. Sigbrit Franke, head of the Swedish National Agency for Higher Education, was quoted in the U.S.-based *Chronicle of Higher Education* saying that ranking Swedish colleges and universities was like comparing a hockey team to the Swedish Radio Symphony Orchestra. "What's best for you," she said, "may not be best for another student." *Asiaweek* has for a few years ranked universities throughout Asia, but the school that was consistently ranked number one, the University of Tokyo, decided to refuse to participate. Hasumi Shigehiko, president of the University of Tokyo, said that the decision will stand "so long as I am president." Thus globalism rocks along, with bad ideas just as likely to be exported as good. *U.S. News & World Report* is now ranking hospitals. If they conduct the studies the same way they rank U.S. colleges, the hospitals that admit the healthiest patients and have the largest financial reserves will be found "best."

There are things you need to understand about the school, however. It is really three schools in one. You must know your field in advance. You do not go to Cooper to experiment around with art and architecture and engineering. Like many engineering and architecture programs, you have to begin working on your degree requirements right from the freshman year. You cannot falter or you will be unable to finish in time. The architecture program is heavily theoretical, and is often mentioned as one of the best in the world. Located in Manhattan, you will also have to cover your living expenses, which can be tremendous. Financial aid is available.

Cooper uses a problem-solving orientation in its curriculum. "We try to look at problems as they really exist, rather than at a problem divorced from the environment," says the dean of admissions. "We address real problems in our society as they are manifest today." Assignments in the past have included how to design an ergonomic and energy-efficient taxicab, and what to do with the recycled glass piling up nationwide. This is an intense school. Students take six and seven courses per semester, and students are in a lab or a studio constantly if they are not in class.

The dean warns, "We won't hold your hand here."

Cooper Union for the Advancement of Science and Art

30 Cooper Square

New York, NY 10003

212-353-4120

admissions@cooper.edu

www.cooper.edu

> **In my younger days, when I was pained by the half-educated, loose and inaccurate ways women had, I used to say how much women need exact science. But since I have known some workers in science, I have now said how much science needs women.**
>
> *—Maria Mitchell, first woman member of the American Academy of Arts and Sciences Hall of Fame*

Homo sapiens has been a separate species for approximately 400,000 years, but civilization, every aspect of it, is brand new. We've had villages for only 11,000 years; before that, there was no human organization larger than a band. We've had writing for about 5,000 years, and it took all of that to make it global. Imagine what *homo sapiens* can do in, say, 500,000 years of civilization—500,000 more years of science and discovery.

On the other hand, we may wipe ourselves out long before then. For the last fifty years the biggest global fear was nuclear annihilation. Now the biggest risk comes from bioengineering. Nature took 3 *billion* years to develop this planet's DNA stockpile, and scientists are now combining it in new and unpredictable ways on a daily basis. The history of plagues and the introduction of nonnative species into new ecosystems is full of catastrophic disasters sparked by just this type of activity. Whether you become a scientist or a social theorist, remember this.

MORE ENGINEERING SPECIALTY SCHOOLS

Wentworth Institute of Technology, Boston, Massachusetts

Webb Institute, Glen Cove, New York (see p. 204)

State University of New York College of Technology, Farmingdale, New York

Southern Polytechnic State University, Marietta, Georgia

South Dakota School of Mines and Technology, Rapid City, South Dakota

Oregon Institute of Technology, Klamath Falls, Oregon

New Mexico Institute of Mining and Technology, Socorro, New Mexico

Milwaukee School of Engineering, Milwaukee, Wisconsin

Kettering University, Flint, Michigan (see p. 168)

Capitol College, Laurel, Maryland

SOME OTHER SCHOOLS OF ENGINEERING TO CONSIDER

Smith College, Northampton, Massachusetts

Rochester Institute of Technology, Rochester, New York

Rice University, Houston, Texas

Rensselaer Polytechnic Institute, Troy, New York

The Military Academies (see next chapter)

The Maritime Academies (see next chapter)

Georgia Institute of Technology, Atlanta, Georgia

The Aeronautics Schools (see next chapter)

> The most popular T-shirt at MIT right now is "Everything I ever needed to know I learned from *Star Trek.*"

MOST MILLIONAIRES COME FROM THE MIDDLE OF THE PACK

Who wants to be a millionaire? Conventional wisdom says it's the students who get straight As, blow the roof off the SAT, and go to Ivy League colleges. Or maybe it's the children born into wealthy families with brilliant connections. Neither is typical, says Thomas J. Stanley, who surveyed 1,300 millionaires for his book, *The Millionaire Mind* (Andrews McMeel, 2000). The average millionaire made Bs and Cs in college, Stanley says. Their average SAT score was 1190—not good enough to get into many top-notch schools. In fact, most millionaires were told they were not intellectually gifted, not smart enough to succeed. Attending a top-rated college ranked twenty-third as a cause for wealth accumulation, and doing well in college ranked even worse, at thirtieth.

—Associated Press (San Francisco Chronicle)

WARNING: Choosing an engineering college, or even an engineering major, frequently involves a commitment to your major from the freshman year. These schools are not designed so much for exploring your interests, but mastering an interest that you have already selected. Changing your major can result in an inability to graduate on schedule. Just something to think about.

MURPHY'S LAW

Every engineer needs to know what Murphy's Law actually is: "If there is a wrong way to do something, somebody, sooner or later, will do it that wrong way." So Murphy's Law is about failure analysis, and foreseeing and planning for human misuse of any product.

80/20 RULE

While we're on it, the 80/20 Rule is a fallacy. Having 80 percent of X in no way entails 20 percent of any given Y. Examples: 80 percent of accidents are caused by 40 percent of drivers, or 29 percent of drivers, or 32 percent of drivers, or 10 percent of drivers, or whatever. Start thinking about this. Ninety percent of the crime is committed by 10 percent of criminals? Maybe, but I doubt it. This is the type of sloppy thinking that is not allowed in science, engineering, and if there is a God, journalism. Let us all pray.

THINK SMALL COLLEGES DON'T HAVE MUCH CLOUT? Think it's better to go to a huge college with famous professors (even though you'll never meet them)? Recently Principia College, a unique liberal arts school with *fewer than 600 students total enrollment* decided to find out where their graduates go. Here is where their graduates have been going, either as graduate students or later as faculty: Cambridge University (UK), University of Oxford (UK), Harvard University, Cornell University, Columbia University, The Wharton School of Business at The University of Pennsylvania, Yale University, Dartmouth College, The University of Chicago, Stanford University, Massachusetts Institute of Technology (MIT), Harvard Law School, Stanford Law School, Harvard Business School, Kellogg Graduate School of Management at Northwestern University, California Institute of Technology (Caltech), Duke University, The Juilliard School, The Sloan School of Management at MIT, Washington University in St. Louis, Queen's University (Canada), University of Illinois, Art Center College of Design, University of California at Los Angeles (UCLA), George Washington University, Yale Law School, College of William and Mary, The Fletcher School of Law and Diplomacy at Tufts University, The Brookings Institution, The Center for Strategic and International Studies, The Anderson School of Business at UCLA, Rutgers-The State University of New

Jersey, Ohio State University, Indiana University, University of Wisconsin, University of Colorado, Rice University, Fordham University School of Law, Northwestern University, University of Alaska, Tufts University, Louisiana State University, DePauw University, College of St. Catherine, University of Pittsburgh, University of Dayton, Georgia Institute of Technology (Georgia Tech), The Tyler School of Art (Rome), University of Michigan, Johns Hopkins University, University of Virginia, Woodrow Wilson Department of Government and Foreign Affairs at The University of Virginia, The University of Michigan Law School, Manhattanville College, The American University Graduate School of International Management, University of Bristol (UK), Sophia University (Japan), Kyoto University (Japan), The Savannah College of Art and Design, SUNY-Buffalo, University of Texas, University of Massachusetts, New York University, Victoria University (New Zealand), Emory University, Queensland University (Australia), Monterey Institute of International Studies, The Nitze School of Advanced International Studies at Johns Hopkins University, Boston College, Parsons School of Design, University of Puerto Rico, Willamette University, Stetson University College of Law, University of Minnesota, Washburn University School of Law, Middlebury College, Michigan State University, Syracuse University, University of Vermont, The Ivey School of Business at The University of Western Ontario (Canada), Ripon College, Florida State University, Hamline University, Mount Holyoke College, University of Nebraska, University of Reading (UK), Loyola College, University of Alabama, University of Kentucky, Kansas State University, The George Bush School of Government and Public Service at Texas A&M University, Washington State University, Georgia State University, Gemological Institute of America, The Kennedy School of Government at Harvard University... *and* such education-related institutions as The Challenger Center for Space Science Education, NASA Jet Propulsion Laboratory, Hubbs-Sea World Research Institute, Caribbean Marine Research Center, International Institute for Global Peace, U.S. Agency for International Development, United Nations Institute for Training and Research, National Oceanic and Atmospheric Administration (NOAA), The Smithsonian Institution, The Joffrey Ballet, Royal Society of Arts (UK), The White House Young Astronauts Program, The Supreme Court Law Library, The Nature Conservancy, The National Geographic Society, U.S. Olympic Committee. I think you get the idea. Although Principia College is obviously an impressive institution, all the better small colleges are much bigger than they seem.

Chapter Eight

FLYING, SAILING, AND MILITARIZING

You can be a woman and you can be a man, but you cannot go the United States Military Academy at West Point if you are married.

If you've ever fantasized about being the captain of an oil tanker, or the pilot of a 747, or, for that matter, the space shuttle, then the right school for you might be in this chapter. The military academies are one option, but they're not the only access point to these types of careers anymore. Check out the schools of aeronautics, the Webb Institute of Naval Architecture, and the academies for the merchant marine. Several of these schools are free, and consider this: For the military academies, the job placement rates are always 100 percent. These options are not for everybody, but for the student attracted to one of them, they can be an opportunity for a unique college experience.

THE MILITARY ACADEMIES

If you are patriotic, in good physical condition, self-disciplined, and have kept your drug experimentation to the legal kind, you should consider one of the military academies. And especially if you have a tradition of military service in your family, you should consider one of the military academies. Perhaps you should think of it this way: Do you think you *ever* want to join the military? If the answer is yes, consider going to academy; if the answer is no, skip to the next section.

The academies want you to focus on the fact that theirs is perhaps the best free education in the world. But that is not the most important part of applying to academy. This is: If you are accepted, and if you go, you are joining the military and choosing to have the first part of your career, at least, in the military. Don't forget that, no matter how much the full ride means to you and your family.

DOWNSIDE: These programs are demanding. They're physically tough, mentally challenging, and there's no such thing as taking a year off. They require complete loyalty and all of your attention. If you wash out, it's probably better that you had never gone. They are occasionally racked by scandal (drugs, sex, cheating), which can tarnish

WEBB INSTITUTE OF NAVAL ARCHITECTURE

Also, check out the Webb Institute of Naval Architecture in Glen Cove, New York. It is tuition free, but only accepts a handful of students each year. Note: Webb is not a military academy.

Webb Institute of Naval Architecture • Crescent Beach Road
Glen Cove, NY 11542 • 516-671-2213 • www.webb-institute.edu

every student's reputation even if you're not involved. These degrees are not trans-ferrable between branches. If you decide you don't like the army, the navy is not going to give one whit's care if you are a West Pointer.

MORE UPSIDE: If you go to academy, you will not only enter the affiliated branch of the United States military as an officer, but you will forever be one of the elites in that branch. Whatever your eventual career goals, from politics to engineering to achieving a high rank, this is an illustrious beginning.

These programs have elaborate application procedures, so check out the school's Web site *as early as possible* so you can set everything in motion.

United States Air Force Academy

2304 Cadet Drive

Colorado Springs, CO 80840

719-333-1110

www.usafa.af.mil

United States Coast Guard Academy

31 Mohegan Avenue

New London, CT 06320

860-444-8444

www.cga.edu

United States Military Academy

(usually just called West Point)

Stony Lonesome Road

West Point, NY 10996

914-938-4200

www.usma.edu

United States Naval Academy

121 Blake Road

Annapolis, MD 21402

410-293-1000

www.nadn.navy.mil

> **I seem to have been only like a boy playing on the seashore, and divert-ing myself in now and then finding a smoother pebble or a prettier shell than ordinary, whilst the great ocean of truth lay all undiscovered before me.**
>
> *—Sir Isaac Newton*

When football players wear Super Bowl rings they are partaking of the fine tradition of wearing academic class rings, which started at West Point and spread to every college and high school in the country. It's not entirely clear what this has to do with professional football players, but it's probably a good idea not to argue with any of them.

AVIATION AND AERONAUTICS

Since the First World War the military has kept the commercial aviation industry in pilots. As soon as a war would end, there would be plenty of surplus pilots, and well before that batch was ready to retire, there'd be another. In peacetime the military still turned out loads of freshly trained pilots. Traditionally, 80 percent of commercial pilots were originally trained in the military. But today's smaller military cannot keep up with pilot demand. Even though some airlines are struggling, other airlines are picking up their planes, routes, and passengers. Commercial air traffic has been on a steady increase for decades. So, for the next fifteen years, becoming an entry-level commercial pilot should be a good career choice.

To be licensed in the United States means four years of engineering training and flight school leading to a bachelor's degree and a pilot's license. There are 120 colleges or universities with aviation schools, of varying quality. The best ones combine a strong engineering curriculum with flight training, and the worst ones basically graduate anyone sober who has passed their licensing exams and flight time. If it appeals to you, it can be a good career, involving lifelong learning, cool uniforms, and lots and lots of travel. Most beginners start as copilots for regional airlines. Pay is low to begin with, but can be seriously into six figures for a full captain on international routes. The schools have vastly different infrastructures, so ask pointed questions about flight simulators and other equipment available to students, and be sure to get "available to students" defined precisely. There are too many schools to list, but if this appeals to you, here are a few schools to start your search. Oh, and one final thing: this is one route to becoming an astronaut.

College of Aeronautics
La Guardia Airport
Flushing, NY 11371
718-429-6600
www.aero.edu

Embry-Riddle Aeronautical University
3200 Willow Creek Road
Prescott, AZ 86301
800-888-3728 or 520-708-3728
www.pr.erau.edu

Embry-Riddle Aeronautical University
600 South Clyde Morris Boulevard
Daytona Beach, FL 32114
904-226-6000
www.embryriddle.edu

Western Michigan University
1201 Oliver Street
Kalamazoo, MI 49008
616-387-3530
www.wmich.edu

John D. Odegard School of Aerospace

Sciences at the University of

North Dakota

University Avenue

Grand Forks, ND 58202

800-258-1524 or 701-777-2011

www.und.edu

THE MERCHANT MARINE

If you don't want to join the military, perhaps you'd be interested in the merchant marine. The nation's maritime academies graduate able-bodied seamen and women, engineers, mates, and pilots for U.S. flagships carrying all types of cargo around the globe. The curriculum focuses on engineering and the sciences related to maritime issues (for example, you can study oceanography or meteorology). Just so you know, a typical oil tanker captain's schedule is six months on, six months off, so this is not the same as airline pilots who flit here and there and are back for dinner at least once a week. Also, these jobs can be cyclical, depending at least in part on global trade, but also on U.S. policy related to that trade. In the past, some of the maritime academies had placement rates as high as 100 percent, which is vastly higher than *any* other type of college or university, but that may not be the case by the time you get to the end of your program.

If this appeals to you, following are all the maritime and merchant academies in the United States and Canada. You should know that some of these have really cool programs, like all-sail tall ship training programs, and industrial salvage and repair scuba schools, and so on. Check them out. One thing to realize, however, is that the merchant marine can be pressed into service in case of severe need in wartime, and war zone merchant marines are considered veterans. But if that happens, there'd probably be no New York, so what the heck.

For every accredited college and university in the U.S.
and Canada go to **www.donaldasher.com/colleges**

MARITIME COLLEGES AND ACADEMIES IN THE U.S. AND CANADA

Note: Not all of these are undergraduate degree-granting institutions.

California Maritime Academy
200 Maritime Academy Drive
Vallejo, CA 94590
800-561-1945 or 707-654-1000
www.csum.edu

Canadian Coast Guard College
1190 Westmount Road
Westmount, NS B1R 2J6
Canada
902-564-3660
www.cgc.ns.ca

Great Lakes Maritime Academy
Northwestern Michigan College
1701 East Front Street
Traverse City, MI 49686
800-748-0566 x1200 or 231-922-1200
www.nmc.edu/~maritime

Maine Maritime Academy
Pleasant Street
Castine, ME 04420
800-227-8465 or 207-326-4311
www.mainemaritime.edu

Marine Institute of Memorial University of Newfoundland
155 Ridge Road
St. Johns, NF A1C 5R3
Canada
800-563-5799 or 709-778-0497
www.mi.mun.ca

Massachusetts Maritime Academy
101 Academy Drive
Buzzards Bay
Cape Cod, MA 02532
800-544-3411 or 508-830-5000
ww2.mma.mass.edu

Seattle Maritime Academy
4455 Shilshole Avenue, NW
Seattle, WA 98107
206-782-2647
www.seattlecentral.org/maritime

State University of New York
Maritime College
6 Pennyfield Avenue
Throggs Neck, NY 10465
718-409-7200
www.sunymaritime.edu

Texas A & M Maritime

200 Seawolf Parkway

Galveston, TX 77553

800-850-6376 or 409-740-4854

www.tamug.tamu.edu

U.S. Coast Guard Academy

31 Mohegan Avenue

New London, CT 06320

860-444-8444

www.cga.edu

U.S. Merchant Marine Academy

300 Steamboat Road

Kings Point, NY 11024

800-732-6267 or 516-773-5000

www.usmma.edu

U.S. Naval Academy

121 Blake Road

Annapolis, MD 21402

410-293-1000

www.nadn.navy.mil

Woods Hole Oceanographic Institute

360 Woods Hole Road

Woods Hole, MA 02543

508-457-2000

www.whoi.edu

> **An invasion of armies can be resisted, but not an idea whose time has come.**
>
> —*Victor Hugo*

CoOl BoOks AlErT!

From F to Phi Beta Kappa: Supercharge Your Study Skills by Lance O. Ong (Chromisphere Press)

Are good students made or born? The answer seems clear: They are made. *You can make yourself into a stellar student.* The smarter you are, the greater the likelihood that you were able to coast through school without developing good study habits and without learning how to allocate your efforts strategically. Lance Ong, who literally went from F to Phi Beta Kappa as an undergraduate, has identified time-saving ways to do better in college. Even if you are a genius, you will still have to turn in work and take tests for grades. You may as well earn a high GPA for your efforts and improve your options for graduate school. This is a highly recommended book on study skills.

The Complete Guide to Academic Stardom by James Duban (Trafford Press)

Wanna be a Truman, Fulbright, or Rhodes scholar? You have to start practically from freshman year to prepare to be competitive for these types of honors. Dr. Duban, a college professor and director of the Office for Nationally Competitive Scholarships, takes the position that any excellent student can become competitive with a little planning and preparation. Dr. Duban deconstructs good study skills to teach you how to improve your grades by working smarter, not longer and harder.

MOTIVATIONAL DEFICIENCY? OR JUST PLAIN LAZY?

Do you suffer from motivational deficiency disorder? Well, you're not alone. That's "common laziness," and it was defined by Dr. Ray Moynihan in the *British Medical Journal,* as a joke, and then picked up by the newspapers as fact. So, the next time your parents tell you to clean your room, tell them you suffer from motivational deficiency disorder.

❝ Travel, in the younger sort, is a part of education.❞

—Francis Bacon

CoOl BoOk AlErT!

My Freshman Year: What a Professor Learned by Becoming a Student by Rebekah Nathan (Cornell University Press)

See any older students in your dorm? Maybe one is a spy! Rebekah Nathan, a professor of anthropology, applied to her own university and moved into a freshman dorm. Without telling students that she was a tenured professor on sabbatical, she took real classes and agonized over grades and coursework and the behavior of faculty and other students—just like everyone else. The result is a surprising look at college life from across the generational divide. (By the way, Rebekah Nathan is a nom de plume.)

One of her most interesting findings was that college was harder than professors think. She intentionally took classes in topics distant from her specialty, so she would not be recognized. She found the work outside her area of expertise to be difficult, professors at times arbitrary, and grading to be disassociated from the content of the class. And you're gonna love this: She was busted for drinking alcohol in a public space within 48 hours of her arrival on campus!

One of her findings was sad, however, and that was at the large state university in her study, students almost never talked about course work outside the 49 minutes and 60 seconds of a class. "We would occasionally engage in class debates that seemed ready to spill over into the halls after class. The moment that we walked out of class, though, the subject at hand was abruptly dropped, as if the debate had only been part of a classroom performance. The boundaries of discourse seemed clear. Outside the classroom, students just didn't appear to talk among themselves about the ideas presented in their classes." *Please* use this book to find a better college for yourself than that!

THE WORK COLLEGES

Work colleges differ from co-op colleges in the way they view work itself. Co-op colleges view work as means to an end, as preparation for a career, as a complement to the curriculum, and so on. To perhaps overgeneralize, work colleges view work as a sacrament, as something beyond a means to an end, as something to be pursued, enjoyed, and mastered for its own sake. Work is central to the educational experience at these schools, not a peripheral annoyance or a distraction from studies.

A LIFE OF WORK AND LEARNING

by Dennis Jacobs, project director, Work Colleges Consortium

In the past three years, I have been employed by the nation's seven work colleges. In addition, I have been privileged to conduct research regarding student perspectives on the experience of work. In so doing, I have come to understand the importance of work in the lives of students and the need to enhance and integrate that experience on college campuses. The value of work is largely overlooked in higher education. This is unfortunate as 81 percent of undergraduates work at least part-time during any given year. Undergraduates know, or soon learn, that they must work in order to deal with the financial strain of attending college. The ability to pay influences whether or not they can continue, and affects the quality of their lives while enrolled.

Who we are is shaped largely by our experience of work. Many students have already worked long hours in difficult jobs in order to have the opportunity to go to college. The world of work has made an authentic contribution to what they have learned. Work has shaped their activity and often determined their opportunities.

Work is a vital part of human experience. Educators tend to see work as either contributing to the students' career development or as an unfortunate interference. This devaluing of the students' experience devalues students as well. At the work colleges, educators are reminded that they are in a position to help students understand, evaluate, and integrate this experience. Work is more than career development. People engage in study in order to enhance the quality of their lives. Whether or not work contributes to the advancement of a particular major, it has significance as a context for development of character, understanding, and of critical thinking skills, essential factors in building better communities. The world of work is a relevant part of our students' lives, not only as a contributor to future goals, but also as current experience.

It is within the context of work that graduates test not only their knowledge, but their character. Students understand that there are ethical issues related to the experience of work. Opportunities to examine these issues in an academic setting prepare students for ethical leadership. It is primarily in the contexts of work and family that students integrate academic understanding with out-of-class experience.

Faculty and staff at the nation's work colleges understand the importance of work. They also understand that work can, in fact, interfere with a student's academic endeavors. That is why the work colleges have created programs that balance work experience with quality academic programs. Class schedules and job assignments are designed to reduce conflicts between work and study. All of the work colleges are committed to reducing student debt through work.

The work colleges challenge students to contribute in a real way to college operations and departments. They benefit from being team members rewarded for admirable performance, and from the increased opportunities for representatives of the college to be involved in their development.

Involvement of all resident students in these programs builds an awareness of the needs of the community and an appreciation for the contributions of others. Work is seen as a service to the campus community. Students, thus, gain respect for the dignity of all work as they prepare themselves to lead in this new millennium. Students work in all areas of the colleges, from the mailroom and the kitchen to media service sites, computer centers, and public relations offices. As one work college student put it, "We are this place."

The work colleges create increased opportunity for related discussions and activities through the Work Colleges Consortium. These colleges collaborate to engage in service projects and partnerships, to share ideas about administration of student work programs, to examine academic links, and to promote open exchange regarding the role of work in higher education and in society. The work colleges serve as consultants for other higher education institutions and groups interested in improving student work programs.

Institutional missions and histories shape the work programs differently. Values other than work inform and shape the curriculum, work programs, and campus life. The colleges serve diverse populations and geographic regions. They provide a wide range of academic majors and extracurricular programs. Their educational philosophies are distinctive. Consequently, the work colleges offer a wide variety of experiences. Perhaps one is right for you.

THE WORK COLLEGES

ALICE LLOYD COLLEGE

Pippa Passes, Kentucky

Alice Lloyd offers full-ride tuition packages to students who are expected to go on to become doctors, lawyers, teachers, and other professionals before returning to serve their own hometowns in Appalachia. The college's mission: "At Alice Lloyd, we are preparing leadership for Appalachia." The college was founded by a visionary, Alice Spencer Geddes Lloyd, with quite a personality in her own right.

Alice Lloyd College

100 Purpose Road

Pippa Passes, KY 41844

606-368-2101

www.alicelloyd.edu

BEREA COLLEGE

Berea, Kentucky

Berea College has offered work learning opportunities since its inception in 1855. Currently, they provide full-tuition scholarships for all students who attend, and financial need is a prerequisite for acceptance. The labor grant is part of that scholarship, and all students work on campus. The college serves students from throughout Appalachia, and reserves some 20 percent of its admission slots for outstanding applicants who apply from throughout the world. Academic expectations are high, and Berea grads can be found in industry, education, and government throughout the country.

Berea College

101 Chestnut Street

Berea, KY 40403

800-326-5948 or 606-986-9341

www.berea.edu

> **All work is relevant. All work is valid. Work is not just career development, not just educational, not just an opportunity to provide service, but it is all of these things.**
>
> *—Dennis Jacobs, project director, Work Colleges Consortium*

BLACKBURN COLLEGE

Carlinville, Illinois

Students hold all management positions in the work program at Blackburn. The college offers a minor in leadership, which links work-program processes and opportunities with academic reflection. Its worker-managed teams mimic state-of-the-art management theory vis-à-vis employee empowerment.

Blackburn College
700 College Avenue
Carlinville, IL 62626
217-854-3231
www.blackburn.edu

COLLEGE OF THE OZARKS

Point Lookout, Missouri

College of the Ozarks also offers full-tuition scholarship to all admitted students. Their work program reaches beyond the campus to farms, the fire department, the Red Cross, and a summer camp for needy children. College of the Ozarks, aka "Hard Work U," allows a student to get a first-rate education without accruing a backbreaking load of debt.

College of the Ozarks
Opportunity Avenue
Point Lookout, MO 65726
800-222-0525 or 417-334-6411
www.cofo.edu

GODDARD COLLEGE

Plainfield, Vermont

Based upon a progressivist philosophy, Goddard strives to help students to reflect upon all life experience as a laboratory for learning. The work program provides a unique context for this reflection. As the school's home page says, "Your education at Goddard focuses your attention on the real world needs of community for beauty, justice, goodness and equity."

> **What I hear, I forget; what I see, I remember; what I do, I understand.**
>
> —*Unknown*

Goddard College

123 Pitkin Place

Plainfield, VT 05667

802-454-8311

www.goddard.edu

STERLING COLLEGE

Craftsbury Common, Vermont

Sterling College's campus features a family farm on which all students do "chores." The Dean of Work prefers the title of Dow, which stresses the spiritual and holistic nature of work involvement. Sterling is a very special place.

Sterling College

16 Sterling Drive

Craftsbury Common, VT 05827

800-648-3591 or 802-586-7711

www.sterlingcollege.edu

THE SAGA OF A MOUNTAINTOP SCHOOL

Tiny and innovative, World College West closed down in the summer of 1992 and devolved into a homeless shelter. You wouldn't want this to happen to your alma mater. According to newspaper reports at the time, the homeless particularly enjoyed the gym and weightroom at the former college. The site was later bought by Dr. Y. King Liu, lock, stock, and barrel. He has launched the University of Northern California. This school is not yet accredited, but it "aspires to become a premiere engineering university with substantial programs in the liberal arts and sciences." Curious? Check it out:

University of Northern California • 101 South San Antonio Road

Petaluma, CA 94952 • 707-765-6400 • www.uncm.edu

WARREN WILSON COLLEGE

Asheville, North Carolina

Students contribute 150 hours of volunteer community service as well as work at paying jobs. In addition to the regular curriculum, Warren Wilson periodically offers courses in which students reflect upon the very nature of work.

Warren Wilson College

701 Warren Wilson Road

Asheville, NC 28815

704-298-3325

www.warren-wilson.edu

CoOl WoRd LiSt!

prosopagnosia · anthimeria · brunneous · elucubrate · eudaemonic · logorrhea · succedaneum · smaragdine · argillaceous · paedarchy · hircophobia · cumberground · pogonip · melcryptovestimentaphilia

❝ Fact: Introverts, on average, have higher grades than extroverts. ❞

BERRY COLLEGE

Berry College in Rome, Georgia, also offers all its students on-campus employment, and admits students regardless of need. Approximately 90 percent of Berry students work on campus. Started in 1902 by Martha Berry, Berry College today emphasizes a comprehensive curriculum combined with "high academic standards, Christian values, and practical work experience in a distinctive environment of natural beauty." Berry College claims to have the largest campus in the world, 28,000 acres of fields, forests, lakes, and mountains in northern Georgia, little more than an hour's drive from Atlanta, but a couple of worlds away from urban bustle and strife. The college has its origins in a one-room log cabin school, but today it boasts a central campus patterned after Oxford University's central quadrangle, a gift of car magnate Henry Ford.

Berry College · 2277 Martha Berry Boulevard, NE
Mount Berry, GA 30149 · 706-232-5374 · www.berry.edu

CoOl BoOks ALErT!

Derek Bok is a former and current acting president of Harvard University. He's the beloved and admired one, not the one that left after claiming women were genetically disadvantaged as scientists. In this book, Bok presents a balanced view of the role of colleges and universities and reminds critics that there was no golden era of education, when students worked hard and faculty kept their political views out of view. But if you want to learn what good professors do, as compared to mediocre ones, it's in this book.

Vincent Tinto is the guru of unhappy studentdom. At any given institution, on average, more than one-quarter of the incoming students will not return after the first year. About half the people who enter a college or university will *never get a degree of any kind,* neither associate's nor bachelor's. If any other aspect of our society had such a high failure rate, citizens would revolt! By the way, many students want their parents to believe that everybody is taking five and six years to graduate, but the largest group of students, about 4 in 10, still graduate in four years or faster. Another 25 percent will graduate in five years and 10 percent more in six years. The remaining 25 percent spread out into infinity, or at least the limits of a human lifespan. So like it or not, nationally the norm is still in-and-out in four years. Of course, on many campuses the norm on that campus may definitely be five years or more. That's where we get the newly common term "second-year senior" and its defeatist corollary "first-year senior."

Want out faster? Don't change your major very often, don't work for pay very much, don't develop drug or alcohol or financial problems, go to school all five days of the week, always take more than the minimum class load, get engaged in student activities, and assume at least some leadership roles. Perhaps most important of all, choose a college that will excite and engage you, rather than a place with which you develop no particular bond. Of course, if you find yourself in a school that doesn't inspire you, leaving that college to find a better one is exactly what you should do.

For every accredited college and university in the U.S. and Canada go to **www.donaldasher.com/colleges**

MORE COOL IDEAS

What is a spiritual school? Should you consider a religious or church-affiliated school? This is a very satisfying option for many students, but there are some caveats, as we will cover in this chapter. Also, we'll consider some of the options for nontraditional-age students and single parents, who may not want to go to school where everyone is eighteen and single. Schools of art and music are covered, albeit briefly. This chapter also houses a grabbag of unusual college options, such as schools focusing on textiles, computer games, foreign languages, culinary arts, auctioneering, railroading, stand-up comedy, and surfing, among many others. Finally, what about options for those students who want to consider taking a year off before hitting the college books? Programs ranging from Semester at Sea to Americorps are briefly described, as well as a Web site offering thousands of activities a young person can pursue instead of a freshman year.

THOMAS AQUINAS COLLEGE

The best college class I ever attended, undergraduate or graduate, was at Thomas Aquinas College, a school affiliated with the Catholic faith and with a rigorous great books curriculum. All the students had read and thought about the assignment, a difficult passage in philosophy of religion with which I happened to be familiar. All the students participated equally, the men and the women, and intelligently, which was easy to discern due to the nature of the passage. They backed up their comments with evidence and careful, logical arguments. They were politely influenced by one another's thoughts, with the conversation building in a sequence (instead of that compounded non sequitur that happens when students are simply waiting their turn to say what *they* think). The reading itself was the focus of the class, and any tangents that did come up were gently steered back to the central question by the professor. The professor was a master of the material, and had read the original in Latin, which he occasionally used to discern the most exact meaning of the more esoteric sentences. The students spoke for perhaps 90 percent of the time, the professor only occasionally interjecting guidance. No one knew for sure where the conversation was headed. The hour passed as if it were a moment.

This class had begun with a prayer, for which the professor and all the students but one stood. The one student who did not stand was an atheist, who had chosen this school as an excellent place to get an education, and had said as much to the admission committee, both that he was an atheist and that he thought they offered an outstanding education. They admitted him, he came, and his presence was proof positive that this was an institution of higher learning, a place where critical thinking was the goal, not indoctrination. I shall remember this class, where I was but a guest, for the rest of my life.

A SPIRITUAL COLLEGE? HOW CAN THAT BE?

A spiritual college goes beyond the concerns for a student's intellectual development, or even ethical development, and recognizes that we human beings are spiritual creatures. Spiritual development can, indeed, be a goal of the college experience.

A "spiritual" college will be open to many paths, while a "religious" college is a little different in that it has a commitment to a particular faith. The next page covers religious colleges as an option. First we will consider one of the spiritual colleges.

Naropa College was founded in Boulder, Colorado, in 1974 by Chögyam Trungpa, Rinpoche, a Buddhist teacher. Following a visit to the University of Colorado, he stayed on to teach others, eventually serving as the catalyst for the formation of a new school that ties the Western liberal arts tradition to the Eastern Buddhist heritage. According to Naropa's literature: "Naropa University, accredited by the North Central Association of Colleges and Schools, was inspired by the famous Nalanda University which flourished in India from the fifth to the twelfth centuries. At Nalanda University, scholars, artists, and healers from many Asian countries and religious traditions came to study, meditate, and debate," and that's pretty much what Naropa students do today. Less than 10 percent of students are affirmed Buddhists but respect for the Tibetan Buddhist origins of the college is the norm. "We want to train people to be warriors for compassion, warriors for service," an administrator told me. Certainly, no other college administrator has ever said that to me before.

A student assured me, "The faculty come from all faiths. There's no one way. But you are expected to explore and integrate your intellectual and spiritual side." He said "side," not "sides." At Naropa, you notice things like that.

There are regular majors, regular grades, and so on, but this school could be a very interesting choice. Alcohol and tobacco are not allowed on campus—anywhere. One student told me: "The academic and personal rigors take some students by surprise. Turning inward to face your own ego and family issues, frankly, some students cannot do

---

Schools that claim to promote a religious environment for religious students do not always have that environment. Some students select these schools to please their parents, without personally endorsing the lifestyle they are expected to exemplify. Others choose a college while in a particularly strong period of faith, and later stay on with a religious college after they are no longer as devout. Furthermore, the schools themselves pass through more and less secular and more and less pious periods in their cultural and collective histories.

> **The gods love the obscure and hate the obvious.**
>
> —*Upanishads 4.2.2*

this." I did not find the place to have an overly pious feel, however. The print center was booming to hip-hop music, the coffee shop served meat dishes, and there was *zero* mean/angry/alarmed stuff posted on bulletin boards, something I always check on.

Check it out. It could be right for you.

Naropa University

2130 Arapahoe Avenue

Boulder, Co 80302

303-546-3572

800-772-6951

www.naropa.edu

admissions@naropa.edu

Also, check out this brand new Buddhist-affiliated, open-to-all-faiths school in Southern California, also fully accredited:

Soka University of America

1 University Drive

Aliso Viejo, CA 92656

888-600-7652

949-480-4000

www.soka.edu

info@soka.edu

SHOULD YOU GO TO A RELIGIOUS OR CHURCH-AFFILIATED SCHOOL?

If you are a member of a faith, should you go to a school closely affiliated with that faith? This is certainly an option you should consider. Great reasons to go to a religious school:

- You don't have to explain your religion to nonbelievers.
- You don't have to put up with professors and fellow classmates who insult your beliefs in class (out of class, maybe, but in class probably not).
- You can explore your faith in an environment where such exploration is the norm, rather than something you feel you need to conceal from others.

- Some religiously affiliated schools have outstanding financial aid.

- Your parents will probably endorse your choice.

One warning, however: faith is explored, intellectually, at many religious and religion-affiliated schools. If you cannot articulate, expound upon, support, defend, and otherwise dissect your faith, you may be uncomfortable. It is, after all, a college not a church. Furthermore, you should not think that there is not sexual and substance use exploration at religious schools. This is a naive belief, leading to great disappointment by students who were expecting all the other students at a religious school to be as pious as are they.

I interviewed an atheist who went to a Christian college because it had a great TV studio and students had unlimited access to it. He was admitted and even given an academic scholarship. Nowhere in his application did he discuss his religious beliefs or misrepresent himself, but he did not volunteer this information either. He was delighted with the television studio, and ended up making a student film that won national awards. Nevertheless, he was absolutely miserable for his entire undergraduate career. "I felt like a pariah," he told me. "Once people found out I was an atheist, they ostracized me or tried to convert me. Nobody could leave it alone. I wasn't allowed to just be me. I was always 'that atheist.' Professors and students alike did this. I have only one friend from my entire four years as an undergraduate, and he lives in another state." Caveat emptor.

I have visited some outstanding religious schools, and for those who have strong religious beliefs, they can be the best college choice. Here are a few options:

If you are Catholic, **Thomas Aquinas** in Ojai, California (see p. 220), and **The Thomas More College of Liberal Arts** in Merrimack, New Hampshire, provide outstanding—and rigorous—academic experiences. Neither is exclusively Catholic, but Thomas Aquinas is overwhelmingly so.

Alverno College in Milwaukee, Wisconsin, provides women of all faiths with an

There are no programs concentrating on the needs of single fathers, but if you can get a place in the married and family dorms you can take advantage of on-campus daycare and you'll be the most popular bachelor in town.

innovative curriculum focusing on mastering a specified set of life skills. Alverno prides itself on serving disadvantaged and nontraditional students, including single mothers. (See p. 226 for more on Alverno.)

The twenty-eight **Jesuit universities** are also an option. The affiliation is not overly strong, and most view themselves as liberal institutions of education; nevertheless, and especially if you've attended Catholic parochial schools, it's an option to consider. For a complete list, see www.ajcunet.edu.

If you are Protestant, **Wheaton College** in Wheaton, Illinois, was repeatedly cited in my surveys as a strong liberal arts college with a purposeful Christian atmosphere.

Perhaps less demanding but equally interested in providing a purposeful Christian atmosphere are two schools I visit often: **George Fox University** in Newberg, Oregon, and **Grove City College** in Grove City, Pennsylvania. George Fox was origianlly a Quaker school, but now welcomes all denominations.

There are, of course, many, many others. If you are a Christian Scientist, the best school in the world for you is **Principia** in Elsah, Illinois. It combines a strong liberal arts education with a practicing Christian Science community. The school has a strong endowment, a beautiful campus up on the bluffs overlooking the Mississippi River, and a truly global perspective from the heart of the Midwest. If you are interested in more on Christian religious colleges, both the decision to attend and specific colleges to consider, see Peterson's *Christian Colleges & Universities* (Peterson's, 1999), and talk to your religious leaders about options for your faith.

SPECIAL PROGRAMS FOR NONTRADITIONAL STUDENTS, SINGLE PARENTS, AND WOMEN

Here's a personal tale for you: When I was in high school, my mother was in college. Starting from scratch, she graduated Phi Beta Kappa in three and a half years, was president of the academic honor society for her discipline, and provided an academic role model for her teenage children. My mother loved learning, and every day she'd come home and tell us everything she'd learned that day. At one time there were five full-time students in my household. Were we deprived because our mother went to school while we were growing up? On the contrary, I think we were well served by this experience. My mother didn't bake cookies, but if you brought home a box of rocks with fossils in them, she was always first to recommend that you dump them on the table and find the magnifying glass that came with the big dictionary.

So, no matter whether you are twenty-one or ninety, if you want to go to school there is a way. And, lest you think you are going to be too old by the time you complete that degree, I always quote my favorite wise woman, Dear Abby, who asks, "And how old will you be in four years if you *don't* complete that degree?"

Many colleges and universities have on-site daycare for students and staff. Your status as head of household *is* taken into consideration in financial aid offers. Single mothers often have preferential placement in campus-owned married and family housing. You may be able to get an assignment as a residence hall advisor, where you can be "dorm mom" and save on your expenses.

Here are two programs that focus on the needs of nontraditional women students.

FRANCES PERKINS PROGRAM AT MOUNT HOLYOKE COLLEGE

South Hadley, Massachusetts

This is a program for women twenty-four and older, sometimes *a lot* older, "married, single, divorced, or widowed." Frances Perkins was a Mount Holyoke alumna and secretary of labor under Franklin Delano Roosevelt. She implemented many worker protections that we all take for granted now, such as the minimum wage, child labor restrictions, and unemployment insurance. The Frances Perkins Program at Mount Holyoke College is an opportunity for the scholarly minded woman to complete her degree at the oldest institution of higher learning for women in the United States. The program purports to smooth the transition for women, including those who have not been in a classroom in years. The program is integrated into the larger campus, thereby being able to offer forty-eight different majors.

CoOl BoOks AlErT!

Nontraditional? Over 25? Over 40? Over X? Considering college? Check out Carole S. Fungaroli's *Traditional Degrees for Nontraditional Students* (Farrar, Straus & Giroux). She comes to the conclusion that it's never too late to go to college or pursue advanced education, and that latecomers are benefited in every aspect of their lives (career, personal, social). Finally, check out *Bears Guide to Earning Degrees by Distance Learning* (Ten Speed Press), which identifies all types of degree completion and distance learning programs. If you're three units shy of finishing a bachelor's, even if it's been twenty years, the solution is in *Bears Guide.* One nice thing about *Bears Guide,* it differentiates cleanly between diploma mills and legitimate, accredited options.

> **Life is either a daring adventure, or nothing.**
>
> —*Helen Keller*

Frances Perkins Program at Mount Holyoke College

50 College Street

South Hadley, MA 01075-1435

413-538-2077

www.mtholyoke.edu/acad/programs/fp

ALVERNO COLLEGE

There is no place like Alverno College, a Catholic women's college with a unique curriculum and mission. Alverno is a teaching college, with intense, small classes, and an emphasis on team work and in-class presentations. "There's nowhere to hide at Alverno. It's not cool not to do your work here." The curriculum is designed to establish mastery over self and subject matter. There are over sixty majors and concentrations, but no one graduates who cannot demonstrate mastery of Alverno's "Eight Abilities":

Communication	Social Interaction
Analysis	Global Perspectives
Problem Solving	Effective Citizenship
Valuing in Decision Making	Aesthetic Engagement

Students of traditional age are welcome at Alverno, but many of the students are returnees who work, or are parents, or both. Most live off campus and commute, 85 percent receive financial aid, almost 70 percent are first generation, and almost 40 percent are minority. Alverno does not give letter grades but uses a narrative evaluation process. You don't have to be a top student to get into Alverno, but you will be one by the time you get out.

"History of Rock Music" ranks among the most popular music courses offered at UNC-Chapel Hill. Associate professor John Covach wears his Fender Stratocaster in the classroom and jams along with some of his students on tunes from Elvis Presley, Jimi Hendrix, the Beach Boys, and others. Covach also teaches "The Beatles, Psychedelia, and the British Invasion" and a seminar just for freshmen entitled "Rock and Roll Music: The First Wave, 1955–64."

Alverno College

3400 South 43rd Street

Milwaukee, WI 53234

800-933-3401 or 414-382-6000

www.alverno.edu

These schools also have programs specifically targeting single mothers and/or school returnees who are seeking another chance at a great education:

Bryn Mawr College, Bryn Mawr, Pennsylvania

Agnes Scott College, Decatur, Georgia

Smith College, Northampton, Massachusetts

Randolph-Macon Women's College, Lynchburg, Virginia

Wellesley College, Wellesley, Massachusetts

Many of these programs are designed specifically for the special needs of women with children, and some provide full tuition. Past grades may not be as important as a thoughtful and passionate application.

HERITAGE UNIVERSITY

Minority and nontraditional-age men and women might be very interested in Heritage University in Toppenish, Washington. Heritage is an entire school tailored to the special needs of rural and isolated peoples, such as itinerant farm workers and Native Americans. With a commitment to serving this constituency, Heritage offers a low student-teacher ratio, committed faculty, and a student body that is likely to be making significant sacrifices to pursue an education. The school provides a strong liberal arts environment that stresses academic excellence, cross-cultural learning, and the development of the whole person with professional and career-oriented programs for life and

One of the older democracies in the world is the Cherokee Nation. Early European settlers could not understand their form of government, and referred to the Cherokee leaders as kings and chiefs. There never was, not even once, any person who could be called a Cherokee Princess, even though several are buried in graves so marked by romanticizing Europeans.

work. There is no cynicism or nihilism here, no one angry at the world because they lack meaning in their lives, no rows of Porsches and BMWs in the parking lots.

Heritage University is located on the Yakama Indian Reservation and also offers courses at six regional sites across the state. It has partnerships with the Greater Yakima Chamber of Commerce, Yakima School District, Yakima Valley Memorial Hospital, Yakima Valley Farm Workers Clinic, Yakima Regional Medical and Cardiac Center, Yakama Nation, and Yakima Valley Community College.

Heritage University

3240 Fort Road

Toppenish, WA 98948

509-865-8500

1-888-272-6190

www.heritage.edu

Major universities and commuter campuses often serve the needs of nontraditional students very well. On almost any campus in the nation, the average GPA for older students is higher than that for traditional-age students. The average age of the entire student body at a major state university or commuter campus is often closer to thirty than to twenty, and with the other nontraditional and graduate students, you will see plenty of people in their forties, fifties, and beyond.

New College in Sarasota, Florida, and **Marlboro College** in Marlboro, Vermont, also seem to do well by nontraditional age students; the greater maturity and self-directedness that comes with age are an advantage in these challenging programs.

Also, see the list of Tribal, Indian, and Native American Colleges on p. 242 and the list of Hispanic Colleges, on p. 232.

And finally, you should know about **Florida Atlantic University's Lifelong Learning Society**, "the nation's largest university-based educational program for seniors." Offering a wide range of minicourses every week, this program is available on seven campuses in Florida. Call 561-297-3171 for more information.

Kansas State University in Manhattan, Kansas, has a major in baking science.

MORE COOL IDEAS: SPECIALTY SCHOOLS

Here are a few specialty schools that may be of interest to you:

- **National Labor College,** Washington, DC
- **Philadelphia College of Textiles and Sciences,** Philadelphia, Pennsylvania
- **Institute of Textile Technology,** Charlottesville, Virginia
- **Institute of Paper Science and Technology,** Atlanta, Georgia
- **College of Insurance,** New York, New York
- **John Jay College of Criminal Justice,** New York, New York

MORE COOL IDEAS: COOL CLASSES AND PROGRAMS

Here are a few of the more interesting classes and programs in the U.S. and Rome:

- Identity Theft, Utica College, Utica, New York
- History of the Pig in America, Xavier College, Cincinnati, Ohio
- International Quilt Study Center, University of Nebraska, Lincoln, Nebraska
- Salmon Hatchery, Sheldon Jackson College, Sitka, Alaska
- The Study of Murder, Santa Barbara City College, Santa Barbara, California
- Wigs and Hair, DePaul University, Chicago, Illinois
- Exorcism and Prayer of Liberation, Pontifical Academy Regina Apostolorum, Rome, Italy
- Drunks and Teetotalers: Alcohol in American Society, Carleton College, Northfield, Minnesota
- Technology in the Service of Espionage, Michigan State University, East Lansing, Michigan
- Communication and Shopping Centers, Rowan University, Glassboro, New Jersey
- Forensic Identification, West Virginia University, Morgantown, Virginia
- Peace and Justice Center, St. Norbert College, De Pere, Wisconsin
- Family Violence Center, SUNY Stony Brook, Stony Brook, New York
- Exotic Animal Training Program, Moorpark College, Moorpark, California
- Viticulture and Enology, University of California-Davis, Davis, California
- Continuous Miner Training Simulator, Hazard Community and Technical College, Hazard, Kentucky
- Antique Automobile Restoration, McPherson College, McPherson, Kansas
- Zymurgy: The Art and Chemistry of Brewing, University of Alabama, Tuscaloosa, Alabama

(Sources: Chronicle of Higher Education, U.S. News & World Report, Pittsburgh Post-Gazette, New York Times, and original research)

> **It ain't so much the things we don't know that get us in trouble. It's the things we know that ain't so.**
>
> —*Artemus Ward*

COMPUTER GAME STUDIES

At the time you read this sentence, more than ninety universities have academic concentrations in gaming studies. So if you've spent years perfecting your touch at Blasto! or whatever, you can apply that skill in college while you learn about the cultural impact of computerized games, the computer science behind special effects, and the demographics and psychographics of players. These programs will often have their own game labs on campus, complete with state-of-the-art game stations. According to the *Wall Street Journal*, computer games are a $7.45 billion business, about the same size as the domestic in-theater movie ticket sales, and growing rapidly. When virtual reality becomes a reality, graduates of this program will be poised to rule the world, or at least some version of it.

INTERPRETING AND TRANSLATING

The Monterey Institute of International Studies is primarily a graduate school, but it does have some undergraduates and is seeking to add more. This is one of the only institutions on U.S. soil to train live interpreters and translators, including those working in technical and scientific areas.

Monterey Institute of
International Studies
425 Van Buren
Monterey, CA 93940
408-647-4100
www.miis.edu

> **Satire is a sort of glass, wherein beholders do generally discover everybody's face but their own.**
>
> *—Jonathan Swift*

Virginia Polytechnic Institute and State University, aka Virginia Tech, has a Navy A-6 Flight Simulator as well as its own airport. Embry-Riddle has a Boeing 737–300 Flight Simulator. Purdue claims it has two. Many of the other aeronautical universities have simulators and training planes. (See p. 190. Of course the Air Force Academy has real planes, and lots of them.)

ART

Try these schools:

- **Rhode Island School of Design,** Providence, Rhode Island
- **California Institute of the Arts** (aka Cal Arts), Valencia, California
- **Parson's School of Design,** New York, New York
- **School of the Art Institute of Chicago,** Chicago, Illinois
- **San Francisco Art Institute,** San Francisco, California
- **Cooper Union,** New York, New York
- **Savannah College of Art and Design,** Savannah, Georgia
- **Pratt Institute,** Brooklyn, New York

MUSIC

Try these schools:

- **Juilliard School,** New York, New York
- **Oberlin College,** Oberlin, Ohio
- **Lawrence University,** Appleton, Wisconsin
- **Illinois Wesleyan University,** Bloomington, Illinois
- **Curtis Institute of Music,** Philadelphia, Pennsylvania

Or check out these guides dedicated to arts and music schools: Peterson's *Professional Degree Programs in the Visual and Performing Arts* (Peterson's), or Carole J. Everett's *The Performing Arts Major's College Guide* (IDG Books Worldwide).

COOKING

The culinary arts might be the perfect direction for you to head in.

At the age of fifteen, John Goddard prepared a list of lifetime goals, 127 of them in all. He wanted to explore the Nile, the Amazon, and the Congo; study native cultures in Brazil, Borneo, Kenya, and Australia; climb the Matterhorn and Mt. Ararat; explore the Great Barrier Reef and the Red Sea; and retrace the steps of Marco Polo and Alexander the Great, and write at least one book. He did all these by the time he was in his thirties. Read about it in his book *Kayaks Down the Nile* (Brigham Young University Press). Maybe you should make a list of life goals now too.

While we're on the subject of food: Why are there 10 hot dogs in a pack, and 8 hot dog buns in a pack?

Academy of Culinary Arts

Indiana University of Pennsylvania

125 South Gilpin Street

Punxsutawney, PA 15767

800-438-6424 or 814-938-1159

www.iup.edu/cularts

California Culinary Academy

625 Polk Street

San Francisco, CA 94102

800-229-2433 or 415-771-3500

www.baychef.com

Cambridge School of

Culinary Arts

2020 Massachusetts Avenue

Cambridge, MA 02140-2104

617-354-2020

www.cambridgeculinary.com

Cooking and Hospitality Institute

of Chicago

361 West Chestnut

Chicago, IL 60610

312-944-0882

www.chicnet.org

Culinary Academy of Long Island

141 Post Avenue

Westbury, NY 11590

516-876-8888

www.culinaryacademyli.com

Culinary Arts Institute at the

Mississippi University for Women

302 15th Street

South Columbus, MS 39701

662-241-7472

www.muw.edu/interdisc

Culinary Institute of America

(aka CIA)

433 Albany Post Road

Hyde Park, NY 12538

914-452-9600

www.ciachef.edu

Florida Culinary Institute

2400 Metro Centre Boulevard

West Palm Beach, FL 33407

800-TOP-Chef or 561-688-2001

www.floridaculinary.com

French Culinary Institute

462 Broadway

New York, NY 10013

888-FCI-CHEF or 212-219-8890

www.frenchculinary.com

International Institute of

Culinary Arts

100 Rock Street

Fall River, MA 02720

888-383-2665 or 508-675-9305

www.iica.com

New England Culinary Institute

250 Main Street

Montpelier, VT 05602

802-223-6324

www.neculinary.com

San Francisco Baking Institute

390 Swift Avenue, #13

South San Francisco, CA 94080

650-589-5784

www.sfbi.com

School of Culinary Arts

Baltimore International College

17 Commerce Street

Baltimore, MD 21202-3230

410-752-4710

www.bic.edu/admissions/cularts.html

Western Culinary Institute

1201 S.W. 12th, Suite 100

Portland, OR 97201

800-666-0312 or 503-223-2245

www.westernculinary.com

AUCTIONEERING

Want to go to school for nine days and learn the high art of auctioneering? The Missouri Auction School could be for you. The oldest and largest auction school in the world, it has trained students from Great Britain to Japan, and claims "an international reputation for producing top auctioneers in all fields." The Missouri Auction School trained its first students in 1905, and it's still going strong today. You can learn from the pros about your special areas of interest during in-depth workshops on antiques, autos, real estate, art, machinery and equipment, livestock, business liquidations, and more.

What are diploma mills? They are nonaccredited "colleges" and "universities" that grant degrees for a fee. Sometimes the "student" doesn't have to do any work at all, and sometimes no matter what they turn in it receives the same marks. Recently, a very famous, best-selling author was revealed to have "earned" his doctorate from one of these. He's on TV every day referred to as "Dr. _____." How embarrassing!

On the other hand, an honorary doctorate is a degree awarded to someone who a university admires, respects, or wants to curry the favor of. There's nothing wrong with an honorary doctorate. It's an honor to receive one. However, an honorary doctorate is not and has never been the same thing as an earned doctorate.

The Rev. Theodore M. Hesburgh, C.S.C., president emeritus of the University of Notre Dame, has received 141 honorary degrees, more than anyone else in the world. He has been honored because of his tireless service to others. He deserves the recognition. How admirable!

Missouri Auction School

213 South Fifth Street

St. Joseph, Missouri 64501

800-835-1955 or 816-279-7117

www.auctionschool.com

MODERN RAILROADING

The Modoc Railroad Academy in remote and beautiful Alturas, California, offers training for students who want "to enter the field of modern railroading." Railroad staffs are quite old, on average. While railroads have updated their technologies and are moving record amounts of freight, massive waves of retirement are expected to rock the industry in the next few years. "They anticipate more than 100,000 job openings in the next ten years," according to the Modoc Railroad Academy. The Academy offers an eight-week intensive course leading to entry-level employability. This is a hands-on course, with real railroads, engines, tracks, and, they promise, whistles. It is approved by the Railroad Educational Training Association.

Modoc Railroad Academy

2001 Railroad

Alturas, California 96101

530-233-5515

modocrailroadacademy.com

SCHOOL OF THE BUILDING ARTS

The School of the Building Arts in Charleston, South Carolina, is the nation's first four-year artisan college dedicated to the building arts needed for historic preservation and classical architectural artistry. This is a new school with some growing pains, but it might be a great place if you've always wanted to carve stone or make your own moulding or design an arch or learn the history of mortarless and mortared masonry.

School of the Building Arts

325 Country Club Drive

Charleston, SC 29412

843-762-9423

TOM SAVINI'S SPECIAL MAKE-UP EFFECTS PROGRAM

Want to learn to create monsterish makeup for film and television? Wounds, space aliens, cone heads? How about just how to make tired, old fading Hollywood stars look fabulous, darling, again? Then you might want to look into this special program offered by Douglas Education Center.

Tom Savini's Special Make-UP Effects
Program at the Douglas
Education Center
130 Seventh Street
Monessen, PA 15062
800-413-6013
www.douglas-school.com

COMEDY SCHOOL

Or, for something totally different, why not go to school to learn to be a stand-up comic. The Humber Comedy Center offers a one-year, comprehensive training program in comedy at The American Comedy Institute in New York City or at Humber College in Toronto, Canada. It has an impressive board of advisors: Steve Allen (chairman), Anne Beatts, Irvin Arthur, Mark Breslin, Joe Flaherty, Bruce Jay Friedman, Eugene Levy, Rick Moranis, Jack Rollins, Perry Rosemond, George Shapiro, Dave Thomas.

Humber Comedy Center's
American Comedy Institute
1600 Broadway, Suite 614
New York, NY 10019
212-247-5555
www.comedyinstitute.com

Humber Comedy Center
Humber College
205 Humber College Boulevard
Toronto, ON M9W 5L7
Canada
416-675-3111
creativeandperformingarts.humber.ca/comedy

For every accredited college and university in the U.S. and Canada go to www.donaldasher.com/colleges

> **What is reality, anyway? Nothing but a collective hunch.**
>
> —*Jane Wagner, humorist*

AMERICORPS

Maybe you shouldn't go to college right away at all. Americorps accepts students right out of high school for terms of service from nine months to two years. Call 1-800-AMERICORPS or surf to www.americorps.org. You need to check out the Americorps program you're interested in carefully, however, as they are all different and can change radically from year to year. You'll have to live on almost nothing, cashwise, but you'll gain a lump sum upon completion that can be applied to college tuition. Meanwhile, you can work on the environment or fight poverty or preserve the legacy of this and past generations.

TAKE A YEAR OFF

There's a Web site dedicated to structured time off run by Bob Gilpin out of Milton, Massachusetts. Call 617-698-8977 or 617-696-6297 or surf to www.timeoutassociates.com. You can learn about such opportunities as teaching in Kenya, apprenticing to a glassblower in San Francisco, and serving as a production slave on documentaries in New York. Bob told me he has thousands of such opportunities catalogued, and he works with students and their families to find the right one, sign them up, and oversee the transition. He charges a consultation fee, but for those families that can afford it, he's the known source for this type of thing. For a book on the subject, see Colin Hall and Ron Lieber's *Taking Time Off: Inspiring Stories of Students Who Enjoyed Successful Breaks from College and How You Can Plan Your Own* (Noonday Press). Also check out the Center for Interim Programs at www.interimprograms.com.

SEMESTER AT SEA

Semester at Sea (SAS) accepts students who have completed "at least one full-time semester of college." Although students complete twelve credit hours per semester in SAS, several have told me that this is more like an adventure vacation than a semester at college. It's also pretty expensive at $15,550 single with portal, and a "full financial aid" rate of $4,975. (If you are in need of full financial assistance, where in the heck are you going to come up with $4,975???) Also, going abroad can be dangerous, even under the best-run programs. Although in all fairness, you can get hit by a bus on your way to church.

Semester at Sea

University of Pittsburgh

811 William Pitt Union

Pittsburgh, PA 15260

800-854-0195 or 412-648-7490

shipboard@sas.ise.pitt.edu

www.studyabroad.com

www.semesteratsea.com

As an alternate source, check out:

Sea Education Association

P.O. Box 6

Woods Hole, MA 02540

800-552-3633

www.seaeducation.org

www.sea.edu

EVEN MORE UNUSUAL CLASSES, MAJORS, AND PROGRAMS

- **The Center for Really Neat Research,** Syracuse University, Syracuse, New York
- **The Center for the Study of Popular Television,** Syracuse University
- **Ranch Management,** Texas Christian University, Fort Worth
- **Peace and Conflict Studies,** University of California, Berkeley
- **The Family Violence Education and Research Center,** SUNY Stony Brook
- **Math Ecology,** University of Tennessee, Knoxville
- **Energetic Materials Research and Testing Center** (that means explosives, folks), New Mexico Tech, Socorro, New Mexico
- **The National Superconducting Cyclotron Laboratory**, Michigan State University, East Lansing
- **Equestrian Studies**, Salem-Teikyo University, Salem, West Virginia
- **National Labor College,** Silver Spring, Maryland (an AFL-CIO affiliate where you can learn organizing, labor law, and the history of the labor movement)
- **Surf Camp,** Orange County Marine Institute (not to be confused with the Surf Science Technology Degree Program at Plymouth University, in England, U.K.)
- **The National Center for Bioethics in Research and Healthcare,** Tuskegee University, Tuskegee, Alabama
- **The School of Leadership Studies,** University of Richmond, Richmond, Virginia
- **The Center for Nonproliferation Studies,** Monterey Institute of International Studies, Monterey, California
- *The Simpsons* **Sitcom as Social Satire,** University of California, Berkeley

CoOl BoOk AlErT!

Making the Most of College: Students Speak Their Minds
by Richard Light (Harvard University Press)

After ten years of studying some of the best college students in the nation, and visiting over ninety colleges and universities, Richard Light and his colleagues have discovered what an outstanding college experience looks like. The greatest value in this book is Chapter 3, "Suggestions from Students." Since most of the information here came from Harvard alumni, the advice is most apt for academically serious students. Here are some of their recommendations, affirmed by Dr. Light's wider research:

- Expect college to be different from high school, and plan on adjusting your study skills and work habits to succeed in the new, more challenging environment.
- Get involved outside the classroom; classes are only one part of the college experience!
- Ask a professor to let you assist them her research (the earlier the better!).
- Study in groups; you'll learn more and have more fun. (Students who always study alone have lower GPAs.)
- Seek good advising; if you don't get what you need, try again, and again, and again.
- When you have a problem, *any kind of problem,* seek help resolving it; there is virtually unlimited assistance available if you are willing to go and look for it.
- Develop close relationships with people different from you, that is, people from other races, other countries, or other socioeconomic strata.
- Write a senior thesis or design and conduct an extended independent research project; do this even if no one else at your school does this.

To the above, I would add this one thing: Ask a professor if you can be a teaching assistant for a lab or a class; it looks great on your resume and is good preparation for graduate school. The serious and thoughtful student truly would benefit from looking at this book before college.

CoOl ScHoLaRsHiP!

The Mr. and Mrs. Frederick Beckley Scholarship, more commonly known as the Left-Handed Scholarship, was first awarded at Juniata College in Huntington, Pennsylvania, in 1979. Mrs. Beckley, a former Juniata student, met her husband, Frederick, while playing tennis at the college in 1919, their freshman year. The two were paired because both were left-handed. They married in 1924, and later established the unusual scholarship targeting the 10 percent of the population often slighted in a right-handed society. The Beckley Award is open to any Juniata student who demonstrates financial need as well as academic promise. The only stipulation is that the student must be left-handed.

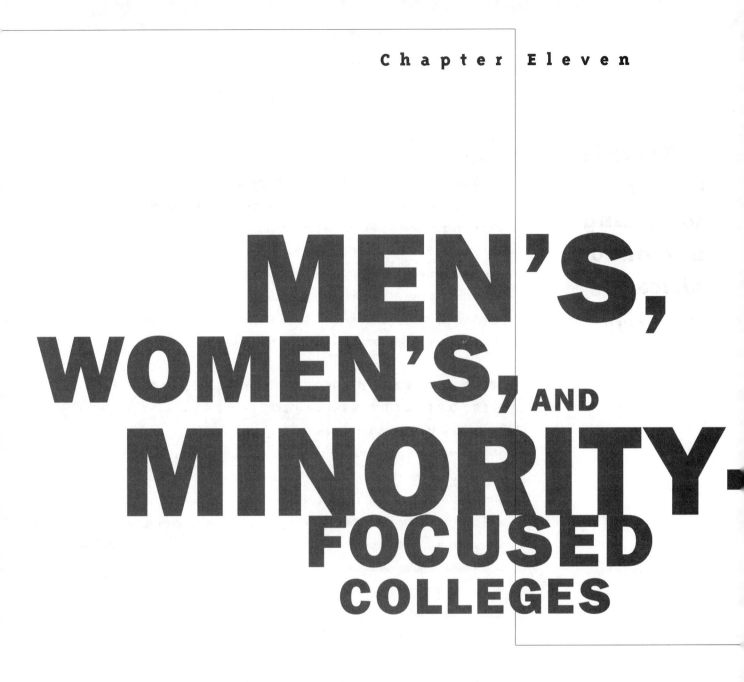

Chapter Eleven

MEN'S, WOMEN'S, AND MINORITY-FOCUSED COLLEGES

There is always something new out of Africa.

—Pliny the Elder

The rationale for attending a men's, women's, or minority-focused institution was presented on p. 49. Also, read the essay in this chapter by Amelia R. Shelby, who explains why she went from an Ivy League school to an historically Black college for graduate school. Her rationale would apply to everyone who has done well but wondered what it would be like to be in the majority for a change. One warning about some of the schools listed in this chapter: Some schools that have traditionally served certain constituencies no longer have very impressive percentages of those populations. In other words, you could go to a school that claims to focus on you, and find you're still a minority. And finally, it can be a great idea to apply to some men's, women's or minority-focused institutions as part of your college choice process, even if you haven't ever thought about this option before. Students at these schools are passionate about them, and that's a clear sign that they have something special to offer.

WHY I *FINALLY* CHOSE TO ATTEND AN HISTORICALLY BLACK COLLEGE

by Amelia R. Shelby, Howard University

Having attended a predominately white secondary school and college, I have come to appreciate my experience at an African-American medical school even more (Howard University, College of Medicine). Although I don't regret the academic choices I have made over the years, I still wonder how my life might have been different if I had gone to an African-American college during those very formative years of my life. Attending African-American universities provides unique opportunities to discover one's own potential without the burden and responsibility tied to the politics of good race relations.

College is a time for discovering one's identity separate from the world you've always known. Like many ambitious young women, I wanted to go to the "best" school that accepted me and found myself at Columbia University in New York City. It was there that I made the realization that "best" is a relative term, and what is best for my high school classmates was not the best for me. I had much in common with my new classmates, but I was constantly reminded of how different I felt in a predominantly white school. In a desperate attempt to reconnect with my own culture I sought out the African-American community on campus. I participated in every campus group that dedicated itself to promoting self-knowledge in the students of color. It was a very important time in my life, but I also found myself investing much of my time to making my school aware that African-American students existed and that we wanted to know about our own history also.

It became perfectly obvious that at Columbia, I could be a talented Black student, but as an African-American at an African-American college, I could rise above labels and excel based on my own talents. Having grown up in a mixed middle-class neighborhood in the Midwest, I was sheltered from the ugly face of racism. I had a large and close-knit extended family and we were known in our community. All of these factors gave me a strong sense of identity and security. However, when I became old enough to go away to school, my world began to change. Like many African-American families in the 1980s, we moved to the suburbs, which was less integrated than the old neighborhood, and I attended a private school. Suddenly I was surrounded by people who drew their opinions about African-Americans from *The Cosby Show* and other equally distorted images available to mainstream Americans through the media. I made friends and became more comfortable with my surroundings, but I still couldn't shake the feeling that I was some kind of an ambassador for—or representative of—the entire black race. If there was a discussion in class about racism, the teacher asked my opinion. If there was a discussion of rap music in the lunchroom, my classmates asked about my musical tastes. I was in the position of educating my teachers, my peers, and my friends, about a culture that I myself knew less and less about. Just as a patient is best treated by the physician who knows him best, so is an African-American student best taught by individuals with whom the student shares a common history.

> **There were two things I had a right to: liberty and death. If I could not have one, I would have the other, for no man should take me alive.**
>
> *—Harriet Tubman*

CoOl BoOk AlErT!

Been There, Should've Done That by Suzette Tyler (Front Porch Press)

This collection of advice from upper-class students for incoming "frosh" is outstanding. It's one of those little books that are deceptively simple and profound at the same time. Although it's not aimed at top students, no student could fail to gain real advantage from reading this book after high school and before the first night in the frosh dorm. Tips on studying, ditching bad profs, negotiating with potentially insane roommates, to withdraw or not to withdraw, how and where to meet the sexually attractive, and preparing for life after college. By following the tips in this book, you won't get to senior year with that weird feeling, "Did I miss something?" Highly recommended.

An "H" by the name refers to the college as being an historically and presently predominantly Black one, and it will probably remain so. A "P" by the name indicates that the college may or may not have been historically Black, although it is predominantly Black at present, but the college also has at some point opened attendance to students of all races and may or may not be actively recruiting those students. Be aware that some of these institutions are as much as 70 percent white, in spite of these designations. Also, several of these institutions consistently rank near the top for total student debt at date of graduation, so ask pointed and comparative questions about financial aid before deciding which historically Black college may be right for you.

> **Never doubt that a small group of thoughtful, committed citizens can change the world. Indeed, it is the only thing that ever has.**
>
> —*Margaret Mead*

Alabama A & M University - H
4107 Meridian Street
Normal, AL 35762
205-851-5000
www.aamu.edu

Alabama State University - P
915 South Jackson Street
Montgomery, AL 36104
334-229-4291
www.alasu.edu

Alcorn State University - H
1000 ASU Drive
Alcorn State, MS 39096-7500
800-222-6790 or 601-877-6100
www.alcorn.edu

Barber-Scotia College - P
145 Cabarnus Avenue, West
Concord, NC 28025
704-789-2902
www.barber-scotia.edu

Benedict College - P
1600 Harden Street
Columbia, SC 29204
803-256-4220
bchome.benedict.edu

Bennett College - H
(all women, United Methodist)
900 East Washington Street
Greensboro, NC 27401
800-413-5323 or 336-273-4431
www.bennett.edu

Bethune-Cookman College - H

640 Drive Mary McLeod

Bethune Boulevard

Daytona Beach, FL 32114-3099

800-448-0228 or 904-255-1401

www.bethune.cookman.edu

Bowie State University - P

14000 Jericho Park Road

Bowie, MD 20715-9465

301-464-3000

www.bowiestate.edu

Cheyney University

of Pennsylvania - H

Cheyney & Creek Roads

Cheyney, PA 19319-0200

800-223-3608 or 610-399-2000

www.cheyney.edu

Claflin College - P

700 College Avenue, NE

Orangeburg, SC 29115

800-922-1276 or 803-535-5097

www.scicu.org/claflin/cchome.htm

Coppin State College - P

2500 West North Avenue

Baltimore, MD 21216

410-383-5400

www.coppin.edu

Delaware State University - H

1200 North DuPont Highway

Dover, DE 19901-2277

302-739-4904

www.dsc.edu

Dillard University - H

2601 Gentilly Boulevard

New Orleans, LA 70122

800-216-6637 or 504-283-8822

www.dillard.edu

Edward Waters College - H

(African Methodist Episcopal)

1658 Kings Road

Jacksonville, FL 32209

904-366-2715

www.ewc.edu

Twenty years from now you will be more disappointed by the things you didn't do than by the ones you did.

—*Mark Twain*

For a scholarly review of the experiences of four thousand Black students at both historically Black colleges and at predominantly white colleges, see if you can find a copy of Walter R. Allen's *College in Black and White: African American Students in Predominately White and Historically Black Public Universities* (SUNY Press).

> **It must be borne in mind that the tragedy in life doesn't lie in not reaching your goal. The tragedy lies in having no goal to reach. It isn't a calamity to die with dreams unfulfilled, but it is a calamity not to dream. It is not a disaster to be unable to capture your ideal, but it is a disaster to have no ideal to capture. It is not a disgrace not to reach the stars, but it is a disgrace to have no stars to reach for. Not failure, but low aim is sin.**

—Dr. Benjamin E. Mays, president emeritus, Morehouse College

Fayetteville State University - P
1200 Murchison Road
Fayetteville, NC 28301-4298
910-486-1474
www.uncfsu.edu

Fisk University - H
1000 17th Avenue, North
Nashville, TN 37208
800-443-FISK or 615-329-8500
www.fisk.edu

Florida Memorial College - P
15800 N.W. 42nd Avenue
Miami, FL 33054
305-626-3750
www.fmc.edu

Grambling State University - P
P.O. Drawer 28
Grambling, LA 71245
318-274-2233
www.gram.edu

Hampton University - H
Hampton, VA 23668
800-737-7778 or 757-727-5328
www.hamptonu.edu

Howard University - H
2400 Sixth Street, NW
Washington, DC 20059
202-806-6100
www.howard.edu

Huston-Tillotson College - P
900 Chicon Street
Austin, TX 78702
512-505-3028
www.htc.edu

Jackson State University - P
1400 J.R. Lynch Street
Jackson, MS 39217
800-848-6817 or 601-968-2121
www.jsums.edu

Kentucky State University - P
400 East Main Street
Frankfort, KY 40601
800-325-1716 or 502-227-6000
www.kysu.edu

Langston University - H
Langston, OK 73050
405-466-2231
www.lunet.edu

LeMoyne-Owen College - H
807 Walker Avenue
Memphis, TN 38126
901-774-9090
www.lemoyne-owen.edu

Lincoln University - H
820 Chestnut Street
Jefferson City, MO
800-521-5052 or 573-681-5000
www.lincolnu.edu

Lincoln University - H

1570 Baltimore Pike

Lincoln University, PA 19352

610-932-8300

www.lincoln.edu

Livingstone College - P

701 West Monroe Street

Salisbury, NC 28144

800-835-3435 or 704-638-5500

www.livingstone.edu

Mary Holmes College - H

P.O. Drawer 1257

Highway 50 West

West Point, MS 39773-1257

www.maryholmes.edu

Meharry Medical College - H

1005 Drive D. B. Todd, Jr., Boulevard

Nashville, TN 37208-3599

615-327-6223

www.mmc.edu

Morehouse College - H

(all men)

830 Westview Drive, SW

Atlanta, GA 30314

800-851-1254 or 404-681-2800

www.morehouse.edu

Morris Brown College - P

643 Martin Luther King, Jr. Drive, NW

Atlanta, GA 30314

404-220-0152

www.morrisbrown.edu

Morris College - P

North Main Street

Sumter, SC 29150

888-778-1345 or 803-775-9371

www.icusc.org/morrise/mchome.htm

Norfolk State University - P

700 Park Avenue

Norfolk, VA 23504

757-823-8600

www.nsu.edu

North Carolina Central University - H

1801 Fayetteville Street

Durham, NC 27707

919-560-6100

www.nccu.edu

Oakwood College - H

(7th Day Adventist)

7000 Adventist Boulevard

Huntsville, AL 35896

800-824-5312

www.oakwood.edu

> **When house and land are gone and spent, Then learning is most excellent.**
>
> *—Samuel Foote*

Paine College - P
1235 15th Street
Augusta, GA 30901-3182
706-821-8320
www.paine.edu

Paul Quinn College - H
3837 Simpson Stuart Road
Dallas, TX 75241
800-237-2648 or 214-376-1000
www.pqc.edu

Saint Augustine's College - P
1315 Oakwood Avenue
Raleigh, NC 27610-2298
919-516-4012
www.st-aug.edu

Shaw University - H
118 East South Street
Raleigh, NC 27601
919-546-8275
www.shawu.edu

Spelman College - H
350 Spelman Lane, SW
Atlanta, GA 30314
800-982-2411 or 404-681-3643
www.spelman.edu

Stillman College - P
3600 Stillman Boulevard
Tuscaloosa, AL 35401
205-366-8817
www.stillman.edu

Talladega College - H
627 West Battle Street
Talladega, AL 35160
800-633-2440 or 256-362-0206
www.talladega.edu

Tougaloo College - H
500 West County Line Road
Tougaloo, MS 39174
800-424-2566
www.tougaloo.edu

Tuskegee University - H
Tuskegee, AL 36088
800-622-6531 or 334-727-8011
www.tusk.edu

Voorhees College - P
1411 Voorhees Road
Denmark, SC 29042
800-446-3351 or 803-793-3351
www.voorhees.edu

Wilberforce University - H
1055 North Bickett Road
Wilberforce, OH 45384
937-376-2911
www.wilberforce.edu

> **Everything can be taken from a person but one thing: the last of human freedoms—to choose one's own attitude in any set of circumstances, to choose one's way.**
>
> *—Viktor Frankl, Auschwitz survivor and psychiatrist*

Wiley College - H

711 Wiley Avenue

Marshall, TX 75670

903-927-3235

www.wiley.edu

Xavier University - H (Catholic)

7325 Palmetto Street

New Orleans, LA 70125

504-483-7388

www.xula.edu

THE UNITED NEGRO COLLEGE FUND (UNCF) MEMBER INSTITUTIONS

Barber-Scotia College

145 Cabarrus Avenue, West

Concord, NC 28025

704-789-2902

www.barber-scotia.edu

Benedict College

Harden and Blanding Streets

Columbia, SC 29204

803-253-5143

bchome.benedict.edu

Bennett College

900 E. Washington Street

Greensboro, NC 27401

800-413-5323 or 336-273-4431

www.bennett.edu

Bethune-Cookman College

640 Dr. Mary McLeod

Bethun Boulevard

Daytona Beach, FL 32114-3099

800-448-0228 or 904-255-1401

www.bethune.cookman.edu

Claflin College

700 College Avenue, NE

Orangeberg, SC 29115

800-922-1276

www.scicu.org/claflin/cchome.htm

Clark Atlanta University

240 James P. Brawley Drive, SW

Atlanta, GA 30314

404-880-6605

www.cau.edu

Dillard University

2601 Gentilly Boulevard

New Orleans, LA 70122

800-216-6637

www.dillard.edu

Edward Waters College

1658 Kings Road

Jacksonville, FL 32209

904-366-2715

www.ewc.edu

> **"You enter to learn, but you go forth to serve."**
>
> *—Jim Mayo, regional director, United Negro College Fund*

Fisk University

1000 17th Avenue, North

Nashville, TN 37208

800-443-FISK or 615-329-8500

www.fisk.edu

Florida Memorial College

15800 N.W. 42nd Avenue

Miami, FL 33054

305-626-3750

www.fmc.edu

Huston-Tillotson College

900 Chicon Street

Austin, TX 78702

512-505-3028

www.htc.edu

Interdenominational Theological Center

700 Martin Luther King, Jr. Drive, SW

Atlanta, GA 30314

404-527-7790

Jarvis Christian College

U.S. Highway 80

Hawkins, TX 75765

903-769-5741

www.jarvis.edu

Johnson C. Smith University

100 Beatties Ford Road

Charlotte, NC 28216

800-782-7303 or 704-378-1000

www.jcsu.edu

Lane College

545 Lane Avenue

Jackson, TN 38301

800-390-7533 or 901-426-7500

www.lane-college.edu

LeMoyne-Owen College

807 Walker Avenue

Memphis, TN 38126

800-737-7778

www.lemoyne-owen.edu

For every accredited college and university in the U.S. and Canada go to www.donaldasher.com/colleges

Confronted by a player with four Fs and one D, Shelby Metcalf, basketball coach at Texas A&M, is purported to have said, "Son, looks to be like you're spending too much time on one subject."

Richard Lederer, humorist

Livingstone College

701 West Monroe Street

Salisbury, NC 28144

800-835-3435

www.livingstone.edu

Miles College

5500 Myron Massey Boulevard

Birmingham, AL 35064

800-445-0708 or 205-929-1000

www.miles.edu

Morehouse College

830 Westview Drive, SW

Atlanta, GA 30314

800-851-1254 or 404-681-2800

www.morehouse.edu

Morris College

North Main Street

Sumter, SC 29150

888-778-1345 or 803-775-9371

www.icusc.org/morris/mchome.htm

Morris Brown College

643 Martin Luther King, Jr. Drive, NW

Atlanta, GA 30314

404-220-0152

www.morrisbrown.edu

Oakwood College

7000 Adventist Boulevard

Huntsville, AL 35896

800-358-3978 or 256-726-7000

www.oakwood.edu

Paine College

1235 15th Street

Augusta, GA 30901-3182

706-821-8320

www.paine.edu

Paul Quinn College

3837 Simpson Stuart Road

Dallas, TX 75241

800-237-2648 or 214-376-1000

www.pqc.edu

Philander Smith College

812 W. 13th Street

Little Rock, AR 72202

501-370-5221

www.philander.edu

Rust College

150 Rust Avenue

Holly Springs, MS 38635

601-252-8000

www.centurytel.net/rust

> **The future was and remains the quintessential American art form. Other nations sit back and let their futures happen; we construct ours.**
>
> —*David Gelernter, Yale University*

Saint Augustine's College
1315 Oakwood Avenue
Raleigh, NC 27610-2298
919-516-4012
www.st-aug.edu

Spelman College
350 Spelman Lane, SW
Atlanta, GA 30314
800-982-2411 or 404-681-3643
www.spelman.edu

Saint Paul's College
406 Windsor Avenue
Lawrenceville, VA 23868
800-678-7071 or 804-848-4268
www.utoledo.edu/~wfraker/stpaul.html

Stillman College
3600 Stillman Boulevard
Tuscaloosa, AL 35401
205-366-8817
www.stillman.edu

Shaw University
118 E. South Street
Raleigh, NC 27601
919-546-8275
www.shawu.edu

Talladega College
627 W. Battle Street
Talladega, AL 35160
800-633-2440
www.talladega.edu

NOBEL-ITY

Faculty from Harvard University give out the Ig Nobel, an award for "Research which Cannot or Should Not Be Reproduced." Recent categories and winners: **Chemistry**, to a Japanese researcher who invented an infidelity-detection spray for wives to spray on their husbands' underwear; **Medicine**, to a Norwegian doctor who did an in-depth study of urine sample containers; **Peace**, to the South African entrepreneurs who invented a flamethrowing anti-carjacking device that burns would-be carjackers alive. In years past, the award was given out by Nobel prizewinners, of which Harvard has plenty.

While we're on this topic, the Nobel Prize is named after Alfred Bernhard Nobel, the inventor of dynamite and other explosives used in war. The Rhodes Scholarship is named after Cecil Rhodes, a ruthless colonialist who consolidated 95 percent of the world's diamond production by working Black South African laborers under slave conditions. One of his dreams was to recover the American colonies for Great Britain. And Duke University, Durham, North Carolina, is named after James B. Duke, the American tobacconist who controlled over 90 percent of the world tobacco market at one time. If you ever strike it rich under questionable circumstances, launch a scholarship or fund a university and in no time people will speak your name with reverence. It is clear that Bill Gates has every intention of doing this. In a hundred years, being a Gates Scholar will be the height of accomplishment, the greatest of scholastic honors.

Tougaloo College
500 West County Line Road
Tougaloo, MS 39174
888-424-2566
www.tougaloo.edu

Wilberforce University
1055 North Bickett Road
Wilberforce, OH 45384
937-376-2911
www.wilberforce.edu

❝I cannot live without books.❞

—Thomas Jefferson

Tuskegee University
Tuskegee, AL 36088
800-622-6531 or 334-727-8011
www.tusk.edu

Wiley College
711 Wiley Avenue
Marshall, TX 75670
903-927-3235
www.wiley.edu

Virginia Union University
1500 N. Lombardy Street
Richmond, VA 23220
804-257-5855
www.vuu.edu

Xavier University
7325 Palmetto Street
New Orleans, LA 70125
504-483-7388
www.xula.edu

Voorhees College
1411 Voorhees Road
Denmark, SC 29042
800-446-3351 or 803-793-3351
www.voorhees.edu

Bill Gates was a college dropout (Harvard). Michael Dell was a college dropout (University of Texas, Austin). Steve Jobs was a college dropout (Reed). On the other hand, Bill Clinton was a top student, and became a Rhodes Scholar. George Washington, Andrew Jackson, Martin Van Buren, Zachary Taylor, Millard Fillmore, Abraham Lincoln, Andrew Johnson, Grover Cleveland, and Harry Truman never went to college at all. Thomas Jefferson started a college, the University of Virginia, which he called an "Academical Village."

This is a very diverse collection of schools, including some that are overwhelmingly Hispanic, and others that merely have Hispanic/Latino Studies programs.

Contents of this list were gathered from the Web site of the White House Initiative on Educational Excellence for Hispanic Americans at the U.S. Department of Education (www.ed.gov/offices/OIIA/Hispanic) and from MOLIS-Minority On-Line Information Service (www.sciencewise.com/molis).

Adams State College
208 Edgemont Boulevard
Alamosa, CO 81101
800-824-6494 or 719-589-7011
www.adams.edu

American University of Puerto Rico
Road #2, KM14
Bayamon, PR 00960
787-798-2022
www.aupr.edu

Atlantic College
Box 1774
Guaynabo, PR 00970
787-720-1022

Barry University
11300 N.E. Second Avenue
Miami Shores, FL 33161
305-899-3000
www2.barry.edu

In Puerto Rico, faculty members, intellectuals, poets, and artistes from all over the island gather annually at the grave of painter and poet Roberto Alberty Torres, known the world over as Boquio. The event is called Baquinoquio. They toast Boquio and then pour drinks on his grave. They tell Boquio stories, many of which leave the crowd nodding and saying, "Si, es Boquio." They recite epic poems in his honor, and they sing songs of praise. On the walk to the cemetery rows of cars will be parked with the trunks open, and in each trunk is a tub of ice, and in each tub is every kind of alcoholic drink, all for anyone who might pass by and all in honor of Boquio. Boquio was an original. He used to stop cars in the street, and yell at the drivers. "What are you doing? Get out! Walk!" Boquio was a college professor for fifteen minutes before the administration realized what a mistake they had made. The dean of the faculty of the Universidad de Puerto Rico was walking across campus one day, and saw Boquio staring up into a tree and talking to himself. Deciding to investigate, he came up to Boquio and looked up into the tree, too. He found the tree full of students. "What are you doing?" he demanded. "Well," said Boquio, "you cannot expect them to understand a tree from down *here.*"

Bayamon Central University
Avenida Zaya Verde Urb. La Milagrosa
Bo. Hato Tejas
Bayamon, PR 00960
787-786-3030
www.ucb.edu.pr

Boricua College
3755 Broadway
New York, NY 10032
212-694-1000

California State University -
Bakersfield
9001 Stockdale Highway
Bakersfield, CA 93311
805-664-2011
www.csubak.edu

California State University -
Dominguez Hills
1000 East Victoria Street
Carson, CA 90747
310-243-3300
www.csudh.edu

California State University -
Fresno
5241 North Maple Avenue
Fresno, CA 93740
209-278-4240
www.csufresno.edu

California State University -
Los Angeles
5151 State University Drive
Los Angeles, CA 90032
323-343-3000
www.calstatela.edu

California State University -
Northridge
18111 Nordhoff Street
Northridge, CA 91330
818-677-1200
www.csun.edu

California State University -
San Bernardino
5500 University Parkway
San Bernardino, CA 92407
909-880-5000
www.csusb.edu

Caribbean Center for Advanced
Studies - Miami Institute of Psychology
8180 N.W. 36th Street, Second Floor
Miami, FL 33166
305-593-1223
www.mip.ccas.edu

Caribbean Center for Advanced
Studies - San Juan Campus
Tanca Street, #151
San Juan, PR 00902-3711
787-725-6500
www.prip.ccas.edu

An invasion of armies can be resisted, but not an idea whose time has come.

—Victor Hugo

> **It's what we think we know already that often prevents us from learning.**
>
> —*Claude Bernard, physiologist*

Caribbean University - Bayamon Campus
P.O. Box 493
Bayamon, PR 00960-0493
787-780-0070
www.caribbean.edu

City College, City University of New York
160 Convent Avenue
New York, NY 10031
212-650-7000
www.ccny.cuny.edu

College of Aeronautics
La Guardia Airport
Flushing, NY 11371
718-429-6600
www.aero.edu

College of Santa Fe
1600 St. Michael's Drive
Santa Fe, NM 87501
800-456-2673 or 505-473-6011
www.csf.edu

Conservatory of Music of Puerto Rico
350 Rafael Lamar Street
San Juan, PR 00918
787-751-0160

Eastern New Mexico University
1200 West University
Portales, NM 88130
800-367-3668 or 505-562-1011
www.enmu.edu

Florida International University
11200 S.W. Eighth Street
Miami, FL 33199
305-348-2000
www.fiu.edu

Heritage College
3240 Fort Road
Toppenish, WA 98948
509-865-2244
www.heritage.edu

Inter American University of Puerto Rico
Aguadilla Campus
Barrio Corrales
Sector Calero
Aguadilla, PR 00605
787-891-0925
www.interaguadilla.edu

Inter American University
of Puerto Rico
Arecibo Campus
Carretera #2, Km. 80.4
Bo. San Daniel
Sector Las Canelas
Arecibo, PR 00614
787-878-5475
www.arecibo.inter.edu

Inter American University
of Puerto Rico
Barranquitas Campus
Bo. Helechal, Carr. 156
Intersección 719
Barranquitas, PR 00794
787-857-4040
www.inter.edu

Inter American University
of Puerto Rico
Bayamon Campus
Carretera 830 #500
Bo. Cerro Gordo
Bayamon, PR 00970
787-279-1912
www.bc.inter.edu

Inter American University
of Puerto Rico
Fajardo Campus Calle
Union-Batey Central
Carr. 195
Fajardo, PR 00738
787-863-2390
www.inter.edu

Inter American University
of Puerto Rico
Guayama Campus, Bo. Machete
Carr. 744, Km 1.2
Guayama, PR 00785
787-864-2222
www.inter.edu/guayama

Inter American University
of Puerto Rico
Metropolitan Campus, Carretera 1,
Km 16.3
Esq. Calle Francisco Sein
Río Piedras, PR 00919
787-250-1912
www.metro.inter.edu

Inter American University
of Puerto Rico
Ponce Campus
Bo. Sabanetas, Carr. 1
Mercedita Station
Mercedita Ponce, PR 00715
787-284-1912
www.inter.edu/programponce.html

> **Until higher education for the most ambitious youth in American society is seen as something other than credentialing—providing a certificate that the individual will be able to exchange for something called a job—the joys and necessities of learning will be rendered in a debased coinage. The best of America's liberal arts colleges recognize that their so-called product is something other than a negotiable instrument designed to guarantee employment.**
>
> —*Stephen R. Graubard*

> **Nothing endures but change.**
>
> *—Heraclitus*

John Jay College of Criminal Justice-City University of New York
899 Tenth Avenue
New York, NY 10019
212-237-8000
www.jjay.cuny.edu

Mercy College
555 Broadway
Dobbs Ferry, NY 10522
914-693-4500
www.mercynet.edu

Mount St. Mary's College
12001 Chalon Road
Los Angeles, CA 90049
310-954-4015
www.msmc.la.edu

National Hispanic University
14271 Story Road
San Jose, CA 95127
408-254-6900
www.nhu.edu

New Mexico Highlands University
National Avenue
Las Vegas, NM 87701
505-454-2711
www.nmhu.edu

New Mexico State University
University Avenue
Las Cruces, NM 88003
800-662-6678 or 505-646-0111
www.nmsu.edu

Northeastern Illinois University
5500 North St. Louis Avenue
Chicago, IL 60625
773-583-4050
www.neiu.edu

Our Lady of the Lake University
411 S.W. 24th Street
San Antonio, TX 78207
210-434-6711
www.ollusa.edu

In spite of alarmist media, violent crime is way down on campuses nationwide. However, arrests for drug and alcohol violations are way up. It might be a good idea to take those campus drug and alcohol policies seriously, and be particularly careful to avoid large, outdoor parties that look like they may be getting out of hand. Arrests can result in a permanent legal record, possible academic suspension, or even a rescission of your financial aid. "Students are definitely being more careful about where they drink. They're saying, 'I don't need the infraction, so I'm going to stay inside and not cause trouble.'" (*Chronicle of Higher Education*) By the way, policies that rescind financial aid as a penalty for rowdiness are blatantly discriminatory against poor and middle class students, while allowing more affluent students to rack up more infractions before facing any real penalty.

**Pontifical Catholic University
of Puerto Rico**

Arecibo Campus

Arecibo, PR 00613

787-881-1212

www.pucpr.edu

**Pontifical Catholic University
of Puerto Rico**

Guayama Campus

5 South Palmer Street

Guayama, PR 00784

787-864-0550

www.pucpr.edu

**Pontifical Catholic University
of Puerto Rico**

Mayagüez Campus

482 South Post Street

Mayagüez, PR 00681

787-834-5151

www.pucpr.edu

**Pontifical Catholic University
of Puerto Rico**

Ponce Campus 2250

Avenida Las Americas

Ponce, PR 00731

787-841-2000

www.pucpr.edu

Saint Augustine College

1333-45 West Argyle Street

Chicago, IL 60640

773-878-8756

Saint Mary's University

One Camino Santa Maria

San Antonio, TX 78228

210-436-3126

www.stmarytx.edu

Saint Peter's College

2641 Kennedy Boulevard

Jersey City, NJ 07306

888-SPC-9933 or 201-915-9000

www.spc.edu

Saint Thomas University

16400 N.W. 32nd Avenue

Miami, FL 33054

305-625-6000

www.stu.edu

San Diego State University

5500 Campanile Drive

San Diego, CA 92182

858-594-5200

www.sdsu.edu

St. Edward's University

3001 South Congress Avenue

Austin, TX 78704

512-448-8500

www.stedwards.edu

**"Finding
out who you
are is the
whole point of
the human
experience."**

—Anna Quindlen

> **Beauty is in the eye of the beholder, and it may be necessary from time to time to give a stupid or misinformed beholder a black eye.**
>
> —*Miss Piggy*

Sul Ross State University
Highway 90
Alpine, TX 79832
915-837-8011
www.sulross.edu

Texas A & M International University
5201 University Boulevard
Laredo, TX 78041
956-326-2001
www.tamiu.edu

**Texas A & M University
at Corpus Christi**
6300 Ocean Drive
Corpus Christi, TX 78412
512-994-5700
www.tamucc.edu

**Texas A & M University
at Kingsville**
955 West University Boulevard
Kingsville, TX 78363
361-593-2111
www.tamuk.edu

**Universidad Adventista
de las Antillas**
Carr. 106 Km 2.2 Int
Mayagüez, PR 00680
787-834-9595
www.uaa.edu

Universidad Metropolitana
Avenida Ana G. Mendez
Km. 0.3
Cupey Bajo, PR 00928
787-766-1717
www.suagm.edu/UMET/main/default.htm

**Universidad Politecnica
de Puerto Rico**
377 Ponce de León Avenue
San Juan, PR 00919
787-754-8000
www.pupr.edu

Universidad del Turabo
Carretera 189
Km. 3.3
Gurabo, PR 00778
787-743-7979
www.suagm.edu

University of Houston - Downtown
One Main Street
Houston, TX 77002
713-221-8000
www.dt.uh.edu

University of the Incarnate Word
4301 Broadway
San Antonio, TX 78209
210-829-6000
www.uiw.edu

University of La Verne

1950 Third Street

La Verne, CA 91750

909-593-3511

www.ulaverne.edu

University of Miami

1262 Memorial Drive

Coral Gables, FL 33124

305-284-2211

www.miami.edu

University of New Mexico

Mesa Vista 3080

Albuquerque, NM 87131

505-277-0111

www.unm.edu

University of Puerto Rico

Aguadilla Regional College

Calle Belt

Aguadilla, PR 00604

787-890-2681

www.upr.edu

University of Puerto Rico

Arecibo Technological University College

Carretera Núm. 953, Km. 0.8

Arecibo, PR 00613

787-878-2830

www.upr.edu

University of Puerto Rico

Bayamon University College

#170 Carretera 174

Minillas Industrial Park

Bayamon, PR 00959

787-786-2885

www.cutb.upr.clu.edu

University of Puerto Rico

Cayey University College

Avenida Antonio R. Barceló

Cayey, Puerto Rico 00736

787-738-2161

www.cuc.upr.clu.edu

University of Puerto Rico

Humacao University College

Bo. Tejas

Humacao, PR 00791

787-850-0000

www.upr.clu.edu

University of Puerto Rico

Mayagüez Campus

Carretera Núm. 2, Calle Post

Mailing address: c/o P.O. Box 5000

Mayagüez, Puerto Rico 00681

787-832-4040

www.w3rum.upr.clu.edu

> **I have made this letter longer than usual, because I lack the time to make it short.**
>
> —*Blaise Pascal*

University of Puerto Rico

Medical Sciences Campus

Centro Médico

Río Piedras, Puerto Rico

Mailing address: c/o P.O. Box 365067

San Juan, PR 00936

787-758-2525

www.rcm.upr.edu

University of Puerto Rico

Ponce Technological University College

Avenida Santiago de los Caballeros

Esquina By-Pass

Ponce, PR 00732

787-844-8181

www.upr.clu.edu

University of Puerto Rico

Río Piedras Campus

Avenida Ponce de León

Parada 38

Río Piedras, PR

Mailing address: c/o P.O. Box 23300

San Juan, PR 00931

787-764-0000

www.upracd.upr.clu.edu:9090

University of the Sacred Heart

Rosales esquina San Antonio

Pda. 26 1/2

San Juan, PR 00911

787-728-1515

www.sagrado.edu

University of Texas at Arlington

701 South Nedderman

Arlington, TX 76019

817-272-2011

www.uta.edu

University of Texas at Austin

One South Mall

Austin, TX 78705

512-471-3434

www.utexas.edu

**University of Texas
at Brownsville - Texas
Southmost College**

80 Fort Brown

Brownsville, TX 78520

956-544-8200

www.utb.edu

News Flash: WASP males are underrepresented at some elite universities. For example, at Harvard, one in five is a non-Jewish European-American male. In the general population in the United States and Canada, more than one in three is a non-Jewish European-American male. On this same issue, certain smaller liberal arts schools have ignored their own failure to attract a diverse student body. Some good small colleges are white, white, white. If this matters to you, be sure to inquire about it.

(Source: U. S. News & World Report)

University of Texas at Dallas
2601 North Floyd Road
Richardson, TX 75083
972-883-2111
www.ut.dallas.edu

University of Texas at El Paso
500 West University Avenue
El Paso, TX 79968
915-747-5000
www.utep.edu

Western New Mexico University
1000 West College Avenue
Silver City, NM 88062
800-222-9668 or 505-538-6238
www.wnmu.edu

Whittier College
13406 East Philadelphia Street
Whittier, CA 90608
562-907-4200
www.whittier.edu

Woodbury University
7500 Glen Oaks Boulevard
Burbank, CA 91510
818-767-0888
www.woodburyu.edu

> ❞❞ **We fear things in proportion to our ignorance of them.** ❞❞
>
> —*Livy*

THE TRIBAL, INDIAN, AND NATIVE AMERICAN COLLEGES

American Indian College of the Assemblies of God
10020 North 15th Avenue
Phoenix, AZ 85021
602-944-3335

American Indian Institute
The University of Oklahoma,
College of Continuing Education
555 Constitution Street, Suite 237
Norman, OK 73072-7820
405-325-4127
www.occe.ou.edu./aii.html

Bay Mills Community College
12214 West Lake Shore Drive
Brimley, MI 49715
906-248-3354
www.bmcc.org

Blackfeet Community College
U.S. Highway 89
Browning, MT 59417
406-338-7755

A majority of these colleges do not grant bachelor's degrees, only associates degrees. Contents of this list were gathered from the American Indian Higher Education Consortium (www.aihec.org) and the WWW Virtual Library-American Indians: Index of Native American Resources on the Internet (www.hanksville.org/ NAresources) Web sites.

These lands are ours. No one has a right to remove us, because we were the first owners. The Great Spirit above has appointed this place for us, on which to light our fires, and here we will remain. As to boundaries, the Great Spirit knows no boundaries, nor will his red children acknowledge any.

—Chief Tecumseh

Cankdeska Cikana Community College
101 College Drive
Fort Totten, ND 58335
701-766-4415
www.little-hoop.cc.nd.us

College of the Menominee Nation
Highway 4755
Keshena, WI 54135
715-799-4921
www.menominee.edu

Crownpoint Institute of Technology
Lowerpoint Road
Crownpoint, NM 87313
505-786-4100
www.cit.cc.nm.us

D-Q University
Road 31
Davis, CA 95617
530-758-0470
www.dqu.cc.ca.us

Diné College
Route 12 at Highway 64
Tsaile, AZ 86556
520-724-6669
www.ncc.cc.nm.us

Dull Knife Memorial College
100 College Drive
Lame Deer, MT 59043
406-477-6215
www.dkmc.cc.mt.us

Fond du Lac Tribal and Community College
2101 14th Street
Cloquet, MN 55720
218-879-0800
www.fdl.cc.mn.us

Fort Belknap College
Highways 2 and 66
Harlem, MT 59526
406-353-2607
www.montana.edu/~wwwse/fbc/fbc.html

Fort Berthold Community College

220 Eighth Avenue North

New Town, ND 58763

701-627-4738

www.fbcc.bia.edu

Fort Peck Community College

Highway 2 East

Poplar, MT 59255

406-768-5551

www.fpcc.cc.mt.us

Gabriel Dumont Institute of Native

Studies and Applied Research

505 23rd Street East

Saskatoon, SK S7K 4K7

Canada

306-934-4941

www.gdins.org

Haskell Indian Nations University

155 Indian Avenue

Lawrence, KS 66046

785-749-8497

www.haskell.edu

Institute of American Indian Arts

1600 St. Michael's Drive

Santa Fe, NM 87504

505-988-6463

www.iaiancad.org

Keweenaw Bay Ojibwa

Community College

107 Bear Town Road

Baraga, MI 49908

906-353-8161

Lac Courte Oreilles Ojibwa

Community College

13466 West Trepania Road

Hayward, WI 54843

715-634-4790

www.lco-college.edu

Leech Lake Tribal College

Route 3

Cass Lake, MN 56633

218-335-2828

www.lltc.org

Little Big Horn College

1 Forest Lane

Crow Agency, MT 59022

406-638-2228

main.lbhc.cc.mt.us

Little Priest Tribal College

601 East College Drive

Winnebago, NE 68071

402-878-2380

www.lptc.cc.ne.us

> **Eighty percent of success is showing up.**
>
> —*Woody Allen*

Native American Educational Services (NAES) College
2838 West Peterson Avenue
Chicago, IL 60659
773-761-5000
www.naes.indian.com

Nebraska Indian Community College
College Hill Road
Macy, NE 68071
402-837-5078

Northwest Indian College
2522 Kwina Road
Bellingham, WA 98226
360-676-2772
www.nwic.edu

Oglala Lakota College
Piya Wiconi Road
Kyle, SD 57752
605-455-2321
www.olc.edu

Red Crow Community College
Junction 505 West
Cardston, AB TOI 1Y0
Canada
403-737-2400

Salish Kootenai College
52000 Highway 93
Pablo, MT 59855
406-675-4800
www.skc.edu

Saskatchewan Indian Federated College
118 College West
University of Regina
Regina, SK S4S 0A2
Canada
306-584-8333
www.sifc.edu

Si Tanka College
435 North Elm
Eagle Butte, SD 57625
605-964-6044
www.sitanka.org

Sinte Gleska University
Spotted Trail Drive
Rosebud, SD 57570
605-747-2263
www.sinte.indian.com

Sisseton Wahpeton Community College
Old Agency
Agency Village, SD 57262
605-698-3966
swcc.cc.sd.us/cc.htm

Sitting Bull College

1341 92nd Street

Fort Yates, ND 58538

701-854-3861

Southwestern Indian

Polytechnic Institute

9169 Coors Road, NW

Albuquerque, NM 87184

505-897-2347

www.sipi.bia.edu

Stone Child College

Rocky Boy Route

Box Elder, MT 59521

406-395-4313

Turtle Mountain Community College

BIA #7, North

Belcourt, ND 58316

701-477-7862

www.turtle-mountain.cc.nd.us

United Tribes Technical College

3315 University Drive

Bismarck, ND 58504

701-255-3285

www.united-tribes.tec.nd.us

White Earth Tribal and

Community College

210 Main Street South

Mahnomen, MN 56557

218-935-0417

Also note that Heritage College and Prescott College have close ties to Native American Nations, and both train teachers to the standard state teaching credential in Native American settings.

MASCOTS

The coolest mascot in the U.S. and Canada is, without a doubt, the Banana Slug, which guides the University of California, Santa Cruz sports teams into battle. The ass from Colorado College of Mines, which they gracefully refer to as a donkey or occasionally even try to pass off as a mule, is another nominee. This rivals Virginia Tech's Hokie Bird, which is actually a turkey. The ugliest is—and there may be some debate here—the Stanford tree, which looks like an oddly shaped Christmas present wrapped by someone's drunken uncle. It is absolutely incomprehensible that anyone would guess what this visual abomination might depict. Another favorite of mine, on the weirdness scale, is Oglethorpe University's Stormy Petrel, *Thalassidroma wilsonii,* a tough and oily seabird with a unique quality: when dried you can light one on fire and use it as a torch. Then, there's always the University of California, Irvine's fighting Anteaters, and Whittier College's Fighting Poets.

Creighton University

Vanderbilt University

Drexel University

USAF Academy

USN Academy

Manhattan College

Yale University

North Carolina State University

Georgia Institute of Technology

USM Academy

(Source: Jim Naughton "Women's Teams in NCAA's Division I See Gains in Participation and Budgets," The Chronicle of Higher Education)

"I am not young enough to know everything." —Oscar Wilde

Sometimes an otherwise distinguished university has an event attached to it that it really wishes would just go away. The University of Michigan's HashBash is such an event. Started years before Nancy Reagan dreamed up that brilliant slogan, "Just Say No," it has become an institution in its own right. The HashBash happens on the first Saturday of April and is sponsored by the Michigan chapter of NORML. The event entails a rally on the Diag at "high noon," with much open-air burning of Rastafarian-size marijuana cigars. Along with speakers for the reform of marijuana laws, featured guests often include people from *High Times* magazine, eighty-year-old glaucoma grandmas protesting for access to medical marijuana, such dope luminaries as Tommy Chong of the renowned Cheech & Chong, and general mayhem. There are peripheral events to the actual rally, such as hippie drum circles all over town, special events at nightclubs, a preponderance of house parties in the evening, and people generally smoking pot everywhere. There is a large influx of people from out of town. The next day everyone goes back to class, and starts studying as hard as before, because you can't make it at the University of Michigan without studying hard, even if you have to study with red eyes.

Similarly, Vassar College's Queer Association has had dibs on the best party of the year, the HomoHop, a "celebration of sexuality and pleasure," which the administration had been uneasy with for years. Recently the sponsors of the HomoHop decided to end the tradition (for now, anyway) due to excessive drinking by straight people.

Alverno College

3400 South 43rd Street

Milwaukee, WI 53234-3922

800-933-3401 or 414-382-6000

www.alverno.edu

Barnard College at Columbia University

3009 Broadway

New York, NY 10027

212-854-5262

www.barnard.columbia.edu

Bennett College

(historically Black)

900 East Washington Street

Greensboro, NC 27401

800-413-5323 or 336-273-4431

www.bennett.edu

Brenau University

One Centennial Circle

Gainesville, GA 30501

770-534-6299

www.brenau.edu

Bryn Mawr College

101 North Merion Avenue

Bryn Mawr, PA 19010-2899

800-BMC-1885 or 610-526-5000

www.brynmawr.edu

Carlow College

3333 Fifth Avenue

Pittsburgh, PA 15213

412-578-6000

www.carlow.edu

Cedar Crest College

100 College Drive

Allentown, PA 18104-6196

800-360-1222 or 610-437-4471

www.cedarcrest.edu

Chatham College

Woodland Road

Pittsburgh, PA 15232

412-365-1100

www.chatham.edu

College of Notre Dame of Maryland

4701 North Charles Street

Baltimore, MD 21210

410-435-0100

www.ndm.edu

Columbia College

1301 Columbia College Drive

Columbia, SC 29203

803-786-3012

www.collacoll.edu

"A ship in port is safe, but that's not what ships are built for."

—*Grace Murray Hopper, mathematician*

Converse College

580 East Main Street

Spartanburg, SC 29302

864-596-9040

www.converse.edu

Mary Baldwin College

Frederick and New Streets

Staunton, VA 24401

800-468-2262 or 540-887-7000

www.mbc.edu

Emmanuel College

400 The Fenway

Boston, MA 02115

617-277-9340

www.emmanuel.edu

Marymount College

100 Marymount Avenue

Tarrytown, NY 10591-3796

800-724-4312 or 914-631-3200

www.marymt.edu

Hollins University

7916 Williamson Road

Roanoke, VA 24020

800-456-9595 or 540-362-6000

www.hollins.edu

Midway College

512 East Stephens Street

Midway, KY 40347-1120

800-755-0031 or 606-846-4421

www.midway.edu

Judson College

302 Bibb Street

Marion, AL 36756

334-683-5100

www.judson.edu

Mills College

5000 MacArthur Boulevard

Oakland, CA 94613-1301

800-87-MILLS or 510-430-2255

www.mills.edu

For every accredited college and university in the U.S. and Canada go to www.donaldasher.com/colleges

The lifetime value of a high school diploma is $1,057,500. The lifetime value of a bachelor's degree is $1,535,100. The lifetime value of a master's degree is $1,795,800. The lifetime value of a Ph.D. is $2,074,800. The lifetime value of a medical degree is $5,810,000. Education creates social and financial mobility in our society. The U.S. Bureau of Labor Statistics tracks income by thousands of categories, and education is one of the few that show up as a lockstep indicator of income. (All figures in 1995 dollars based on average earnings times potential years of employment and assuming no compounding.)

Mississippi University for Women

1100 College Street

Columbus, Mississippi 39701

877-GO2-THEW or 662-329-4720

www.muw.edu

Moore College of Art & Design

Twentieth Street and The Parkway

Philadelphia, PA 19103-1179

800-523-2025 or 215-568-4515

www.moore.edu

Mount Holyoke College

50 College Street

South Hadley, MA 01075

413-538-2000

www.mtholyoke.edu

Mount Mary College

2900 North Menomonee River Parkway

Milwaukee, WI 53222

414-258-4810

www.mtmary.edu

Mount St. Mary's College

12001 Chalon Road

Los Angeles, CA 90049

310-954-4015

www.msmc.la.edu

Notre Dame College

4545 College Road

South Euclid, OH 44121

216-381-1680

www.ndc.edu

Peace College

15 East Peace Street

Raleigh, NC 27604-1194

800-PEACE-47 or 919-508-2000

www.peace.edu

Pine Manor College

400 Heath Street

Chestnut Hill, MA 02467

800-PMC-1357 or 617-731-7000

www.pmc.edu

Randolph-Macon Woman's College

2500 Rivermont Avenue

Lynchburg, VA 24503-1526

804-947-8100

www.rmwc.edu

Regis College

235 Wellesley Street

Weston, MA 02193

617-893-1820

www.regis.edu

> **Every time I catch myself saying, 'Oh no, you shouldn't try that,' I think, 'Yes, I *should*.'**
>
> —*Erica Jong*

> **I think the girl who is able to earn her own living and pay her way should be as happy as anybody on Earth.**
>
> —*Susan B. Anthony*

One of the world's largest collections of newspaper cartoons, comic books, and cartoon art is housed at the Michigan State University Library Special Collections Department.

Saint Mary-of-the-Woods College

3301 St. Mary's Road

St. Mary-of-the-Woods, IN 47876

812-535-5151

woods.smwc.edu

Salem College

Winston-Salem, NC 27108

800-327-2536 or 910-721-2600

www.salem.edu

Simmons College

300 The Fenway

Boston, MA 02115-5898

800-345-8468 or 617-521-2000

www.simmons.edu

Smith College

(Has scholarship for mature women 24+)

Elm Street

Northampton, MA 01063

413-584-2700

www.smith.edu

Stephens College

1200 East Broadway

Columbia, MO 65215

800-876-7207 or 573-442-2211

www.stephens.edu

Stern College for Women at Yeshiva University

(Jewish)

500 West 185th Street

New York, NY 10033-3299

www.yu.edu/stern.html

Sweet Briar College

Sweet Briar, VA 24595

804-381-6100

www.sbc.edu

Trinity College

125 Michigan Avenue, NE

Washington, DC 20017-1094

800-492-6882 or 202-884-9000

www.trinitydc.edu

Ursuline College

2550 Lander Road

Pepper Pike, OH 44124

440-449-4200

www.en.com/ursweb

Playboy once ran an "article" on Women of the Women's Colleges. It was, predictably, controversial. There was no shortage of women to pose, and women to protest. I'm not sure what this means, but there's plenty to deconstruct here. Cultural anthropology, anyone?

Wellesley College

106 Central Street

Wellesley, MA 02481

617-235-0320

www.wellesley.edu

Wells College

Aurora, NY 13026

800-952-9355 or 315-364-3265

www.wells.edu

Wesleyan College

4760 Forsyth Road

Macon, GA 31210-4462

912-477-1110

www.wesleyan-college.edu

William Smith College

639 Main Street

Geneva, NY 14456

315-781-3700

www.hws.edu

> ❝I am always more interested in what I am about to do than in what I have already done.❞
>
> —*Rachel Carson*

THE MEN'S COLLEGES

Deep Springs College

Off California Highway 168

HC72, Box 45001

Dyer, NV 89010-9803

760-872-2000

www.deepsprings.edu

Hampden-Sydney College

College Road

Hampden-Sydney, VA 23943-0667

800-755-0733 or 804-223-6000

www.hsc.edu

Hobart College

639 South Main Street

Geneva, NY 14456

315-781-3700

www.hws.edu

Morehouse College

(Black college)

830 Westview Drive SW

Atlanta, GA 30314

800-851-1254 or 404-681-2800

www.morehouse.edu

Saint John's University

(Catholic)

Collegeville, MN 56321

320-363-2011

www.csbjsu.edu

Wabash College

301 W. Wabash Avenue

Crawfordsville, IN 47933-0352

765-361-6100

www.wabash.edu

> ❝In the fields of observation, chance favors only the mind that is prepared.❞
>
> —*Louis Pasteur*

INDEX

C

T

Donald M. Asher is one of America's premier career consultants, specializing in the hidden job market and the self-directed job search, and a nationally recognized speaker at colleges and conferences coast to coast.

He is also the author of nine other books, all published by Ten Speed Press:

Who Gets Promoted, Who Doesn't, and Why
How to Get Any Job with Any Major
Asher's Bible of Executive Résumés
The Overnight Résumé
From College to Career
Graduate Admissions Essays
The Overnight Job Change Strategy
The Overnight Job Change Letter
The Foolproof Job-Search Workbook

In addition, Donald Asher is a contributing writer for the *San Francisco Chronicle, San Francisco Examiner,* the *Wall Street Journal*'s CareerJournal.com and CollegeJournal.com, Monster's monstertrak.com, *The National Business Employment Weekly, Managing Your Career Magazine, NACE Journal, WACE Spotlight,* jobstar.org, wetfeet.com, MSN Encarta, and many other publications and career sites.

Also by Donald Asher

How to Get Any Job with Any Major
Career Launch and Re-Launch for Anyone Under 30 (or How to Avoid Living in Your Parents' Basement)

So, you think your choice of major will determine your career path? Think again!

Lisa Kudrow was a biology major.
Alan Greenspan was a music major.
Albert Einstein was a high-school drop-out.

So where do the great jobs that lead to career success come from? It comes from an alignment of passion with preparation. In HOW TO GET ANY JOB WITH ANY MAJOR, college and career guru Donald Asher explains how to discover *your* passion while getting the preparation you *really* need. It is the first book that definitively answers:

- **What's the difference between "getting a job" and "launching a career"?**
- **Which skills do employers value most? (They're *not* what you think!)**
- **Why do employers hire people like you?**
- **Which non-technical skills are high-tech companies actually looking for?**
- **Why do some people get promoted again and again?**
- **How do you prove you have skills that don't show up on your transcripts?**
- **How do you identify your passion if you're confused?**
- **How can you get influential people to use their influence to help you?**
- **Are chance and luck major factors in most successful careers?**
- **What experience do you have now that will help you get into grad school later?**
- **What should you do if you're a graduate and living in your parents' basement?**
- **What should you do if you're a junior to make sure you *don't* end up in that basement after you graduate?**

HOW TO GET ANY JOB WITH ANY MAJOR offers the most creative and innovative thinking on career launch and re-launch to date.

$14.95 paperback (Can $21.95)
ISBN-13: 978-1-58008-539-7
ISBN-10: 1-58008-539-3

Also Ten Speed Press titles are available at bookstores or by ordering directly from the publisher:

Ten Speed Press • P.O. Box 7123 • Berkeley, CA 94707
800-841-BOOK / www.tenspeed.com